QuickC Programming

QuickC Programming

Jack Purdum

SAMS

A Division of Macmillan, Inc.
11711 North College, Suite 141, Carmel, IN 46032 USA

To Dad and Jean

International Standard Book Number: 0-672-22721-5
Library of Congress Catalog Card Number: 90-61919

Acquisitions Editor: *James S. Hill*
Development Editor: *Greg Croy*
Technical Editor: *Alan Plantz*
Production Editor: *Katherine Stuart Ewing*
Copy Editors: *Susan Christophersen* and *Jodi Jensen*
Cover Art Direction: *Glen Santner*
Illustrators: *Don Clemons* and *Tami Hughes*
Compositor: *Douglas & Gayle, Limited*
Production Assistance: *Dennis Sheehan*
Indexer: *Sharon Hilgenberg*

Printed in the United States of America

Trademarks

Overview

Contents

11 Tying It All Together

12 Debugging Programs

Preface

Back in the late 1970s, when I first started using C on a regular basis, it was still pretty rare to find someone who had a personal computer. The deluxe system in those days had 64K total memory and maybe a floppy disk system with two drives. As often as not, you built your system from a kit. The only C compiler for these small machines was Small C, written by Ron Cain. Many of the data types were missing, but you could write small programs in C.

My, how things have changed.

Today's systems have a megabunch of memory, a bazillion bytes of disk storage, and a color monitor with resolutions approaching those found on color TV sets. The processing power that took up an entire room when I was in graduate school now fits on a small table, with room to spare. For any of this to mean much, software has to keep up with the changes in hardware. What has happened in the C compiler market in the past five years or so seems to bear this out.

Microsoft's QuickC compiler is one of several still remaining in the PC C compiler market. Several years ago, more than two dozen C compilers were available for MS-DOS machines. Now, perhaps a half dozen are left. The ones that have survived, however, are incredibly powerful and loaded with features. I think your choice of the QuickC compiler is a good one, for several reasons. First, QuickC is full-featured, provides reasonably quick turn-around time (i.e., the time required to compile and link the program), and generates good code. Second, QuickC is reasonably priced. A compiler with QuickC's features would have cost more than five hundred dollars three or four years ago. QuickC is a bargain. Finally, QuickC provides a smooth migration path to Microsoft's commercial compiler, Microsoft C, Release 6.0. Your experience with the QuickC compiler will make the move to the Release 6.0 compiler relatively easy.

The goal of this book is to teach you C, not how to use all of QuickC's many features. You can use the QuickC documentation to learn about QuickC's features. Although you will learn how to use many of QuickC's features, the primary reason for using any given feature is to make learning the C language easier. For example, you will use the QuickC debugger rather early in the book. However, the debugger is used as a teaching tool more than as a "pure" programming tool. Using the debugger lets me show you things rather than just talk about them. Experience has shown that once something is seen or visualized, it is easier to understand and remember. I use this approach wherever possible so that you can learn the language more quickly and with greater understanding.

The book is based on QuickC, Release 2.5. Although this release has features not found in earlier releases, most of these are sufficiently minor, allowing this book to be used with earlier QuickC versions. Chapter 1 lays some groundwork, and then chapters 2 through 10 discuss the C language in detail. By the time you finish Chapter 10, you should be able to write just about any type of C program you wish. Chapter 11 builds a complete program using many of the topics covered in earlier chapters. Chapter 12 covers program debugging with an emphasis on using the QC debugger. Chapter 13 covers a few odds and ends plus several other programming tools provided with the QC compiler. Chapter 14 concentrates on how to work with a PC display screen using the QC compiler. Chapter 15 discusses the graphics programmming functions supplied with the QC compiler.

As always, a number of people have contributed to this book. The people at Microsoft provided a beta version of QuickC 2.5, which made it possible for me to cover some of its latest features. Special thanks to Davie Reed who provided a nontrivial assembler function to interface with QuickC. I would also like to thank Dave Cooper, Chris DeVoney, Don Dudine, Carl Landau, Chuck Lieske, Jim Rheude, David Schmitt, and Robert Ward for their support, friendship, and ideas that have contributed to this book in many different ways. Finally, a special thanks to the editors and graphic artists who took mangled verbiage and stick figures and turned them into something readable.

1

Introduction

In this chapter you learn

Standard versus ANSI C

Why this book is different

Compilers versus interpreters

This chapter provides information about C in general and how QuickC fits into the C environment. If you have not worked with a compiled language before, this chapter also offers some thoughts on how a compiler compares to an interpreter. Although individual compilers are different, I think you will like the power that Microsoft's QuickC gives you.

Old C, ANSI C, and QuickC

C has come a long way since its beginnings in the early 1970s. The development of C by Dennis Ritchie and Ken Thompson at Bell Labs produced a language that is elegant in design, robust in operators, and powerful despite its relatively few key words. Still, no language is perfect and changes have occurred over the years. Indeed, so many enhancements were made to C, many programmers were concerned that dialects of C (à la BASIC) would fragment the language. To prevent such a fate, a small group of C benefactors (led by Jim Brodie) petitioned the American National Standards Institute (ANSI) to form a committee to develop a standard language definition for C. The result was the formation of the ANSI X3J11 committee to develop a standard for the C language.

The X3J11 committee produced a language definition and submitted it for final public review in 1988. Although the standard seemed to be accepted, one person raised questions that prevented the formal adoption of the X3J11 public review document. The standard was finalized in 1989. Microsoft's QuickC Release 2.5 compiler implements all of the X3J11 document that is possible in an MS-DOS environment. For all practical purposes, therefore, QuickC is an "ANSI compatible" compiler (that is, it follows the X3J11 specification for the C language).

The Need for a Standard C Language

Why did dozens of high-powered C programmers donate their time for three years to produce a standard language definition for C? In a nutshell, it was so the work they did with company ABC's compiler could be compiled with company XYZ's compiler without having to change the source code. With a "standardized" language, you can take a program to a new hardware environment without having to change things much. That is, the source code becomes "portable" among different computing environments.

Obviously, you are about to learn C on hardware designed to run MS-DOS. However, if you develop some super program and want to move it to some other hardware environment, having the program written in C makes moving to that new environment easier than most other languages. At the extreme, think how hard it would be to take a program written in 80286 assembler code and move it to a machine using the 68000 chip family!

The benefits of a standard language definition are not limited to moving programs among different machines. At one time, about two dozen different companies were selling C compilers for the IBM PC-type machines. Think how frustrating it would be to read an article about a program you couldn't compile because you didn't have the same compiler that the author used. The work of X3J11 reduces such problems even more.

I will discuss other advantages of a standardized language as we dig deeper into C.

The Ways This Book Is Different

A number of C books are on the market, several written specifically for QuickC, so why write another one? After all, covering the C language has been done before. I think as you read this book, however, you will find several aspects that make it different.

First, some QuickC books are designed to show how to run the QuickC compiler. Teaching C is a secondary concern. Not so here. My primary purpose is to teach C, using QuickC as the compiler of choice.

Second, QuickC runs in a known environment. That is, QuickC runs on an IBM PC or compatible machine using MS-DOS. This means that you and I have very similar hardware and software resources available to us. Likewise, we will be using the same compiler. With these common resources, you can repeat what is found in the book without worrying about hardware-software incompatibilities.

Third, in this book, you learn C from two different points of view: that of a programmer and that of a compiler. My teaching experiences have convinced me that if you understand how the compiler views a C statement, it is easier to understand why the statement does what it does. Don't worry — this is not difficult to do. (In fact, I assume that you know nothing about how a compiler works. I'll teach you what you need to know.)

Finally, the QuickC Debugger can be used as a teaching tool. Most books postpone discussing the Debugger until the last few chapters. Like most of us, however, you may incur program bugs from the beginning stages of your C experience. Knowing how to use the QuickC Debugger from the outset helps. Also, the QuickC Debugger gives you a more "visual" means of learning C, so you use it often. As you progress through the text, you tackle more sophisticated tasks using the Debugger. As a teaching tool, the Debugger can be extremely valuable even using only two or three of its features.

Things You Should Do

Before you start learning C, there are several things I assume about you. First, I assume that you have installed the QuickC compiler following the directions found in the *Up and Running* booklet supplied with your compiler. Although Release 2.5 has several new options available, you can use the default settings for now.

Second, I assume that you will type the source code examples provided in the text. (I tried to keep these examples as short as possible to minimize this burden.) I realize there is a terrific temptation to skip this, but running the sample programs is a valuable learning experience. Tracking down a misplaced comma or semicolon in a program that you know works is a manageable way to begin your C debugging experience. The old adage "learn by doing" contains a lot of truth. Therefore, I hope that you will read this book while you sit at your computer. You will learn C much faster if you do.

Third, I assume that you don't have to learn C by next weekend. Take your time, experiment with the sample programs, and don't proceed to the next chapter until you feel comfortable with the content of the current chapter.

Fourth, you should read all of the book. Even though you may have some special topic of interest in C, I hope you will read this book from cover to cover. It follows a sequence that builds on the material presented in previous chapters. For example, if you think the terms "definition" and "declaration" have identical meanings in C, you're wrong. If you skip around in the book, you might miss the distinction between the two terms, and you and I won't be viewing things from a common ground. It's your book; read all of it.

Finally, C is a powerful language that allows you to do just about anything you wish (and some things you may not wish). One of the reasons C is so powerful is that few restrictions are placed on how you use it. With this freedom, however, you can do some pretty dumb things. Indeed, probably all C programmers have inadvertently written their names into the middle of the operating system at one time or another. I assume that you are undaunted by such events and will view them as learning experiences.

Compilers Versus Interpreters

If you are like some newcomers to C, you may have programming experience with an interpreted language, such as Microsoft BASIC (which probably came with your computer). Program development using an interpreter, however, is different from using a compiler. Also, execution of a compiled program is different from execution using an interpreter.

With an interpreter, you write the source code for the program using the text editor supplied (usually) with the interpreter. When you finish writing the program, type RUN and the program executes. For example, suppose the program is as follows:

```
10 PRINT "Hello"
```

When you type RUN, the interpreter inspects the first line of the program and finds the BASIC keyword, PRINT. The interpreter then scans its list of keywords (that is, words with special meaning in that language). Because PRINT is a keyword in BASIC, the interpreter sends control to the section of the interpreter that processes the PRINT keyword. The PRINT processing section inspects what comes after the PRINT keyword in the source program to find out what to do next. In our example, the program simply prints Hello on the screen.

Notice that the interpreter spends most of its time scanning each line of your program for keywords; then it branches to whatever section is responsible for processing that particular keyword. Finally, it goes back to the program to process the information associated with the keyword. Therefore, the interpreter spends most of its time in a scan-search-branch sequence as the program executes.

Unlike an interpreter, a compiled program does not use the scan-search-branch sequence. The speed of execution for a compiled program is much faster as a result. Indeed, speed is the primary advantage of using a compiler rather than an interpreter.

In a totally unfair test, I wrote a short program in Microsoft's BASIC and QuickC that incremented a variable from 0 to 64000. The BASIC program took 58 seconds to execute whereas the C version ran in .66 seconds. Although most programs don't exhibit this much difference at runtime, you can expect a compiled C program to run four to six times faster than a similar program written with a BASIC interpreter.

You pay for this speed increase, however. Writing a C program requires several steps. The first step involves writing the source code for the program, probably using the editor supplied with the QuickC compiler. When you save the source code, it is stored as an ASCII (that is, American Standard Code for Information Interchange) file on disk. A common C practice is to use the file extension of .c for C source code files. Therefore, if your program is named test, you would store it on disk as test.c. (Because C source files are stored in ASCII, you can use the MS-DOS TYPE command to display their contents on the screen.)

In the second step, the source program is compiled using the QuickC compiler. The output from the compiler is a file that is stored as an object, or .obj, file. That is, if the source code for the program is test.c, the output of the compiler is test.obj. Such object files are binary files that contain information needed by the next step in the compilation process. However, because .obj files are stored as binary files, you cannot use the MS-DOS TYPE command to list their contents on the screen. (You can try listing .obj files with the TYPE command, but what you see probably won't make much sense and a lot of beeping is likely to be going on, too!)

The third step uses another program, a "linker," to combine the contents of the test.obj file with any other modules needed to form an executable program. This program is supplied with the QuickC compiler package and is stored on your disk as link.exe. The output of the linker is test.exe, which is a program that can be run under MS-DOS.

Note that the output of the linker is a stand-alone program and, unlike an interpreted program, does not require another program to run. In the example, test.exe contains machine language instructions that are directly executable by the computer. Unlike an interpreter with its "scan-search-branch" method of execution, compiled programs are like inline assembler codes that execute at the full speed of the machine.

The cost of the improved speed of a compiled program is the additional steps imposed in the compile-link cycle relative to that required by an interpreter. As a result, the turnaround time (that is, the time required to go from the source code to an executable program) is usually longer when you use a compiler rather than an interpreter. The QuickC compiler, however, is relatively fast in both compilation and linking, so the additional time is not too great. For the typical program in this text, the compile-link time is less than 15 seconds on an AT-type machine.

Thinking Versus Writing

Back in my teaching days, I often gave a programming assignment and sent the students to the lab. Most of the class would start beating on the keyboard to complete the assignment, but one or two students stayed in the classroom, jotted a few notes, and then strolled to the lab five or ten minutes later. The students who stayed behind to think through the assignment before coding the solution consistently produced better programs in less total time than did the rest of the class.

In the "old" days, you wrote your program and submitted it to an operator on punch cards. If you were lucky, you got the results back the next morning. You could lose a full day just by misplacing a single comma. To save time in the long run, a lot of time was spent going over a program before submitting it.

In today's relatively fast hardware-software computing environment, it's tempting to hack away at a problem without giving the program much thought. After all, no day-long waits are required anymore. Still, as you gain experience and your programs become longer and more complex, the time spent designing the program becomes more and more valuable. The value of time is even greater in a compiled environment because of the compile-link overhead relative to an interpreter.

In this text, I often create a situation that leads to a program example. As you read these "set-up" situations, try designing your own solution to the program before reading the solution in the book. Then compare the two solutions. If they are different (normally, they would be), ask yourself why the program was written the way it was. Do the program differences noticeably alter the performance of the program? If so, why? This approach gives you valuable design experience and a deeper understanding of C.

Well, enough of the preliminaries. Now start learning how to program in C.

2

Getting Started

In this chapter, you learn

To run the QuickC compiler

To use the QuickC editor to write a simple C program

The major elements of a C program

Several C programming style conventions

Running the QuickC (QC from now on) compiler is very simple thanks to its intuitive menuing system and on-line help features. The editor uses keystroke sequences that are very much like the popular WordStar text editor. With relatively few commands, you can move around quickly in the C source program. Next, you write a short C program and examine it in some detail. All C programs have certain things in common that you study in this chapter. Finally, you consider some programming style conventions that have emerged over the years. Many of these conventions have been adopted by programmers because they make writing and debugging C programs easier.

Starting QC

As I stated in Chapter 1, I'm assuming that you have installed the QC compiler and are ready to run it. Although some of you may be using the compiler on a floppy disk system, I'm also assuming that the QC compiler is on a hard disk named drive C. If you are using a floppy disk system, the instructions found in this text won't vary much. You should follow the same sequence as those who are using a hard disk.

To start the QC compiler, type QC and press the Enter key.

`C>QC`

In a moment or two, your screen looks similar to that shown in Figure 2-1.

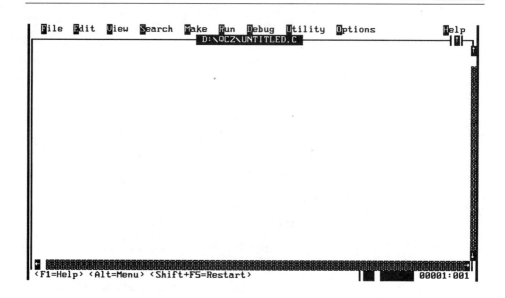

Figure 2-1. Initial QC Screen

The QC compiler is now running, and the cursor sits near the upper left corner of the *source window*, waiting for you to start entering the source code for the program. Because the cursor is in the source window, the compiler is in the *editor mode* of operation when the compiler is first run.

Instead of typing a program at this point, let's set things up so you and I have a similar configuration for the QC compiler.

Moving from the Source Window to the Menu Bar — Alt

Now move from the source window to the top line of the screen. The top line is called the *Menu Bar*. To move from the source window to the Menu

Bar, press the Alt key. (On most keyboards, the Alt key is near the left end of the space bar.) If you touch the Alt key, the cursor moves to the first menu name on the Menu Bar (that is, the word `File`).

Notice that the Alt key shows you which single-letter keystroke can be used to activate a given menu item. On the Menu Bar, pressing the Alt key highlights the F, E, V, S, M, R, D, U, and O keys, which correspond to the menu items shown on the Menu Bar. Select a menu item from the Menu Bar using these highlighted keys.

(Mouse users: You can also select menu items from the Menu Bar by clicking the left mouse button on the desired item in the Menu Bar. I assume, however, that you are not using a mouse.)

Moving from the Menu Bar Back to the Source Window — Esc, Alt

To move back to the source window, touch the Escape key. The Escape key normally is shown as Esc on the keyboard. Unfortunately, the Escape key may be in one of several places depending on the type of keyboard you use. In most cases, it is near the upper left corner of the numeric keypad on the right side of the keyboard. Another way to move back to the source window is by touching the Alt key a second time. Either method works.

If the cursor is located on the Menu Bar, and you touch the Esc key, the cursor moves back to the source window. The cursor remembers where you were in the source window. Therefore, touching Esc moves you back to your previous position in the source window.

Using Options from the Menu Bar

The QC compiler has a number of elements that you can configure to suit your own needs. As you become familiar with the QC compiler, you may want to set these according to your own preferences. For now, however, let's set them so that you and I are working in an identical environment.

Press the Alt key to see the cursor move from the source window to the Menu Bar. Note that pressing the Alt key highlights the first letter of menu names. These letters are used to display menus.

While holding the Alt key, press the O key to activate the Options menu. In case this is the first time you have run QC, refer to Figure 2-2 to see how this menu appears.

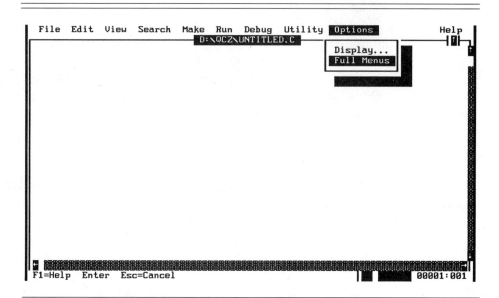

```
   File  Edit  View  Search  Make  Run  Debug  Utility  Options          Help
                     D:\QCZ\UNTITLED.C                   Display...
                                                         Full Menus




















 F1=Help  Enter  Esc=Cancel                                    00001:001
```

Figure 2-2. Using the Options Menu

The Options item allows you to alter things concerning the display and menus. I call these pull-down menus *submenus*. Therefore, Display and Full Menus are submenus of the Options menu.

The Display Item of the Options Submenu

To change one of the items associated with the display screen, press the D key. (Note that because the Display menu item is already highlighted, you can also press Enter to activate the Display menu item.)

Once you have selected the Display item, the screen looks like that shown in Figure 2-3.

A *dialog box* is displayed. Most dialog boxes present one or more options from which to select. The dialog box you see on the screen shows the various options associated with the Display submenu.

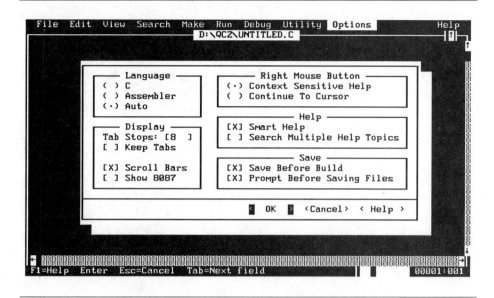

```
   File  Edit  View  Search  Make  Run  Debug  Utility  Options          Help
                           D:\QC2\UNTITLED.C

      ┌──── Language ────┐  ┌──── Right Mouse Button ────┐
      │ ( ) C            │  │ (·) Context Sensitive Help │
      │ ( ) Assembler    │  │ ( ) Continue To Cursor     │
      │ (·) Auto         │  └────────────────────────────┘
      └──────────────────┘  ┌──────── Help ──────────────┐
      ┌──── Display ─────┐  │ [X] Smart Help             │
      │ Tab Stops: [8  ] │  │ [ ] Search Multiple Help Topics │
      │ [ ] Keep Tabs    │  └────────────────────────────┘
      │                  │  ┌──────── Save ──────────────┐
      │ [X] Scroll Bars  │  │ [X] Save Before Build      │
      │ [ ] Show 8087    │  │ [X] Prompt Before Saving Files │
      └──────────────────┘  └────────────────────────────┘

                            ◄  OK  ►   <Cancel>  < Help >


  F1=Help  Enter  Esc=Cancel  Tab=Next field                   00001:001
```

Figure 2-3. The Display Options

Two Ways to Select Items in a Dialog Box

1. Identifying Active Keys: Active keys are shown in a contrasting color or in reverse video. The letter T is the active letter for changing the tab setting, so press the T key.

   The cursor appears in the Tab Stops field waiting for you to enter a new value. My personal preference is to set my tab stops for three spaces rather than the default setting of eight. Three tab stops is enough to show proper program indentation, but not so long that long program lines are "folded" unnecessarily. Press the 3 and Enter keys to change the tab stop setting from 8 to 3. (This can be changed at any time, if you wish. When you press Enter, the Display dialog box disappears and the cursor returns to the source window. If you decide you don't want to make any changes to the Display dialog box, press the Esc key. Esc acts as an abort key and control returns to the source window.

If you wish to change other elements (for example, colors) in the Display item of the Options menu, select the Options item from the Menu item and repeat the process.

2. The Tab Key: A second way to move about in a dialog box is to press the Tab key until you have moved the cursor to the desired item in the dialog box. (The Tab key normally is next to the Q key and is shown as a left- and right-pointing set of arrows.)

If you press Shift-Tab, the cursor moves to the previous field. In other words, the Shift-Tab key sequence is a means to move backward in a dialog box.

Methods to Change Items in a Dialog Box

If you wish to change another item in the Display dialog box, several possible means might be used.

1. Changing Numeric Fields in a Dialog Box: When you changed the Tab Stops field, you entered a digit (for example, 3) to change the Tab Stop setting. You must press Enter to record the change.

2. Changing On-Off Options in a Dialog Box: In some cases, the only option is to have a choice turned on or off. If an x appears in a dialog box field, it is an on-off (or possibly a yes-no) option. If the cursor is sitting on the X, pressing the space bar changes the current status of the option. For example, if you don't want to see scroll bars on the screen, move to the Scroll Bars field and press the space bar once. The X disappears. The absence of the X means the option is off. Press the space bar again and the X reappears, indicating that the option is in the on state again.

There is a second way to toggle on-off options. Simply press the highlighted key to toggle the option. For example, if the X appears in the Scroll Bars window, touching the S key (that is, the active key for the Scroll Bars option) toggles the Scroll Bars option off and the X disappears. Touching the S key a second time restores the X, and the scroll bars are in the on state again.

3. Changing Buttons in a Dialog Box: Other fields in a dialog box may have a list from which you can choose. You can use the arrow keys (for example, the 2, 4, 6, and 8 keys on the numeric keypad) to move

among items in the list. As you press the arrow keys, the button (sometimes called a *radio button*) moves in the direction of the arrow key.

Pressing the down arrow when you are at the bottom of a list causes the button to reappear at the top of the list. Multiple choice button selections have this wrap-around feature.

To select the desired choice, you may either press Enter to set the choice, or use the Tab or active key to move to a different field. If you press the Enter key, QC assumes you are finished with this dialog box and control returns to the source window. If you want to change some other field in the dialog box, use the Tab key to move to the next field to be changed, or press the Alt key and use the active letter to move to that field.

By the way, Release 2.5 lets you change the color of virtually all borders, backgrounds, menus, and active keys you see on the screen. If you are using Release 2.5 and select the Color option (using the Alt-O-C option sequence from the edit window), a dialog box appears and looks like that shown in Figure 2-4.

Figure 2-4. Dialog Box for Setting Colors (Release 2.5)

15

At the top of Figure 2-4 is a set of predefined color options. You may want to try these before testing different color combinations. If you don't like any of the predefined color options, you can set each screen element that appears in the left column of the dialog box. (Use the cursor keys to scroll the list up or down.) The middle column presents the foreground color options, and the right column is the background color. Use the Tab key to move to the next field and the Shift-Tab key combination to move to a previous field. If you want to see what your color scheme looks like, press the Tab key until the cursor appears in the Redraw field near the bottom of the screen (see Figure 2-4). Press Enter and the new colors are displayed.

If you don't like the new colors, either reset them to different values or press the Escape key to abort all changes.

Not Making a Choice in a Dialog Box — Esc

Suppose that you inadvertently get into a dialog box you don't want to change. What now? Normally there are two options available to you. First, use the Tab key to move to the Cancel option near the bottom of the dialog box, or press the Escape (Esc) key. Either method bails you out of a dialog box.

I assume that you have made any and all changes you wish to make concerning the Display submenu and that you have pressed the Enter key. The screen looks like that shown in Figure 2-1 once again.

Full Menus

You can do more with the Options item in the Menu bar. Again press the Alt-O combination to activate the Options menu item. Now press the F key to select the Full Menus option. The Full Menus option is designed to give you as much information as possible when a menu is presented on the screen. Because you are just getting started with QC, this is a good choice for the time being. When you feel comfortable with QC, you can always select the Full Menus options a second time to return to the abbreviated versions of the menus.

If you have not yet done so, press the F key. The cursor returns to the source window. Pressing Alt-O now, you see that the Options submenu has changed from a list of two options to five. You need not be concerned with these new options right now; I simply want you to see the impact of the Full Menus option on the screen.

Using the QC Editor

You are now ready to type your first program. You should type the program shown in Listing 2-1. For the time being, use the arrow, backspace, and Delete keys to correct any mistakes you make.

Listing 2-1. Your First Program

```
/*              This is your first C program  */

#include <stdio.h>

main()
{
   printf("This is my first C program\n");
}
```

When you finish typing the program into the source window, the cursor is sitting after the last brace (that is, the } character) at the end of the last line. In the discussion that follows, I use the carat character (^) to signify pressing the Control (Ctrl) key. (The Control key is located to the left of the A key on most keyboards.)

Move Up One Line — ^E

Pressing the Control and E keys at the same time moves the cursor up one line in the program. Holding the Control key down and tapping the E key several times moves the cursor up one line per tap.

Move Down One Line — ^X

Assuming that the cursor is sitting somewhere near the middle of the program now, press the Control and X keys at the same time. The cursor moves down one line. If you hold the Control key down and tap the X key, the cursor continues to move down one line each time the X key is tapped.

Move Right One Character — ^D

Pressing the Control and D keys together moves the cursor one character to the right. Each press of the D key moves the cursor to the right provided the Control key is held down.

Move Left One Character — ^S

Pressing the Control and S keys at the same time moves the cursor to the left one character. Again, each press of the S key moves the cursor one character to the left as long as the Control key is also held down.

Note that you can accomplish the same cursor movements using the arrow keys located on the keypad. However, most people find the key sequences presented here faster because their hands do not have to move from the typing keys to the keypad. With a little practice, these keystrokes will become second nature to you.

Move One Word Right — ^F

Obviously, advancing one word at a time rather than character by character is a faster way to get near the end of a line. Pressing the Control and F keys at the same time moves the cursor a word to the right. *Word* has a rather loose connotation in this context. For example, if you move to the beginning of the line

```
#include <stdio.h>
```

in Listing 2-1 and press ^F, the cursor moves to the s in stdio.h rather than to the < character. Pressing ^F again moves the cursor to the letter h. You will quickly learn which characters are "skipped" when you press ^F. If you press ^F at the end of a line, the cursor moves to the first word in the next line (providing there is a next line).

Move One Word Left — ^A

A ^A sequence causes the cursor to move one word to the left. Its behavior is consistent with that found when using ^F, except that the cursor movement is to the left. If you are at the start of a line, a ^A moves the cursor to the last word on the line above.

Rapid Cursor Movement; The ^Q? Sequences

When the cursor is at the top of the source window and you need to correct something in the bottom line of the window, pressing ^X a dozen times to get there is a pain. A faster way is the ^QX sequence. Hold the Control key down and press first the Q key and then the X key. The cursor immediately moves to the last line in the source window.

An easy way to remember this is to think of the key sequence as a quick series of the ^X presses, hence the use of the Q key in the Ctrl-Q-X sequence.

To move back to the top, use ^QE. As you can see, the Q sequences are consistent with the single-character cursor movement keys. A summary of the cursor movement keys is shown in Table 2-1.

Table 2-1. Cursor Movement Sequences

Key Sequence	Effect
^E	Move up one line
^X	Move down one line
^QE	Move to top line in the source window
^QX	Move to bottom line in the source window

continues

Table 2-1. Cursor Movement Sequences (continued)

Key Sequence	Effect
^D	Move right one character
^S	Move left one character
^QD	Move to the end of the line
^QS	Move to the beginning of the line
^F	Move right one word
^A	Move left one word

If you are uncomfortable with the key sequences in Table 2-1, you can always use the arrow keys. However, learning the control sequences is worthwhile because your typing speeds up once you have learned them. Note that the Home key moves the cursor to the beginning of a line whereas the End key moves the cursor to the end of the line.

Toggle Insert-Overstrike Modes — ^V

The default status for the QC editor is the insert mode. That is, if the cursor sits in the middle of a word, any keystrokes you make are inserted into the middle of that word. The cursor shape is a thin line when you are in the insert mode.

Occasionally, however, you might like to type over a sequence of characters. This is called the overstrike mode. In this mode, if the cursor is in the middle of a word and you start pressing keys, the characters of the old word are overwritten by the new ones. New characters are not inserted into the word. In this mode, the cursor is a large block shape.

Each time you press the ^V sequence, the cursor shape changes, indicating that you are toggling between the insert and overstrike modes.

There are many other features found in the QC editor. (These features are summarized in the *Up and Running* appendix.) For now, however, you can use the key sequences discussed here to accomplish most of the work you need to do. I discuss other editor features in subsequent chapters.

The Parts of a Program

I assume that you have typed the program from Listing 2-1 and that it is visible in the source window. Now it's time to inspect each element of the program.

Comment Character Pairs — /* */

The first line in the program is

```
/*                    This is your first C program   */
```

This is an example of a comment in C. Comments typically are short sentences that remind you about something in the program. In this example, the comment identifies the program.

Comments begin with a backslash-asterisk pair of characters (/*) and end with an asterisk-backslash pair (*/). Everything between these two character pairs is ignored by the compiler. Because comments have no impact on the size or execution speed of the compiled program, feel free to use them liberally in your programs.

Comments are not limited to a single line. This means that you could have written the program comment as

```
/*
    This is your
    first C program
*/
```

This comment style has no impact on the program. Feel free to use the style you prefer.

The ANSI X3J11 committee did, however, add one restriction with respect to the use of comments. You can no longer *nest* comments. That is, you cannot have a comment within a comment. Therefore, something like

```
/*
    /*
        This is your first C program
    */
*/
```

is no longer allowed under the ANSI definition for C. QC tells you this if you attempt to nest comments.

Comments have one other use besides program documentation. You can use them to remove a line from a program. For example, if you change part of the program in Listing 2-1,

```
main()
{
    /*
    printf("This is my first C program\n");
    */
}
```

you have, in effect, removed the `printf()` line from the program. The reason is that the compiler ignores everything between the comment characters. Therefore, comments provide a convenient means of removing a line from the program when it is compiled. The line, however, is easily restored by simply removing the comment characters. This saves you retyping the line when you want to put the line back into the program. You will likely use this technique often when testing or debugging a program.

The *#include* Preprocessor Directive

The line that reads

```
#include <stdio.h>
```

is called a preprocessor directive because it tells the compiler to read a file named `stdio.h` into the program. (Ignore the < and > characters for the moment.) Actually, the preprocessor can be thought of as a separate program that inspects the source code prior to program compilation. The preprocessor is capable of performing certain *textual* substitutions and file processing actions. The `#include` preprocessor directive tells the preprocessor program to read a text file named `stdio.h` into the program at the point where the `#include` appears in the program. Therefore, any information in the `stdio.h` file is inserted into your sample program.

If you installed your compiler using the QC defaults, you have a subdirectory named INCLUDE. If you examine the contents of this subdirectory, you see that more than two dozen different files end in .h. These files are called *header files*, probably because they are often `#include`d at the head of the program. These header files contain certain overhead information necessary for the compiler to complete its task.

(Header files supplied with the compiler use the .h file extension, but this is not etched in stone. If you create header files of your own later on, they can be used with the `#include` preprocessor directive even though they do not end in .h.)

I discuss other elements of the preprocessor later on. For now, just remember that an `#include` preprocessor directive causes the named file to be read into the program.

C Functions

If you omit the line beginning with `printf()` from the program, it reads

```
main()
{

}
```

In its simplest terms, the preceding lines define a C function named `main()`. The parentheses after the function name are used to hold any data item(s) that might be passed to the function from some other part of the program. If the function needs information from other parts of the program to complete its task, that data would be defined between the opening and closing parentheses following the function name. Formally, anything appearing between these parentheses is called a *function argument*. In our simple program, `main()` doesn't need any "outside" information, so there are no function arguments defined within the parentheses. Although no information is passed into `main()` within the parentheses, the parentheses are still required.

On the next line and below the word `main()`, you find an opening brace ({). The *opening brace* marks the beginning of the body of the `main()` function that is being defined. The *closing brace* (}) in the last line of the program marks the end of the function named `main()`. Everything between the opening and closing braces is part of `main()`'s *function body*. Figure 2-5 summarizes this information.

The function named `main()` has very special meaning in C for several reasons. First, program execution always begins with the function named `main()`. No matter how many lines you see before or after the `main()` function definition, the program begins execution with the first program statement found in the function body of `main()`.

The second reason `main()` is special follows from the first reason. Every program must have a function named `main()`. This seems obvious. If program execution begins with `main()`, you must define a `main()` function somewhere in the program.

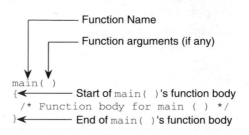

```
main( )
{ ◄──────── Start of main( )'s function body
    /* Function body for main ( ) */
} ◄──────── End of main( )'s function body
```
Function Name
Function arguments (if any)

Figure 2-5. Parts of a Function Definition

Note: In C, all variable and function names are case-sensitive. That is, if you define a function named Main(), or MAIN(), or maiN(), they are not the same as main(). Therefore, if you typed the main() function definition as Main(), or MAIN(), or maiN(), the program could not be run because no main() function exists from which to begin execution. Most C programmers prefer to use lowercase letters for function and variable names.

Statements in C

Now that you know something about functions, look at the single line that comprises main()'s function body.

```
printf("This is my first C program\n");
```

Notice that the line ends in a semicolon. In C, *all program statements end with a semicolon*. In more formal terms, a statement is a C instruction and usually consists of one or more expressions followed by a semicolon.

What Is *printf()*?

So what is printf()? As you might guess, printf() is a function used to print information on the screen. In the example, it prints out a string of characters that display the message, This is my first C program. A sequence of characters surrounded by double quotation marks is called a *string constant*. (Some programmers prefer the term *string literal*.) Programmers often refer to such string constants with the single word *string*.

The Newline Character

What are the \n characters that appear near the end of the string? The compiler views these two characters as just one character, so the backslash immediately followed by a lowercase n is called the *newline character*. Whenever the C compiler sees a backslash in a string constant, the backslash is interpreted as an escape sequence indicating that the next character should be viewed in a special way. Escape sequences are used to gain access to special nonprinting characters. The \n, or newline character, causes whatever might follow this character to be printed on the next (new) line. (If you are familiar with BASIC, the newline character is much like a lone PRINT statement.)

Other common escape sequences are '\t', '\b', and '\f', which stand for the tab, backspace, and formfeed characters. You will discover other escape sequences later in the book.

Closer Inspection of *printf()*

Notice that printf() looks very similar in form to the first line of the main() function, as shown in Figure 2-6.

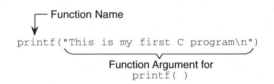

Figure 2-6. Elements of printf()

As you can see in Figure 2-6, the name of the function is printf(), and it has a single function argument in the form of a string constant (that is, the message to be displayed on the screen). The question now becomes, Where is the function body for printf()? To answer this question, we need to discuss something called the C standard library.

The C Standard Library

With the QC compiler, you get a large number of prewritten functions that can be used in your programs. One of these functions is named `printf()`. Now, place yourself in the compiler's shoes to see what it does when it finds one of these functions.

When the compiler examines your source code and sees the `printf()` statement, it makes a note to itself to keep an eye out for a definition for `printf()`. Simply stated, because the compiler cannot find the source code for `printf()` in the program in Listing 2-1, the compiler leaves a message that states in effect, "I cannot find the `printf()` code in the program, so it's up to someone else to find the missing code for `printf()`."

The result of the compiler's compiling the program is a disk file called an *object file*. For the QC compiler, object files end in .obj. That is, if the source code program is called TEST.C, QC produces an object file named TEST.OBJ.

Finally, a different program called a *linker* is run, using the object file as its input. When the .obj file is inspected by the linker, the linker finds the messages from the compiler about the missing source code for `printf()` and looks through the standard C libraries for the missing functions. Because `printf()` is part of the standard library, the linker takes the `printf()` code from the standard library files and shoves it into the appropriate spot in your program. (A QC library file ends in .lib. Examples can be found in the LIB directory on your disk.) When the linker finishes putting all the pieces together, an executable program (*.exe) program results. The linker has extracted the missing code for `printf()` from the standard C library.

The QC standard library contains over 400 functions that are available to you for your programs. These functions are described in Appendix B of the *C for Yourself* book included with your compiler.

Think of it! You have over 400 minitasks already solved for you in the standard C library. Indeed, much of C programming involves little more than collecting the appropriate standard library functions together in the proper order to accomplish a given task.

The concept of writing reuseable functions is an incredibly efficient way to solve programming tasks. As you gain more experience writing C programs, you will begin to collect your own set of functions that can be used in other programs. The more C code you write, the easier subsequent programs become. As you progress through this book, I will point out various things you can do to make your functions more "reuseable."

Compiling Your First Program

Now that you know something about a C program, you can actually compile and run your first program. Although there are a number of ways to compile a program, perhaps the easiest to remember is to press the F5 key. The F5 key causes the compiler to compile and link the program if it has not already done so. When the compile-link process is finished successfully, the program is automatically run as part of the F5 command.

If the cursor is in the source window, touch the F5 key. Immediately a dialog box appears, giving you status information about the compile and link process. If the compile was successful (and it will be unless you made a typing error), the QC screen, as seen in Figure 2-1, disappears and the MS-DOS screen appears.

Your program runs and the message is displayed on the screen. After the program ends, QC displays the time the program took to execute, plus some other information (which you can ignore for now).

Notice that after the program is run and you press any key, the cursor returns to the source window. Press the F5 key again. This time, no compilation dialog box appears; the program simply runs again. The reason is that QC knows the program has already been compiled and no changes have been made to it. Therefore, there is no need to recompile it. If you added an empty line to the program and pressed F5, QC would recompile the program because something was changed in the program's source code (even though it was only the addition of an empty line).

Forcing a Program Bug

One good way to begin learning how to debug a program is to put a bug in the program and see what the compiler does with it. Move to the end of the line containing the `printf()` function and remove the semicolon at the end of the line. Now press the F5 key to recompile the program. (I assume that the program is named UNTITLED.C.)

In a few moments, an error window appears near the bottom of the screen with the message

```
untitled.c(6): error C2143: syntax error: missing ';' before '}'
```

Most error messages follow this format. Figure 2-7 identifies part of the error message.

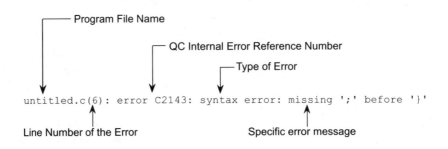

Figure 2-7. Format of QC Error Message.

Reading from left to right, you first find the name of the source file that contains the error. This is more useful than you might think. The reason is that you can write a program as a collection of a dozen or more source files and compile them at one time. Because the QC compiler zips through things pretty fast, knowing the source file on multiple compiles can be quite useful.

After the source file name comes the line number where the error occurred, surrounded by parentheses. The QC compiler's internal reference number for the error comes next. This is done because slightly different program errors may produce identical error messages. Knowing the internal reference number tells the Microsoft people exactly where in the compiler's parser the error message was generated. Normally this isn't very useful to you, unless things get so baffling that you are forced to call Microsoft for help.

In 99.9 percent of the cases, you can track the bug down by yourself. Robert Ward's book, *Debugging C* (no longer in print, but it can be ordered from *The C User's Journal*), offers a formal methodology for debugging any type of program. If, however, you do call Microsoft for help, you should gather as much information about the bug before calling. Indeed, you will find a more willing ear if you can reduce a program bug to a repeatable error that occurs in a program with a dozen or less lines of source code than if you simply tell them you have a bug "somewhere" in your 55K source file. Calling the compiler vendor about a bug should occur only if you are about to throw your computer out the window.

Next, the error message tells you the type of error that was found. Typically there are two flavors of errors: syntax and semantic. A *syntax error* occurs when your code fails to observe the rules of C, such as omitting a semicolon. A *semantic error* occurs when the code adheres to the rules of C, but the statement is being used out of context. For example, an English sentence has a noun and a verb. Consider the sentence, The cat barked. The sentence obeys the rules of English; it is syntactically correct because there is a noun and a verb. But, cats don't bark. There is a semantic error because either the noun or verb is being used out of context. Changing the sentence to either, "The cat mewed," or "The dog barked," removes the semantic error.

In the early stages of your programming experience, you will probably receive syntactic error messages from QC. As you gain experience, you will move on to bigger and better errors. Everyone does.

C Programming Style

When you debug C programs, you will find that the the debugging process can be made easier or more difficult depending on the C coding style used to write the program. Unlike some languages, C is not context sensitive. That is, it doesn't much care about the coding style that is used to write the program. For example, our sample program could be written

```
#include <stdio.h> main(){printf("This is my first C program\n");}
```

and the QC compiler will not complain at all. With such a simple program, coding style may not matter much. As program complexity increases, however, the style you use does impact on the testing-debugging cycle.

What follows are some suggestions about coding style. There is no "correct" C coding style. You need, however, to select a style and use it consistently. If you are involved with programmers who work as a group on a given project, you collectively must select one coding style for the entire group; it makes maintaining the program much easier down the road.

Braces

As we saw in Listing 2-1, braces mark the start and end of a function body. When defining the limits of a function body, almost every C programmer uses the style shown in Listing 2-1. That is, the opening brace for the function body is flush with the leftmost edge of the source window. The closing brace for the function body is also flush with the left edge of the source window.

Certain C keywords are often used with braces. Without discussing these keywords at this point, I can show the style that might be used. For the time being, I let dots represent the missing details that are to be covered in later chapters.

Braces, Multiple Statements, and Indentation

One form of C loop structure is the `for` loop. As you saw earlier in this chapter, C statements end with a semicolon. If you wish to have a `for` loop control more than one statement, you must use braces to group the statements into a *statement block*. The style used in this book for the placement of braces in a `for` statement block is

```
for (...) {
   .
   /* Multiple C statement here */
   .
}
```

Notice that the opening brace for the statement block is on the same line as the `for` statement, and the closing brace is aligned with the f in the keyword `for`. The statements contained within the `for` statement block are indented one tab stop. Because we have set the QC tab stops to three spaces, each statement within the statement block is indented three spaces.

Some programmers prefer the following style:

```
for (...)
{
   /   .
   /* Multiple C statement here */
   .
}
```

The only difference is that the opening brace for the statement block appears below the `for` keyword rather than on the same line. This style is consistent with the style used for function definitions. However, it restricts the amount of code you can view in the source window at one time because of the extra line this style uses. The statements within the statement block are still indented one tab stop with this style, too.

The style you select for the placement of braces is not that important. What is important is that you select a style and use it consistently.

Multiple Levels of Indentation

Obviously, you will have `for` loops defined within functions later on as you gain experience. The following example shows how multiple levels of indentation might be written.

```
main()
{
    .

    for (...) {
        .
      for (...) {
            .
          /* Statements for innermost for loop */
            .
      }              /* End of innermost for statement block  */
            .
    }                /* End of outermost for statement block  */
}                    /* End of main() function block          */
```

Notice how the first `for` loop is indented one tab stop within the `main()` function body. The second `for` loop is indented two tab stops within the `main()` function body (that is, one tab stop more than the first `for` loop). Now you can see why I changed from eight spaces per tab stop to three spaces. With eight spaces per tab, the source lines soon overshoot the right edge of the source window. Although the QC editor scrolls to the right as you type in a long line, you lose visual contact with those statements near the left edge of the source window. Other program editors fold the text to the line below when the right edge is reached. In either case, a partially visible or folded source code line is more difficult to read than one that is not folded.

As a general rule, you should indent one tab stop for the statements that appear in a new function or statement block.

Programming Style and Variable Names

C syntax rules allow you to use upper- and lowercase letters, digit characters, and the underscore character in a function or variable name. However, a variable or function name cannot begin with a digit character. Also, only the first 31 characters of a variable or function name are considered significant. Variables may have more than 31 characters, but they must be distinguishable (that is, unique) within the first 31 characters. Otherwise you will receive a `variable multiply defined` error message.

Another rule is that a variable name cannot be the same as a C keyword. This is probably obvious to those of you who have programming experience, but it is a common source of confusion for beginning C programmers who do not know the C keywords. Therefore, the following list presents the C keywords for the QC compiler; these should not be used as variable or function names.

auto	enum	near	union
break	extern	pascal	unsigned
case	far	register	void
cdecl	float	return	volatile
char	for	short	while
const	fortran	signed	_fastcall
continue	goto	sizeof	_export
default	huge	static	_loadds
do	if	struct	_saveregs
double	int	switch	
else	long	typedef	

NOTE: In the strict ANSI C definition, the keywords: cdecl, far, fortran, huge, near, pascal, _fastcall, _export, _loadds, and _saveregs are not true keywords, but have been added to the QC compiler by Microsoft. Therefore, these keywords may not be available with other compilers.

With the naming rules presented thus far, valid variable or function names might be

room_size port123 Alpha _secret

Examples of variable or function names that are not legal might be

8_levels @cost -discount default

The first three names are not legal beause the first character in each example violates the rules for variable and function names. The last example (that is, default) is not legal because it is a C keyword.

Another potential naming problem occurs when you decide to name a variable the same name as that of an existing standard C library function. For example, `printf()` is a standard C library function. If you try to create a variable by the same name, a conflict arises. With over 400 QC library functions available, it is not practical to list all of the function names here.

If you do define a variable using the name of a library function and then try to call the function, the compiler tells you that the variable "is not a function." Therefore, if you define a variable named `printf` and then try to print a message using the function `printf()`, the compiler says, "printf is not a function." That's your clue that you have selected a variable name that collides with a standard library function name. Obviously, you need to change the variable name.

If you happen to use a variable name that is a name for a standard C library function but do not call the function in the program, the program compiles without problem. Only when you try to use the same name in a different context (for example, use it as a variable and then call it as a function) does the compiler call attention to the error.

Aside from the rules mentioned previously, you are free to name variables and functions as you wish. However, C programmers follow certain style conventions. First, variable and function names usually use only lowercase letters. Many dialects of BASIC force you to use uppercase letters. If you are familiar with Pascal, you have seen variables named using the style

`DirectPortAddress`

where capital letters are used to make the variable name easier to read. Because C programmers avoid uppercase letters in variable names, the same variable name in C would be written

`direct_port_address`

where the underscore character makes the variable name more readable.

A second style consideration is that only symbolic constants are written in uppercase letters. As the book progresses, I discuss what a symbolic constant is. At this point, however, you might look in the `stdio.h` header file and see the following examples of symbolic constants:

`BUFSIZ    EOF    SEEK_END    FILENAME_MAX`

As you might expect, symbolic constants in C are often used to give a name to some magic number or limit used in a program. I mention them here to discourage you from using uppercase letters in your programs.

(By the way, you can view a header file from within the QC editor by selecting the View option from the Menu Bar. Now select the Include option from the View submenu. When you are asked to type the name of the header file, make sure you supply the full path name, too (for example, c:\qc\include\stdio.h). If the program currently in the source window has not been modified since it was last saved, the `stdio.h` header file appears in the source window. If the file in the source window is not up to date, you are asked whether it should be saved before the `stdio.h` header file is displayed in the source window.)

If you place the cursor on the header file name in the source window and select the View-Include option, the header file is automatically loaded into the source window. This is a much faster way to view a header file because you do not have to type the path and file name.

A third style convention concerns the use of the underscore (_) character. The most common use of the underscore character in variable and function names is to make a variable name more readable by giving the illusion of spacing within the variable name.

There is a second stylistic use of the underscore character as well. Prior to the ANSI standard for C, vendors often created special variables for use in your program that were an integral part of their compiler. The vendor had to be careful when selecting names for these variables to avoid conflict with variable names the programmers might use in their own programs. Over the years, programmers and vendors reached a *de facto* agreement whereby variables used by the compiler vendor would always start with a leading underscore character. Because the programmers were aware of this vendor naming convention for variables, they avoided using a leading underscore character in a variable or function name.

Although the ANSI standard has reduced the need for "vendor variables," most C programmers still sparingly use a leading underscore in a variable or function name. For now, I encourage you to avoid using the underscore as the first character in a variable or function name. (I explain potential uses for a leading underscore character in a variable name later in the book when I talk about scope rules and data privacy.)

Conclusion

In this chapter, I have covered how to use the QC compiler and some of its editing commands. You have also seen how functions are defined and what their major parts are. Finally, you know the rules and conventions for naming variables and functions, plus some of the conventions and styles used by C programmers. With this information under your belt, you can start learning C in earnest.

3

Basic Data Types

This chapter covers the following topics:

The basic data types provided by C

The definition of a data item for use in a program

The concepts of `lvalues` and `rvalues`

The distinction between the C terms `define` and `declare`

Modifiers for the basic data types

Expressions, operators, and operands

Operator precedence

Introduction to the QC Debugger

The material in this chapter is crucial to your understanding of more advanced topics in C. Take your time and experiment; this chapter is the foundation on which everything else in C is built.

C Basic Data Types

C offers a wide range of data types that may be used in your program. These basic data types and their range of values are presented in Table 3-1.

Table 3-1. QC Basic Data Types

Data Type	Permissible Range of Values
char	-127 – 127
int	-32,767 – 32,767
float	1.175e-38 – 3.4e+38
double	2.225e-308 – 1.797e+308

The formal term for data types (as shown in Table 3-1) is *type specifier*. A type specifier is a C keyword used to define a data item. As you will see in later chapters, you can build additional data types from the list presented in Table 3-1. For the moment, however, let's examine those presented in Table 3-1.

char

The QC compiler uses eight bits (one byte) to store the char data type. Because each bit may be either on (that is, 1) or off (that is, 0), there are 256 bit combinations possible (that is, 2 raised to the 8th power). The QC compiler, however, uses the high bit (that is, bit seven) as a sign bit. As a result, a char has a range of plus or minus 127.

As an aside, some programmers pronounce char to rhyme with "char," as in "to char a steak." Other programmers pronounce char to rhyme with "care" (as in character). Personally, I think "care" is more pleasing to the ear than "char," but both are widely used.

int

As you might guess, int is the C keyword for the integer data type. On the QC compiler, an int uses two bytes (16 bits) for storage. Because an int may assume either positive or negative value, only 15 bits are used for the value. The 16th bit is the sign bit. Therefore, the range of values for an int corresponds to plus or minus 2 raised to the 15th power.

The actual size of an integer data type in C depends on what is "natural" for the host machine. Because PC-type machines may use 16-bit registers for data, that is the natural size of an `int`. On other machines where 32-bit registers are the norm (for example, the Macintosh), an `int` may require 32 bits for storage. Be aware, therefore, that for an `int` to use 16 bits in all environments is not cast in stone. Realizing this may make porting a program to a different machine somewhat easier.

float

A `float` data type is used to store floating point numbers (for example, numbers with a decimal fraction, like 3.14). The storage required for each `float` is four bytes. Whereas the range of values for a `float` is fairly large, the precision (for example, the number of useful digits) is limited to six digits.

double

The `double` data type is also used for floating point numbers, but requires eight bytes for storage. Because of its greater storage requirements, a `double` has 15 digits of precision.

Although the ANSI standard now permits true `float` math operations, QC (and most C compilers) performs all math operations (for example, addition, subtraction, etc.) using double-precision math. This means that, although you might define a data type to be a `float`, if you perform a math operation on the data item, the compiler generates code to promote the `float` to a `double`, performs the math operation, and then generates code to demote the result back to a `float`. Obviously, the code to perform the promotion-demotion of a `float` consumes code space and time. Therefore, most C programmers prefer using the `double` data type in programs that perform many floating point calculations.

(Release 2.5 of QC allows functions to return a `float` data type; that was not possible with earlier releases. Release 2.5 also supports a `long double`, which is an 80-bit value.)

Epsilon

Because the QC compiler stores floating point numbers as binary values in memory, some floating point numbers cannot be represented with exact precision (for example, one-third). There is a potential danger, then, when comparing two floating point values. The magnitude of this potential error is called the *epsilon* value.

#define and Epsilon

The epsilon value is the smallest number that, when added to 1.0, can be distinguished from the value 1.0. For example, in the float.h header file, we see the following curious line:

```
#define FLT_EPSILON   1.192092896e-07
```

The #define is another preprocessor directive that defines the word FLT_EPSILON to have the same meaning as 1.192092896e-07. Therefore, whenever the preprocessor sees the word FLT_EPSILON in a program, it replaces that word with the characters 1.192092896e-07, so the #define preprocessor directive causes a *textual substitution* of FLT_EPSILON with the ASCII characters 1.192092896e-07. This is an example of a *symbolic constant* to which I referred in Chapter 2.

Note that symbolic constants are normally specified in uppercase letters. If you #include the file named float.h in your programs, use the symbolic FLT_EPSILON to represent the characters 1.192092896e-07. When the program is compiled, QC changes the character digits 1.192092896e-07 into a floating point number with that value.

The interpretation of FLT_EPSILON is that, if you take the value 1.0 and add 1.192092896e-07 to it, the compiler knows that the value is no longer 1.0, but something slightly larger that 1.0. On the other hand, if you add something smaller than FLT_EPSILON to 1.0, the compiler cannot distinguish the result from 1.0. Therefore

```
x = 1.0 + 1.192092896e-07
```

results in a value for x that QC recognizes as being greater than 1.0. On the other hand,

```
x = 1.0 + 1.192092896e-08
```

produces a result for x that appears to be the same as 1.0. (Note that I changed the size of the exponent.) The epsilon value for a double is significantly smaller (that is, about 2.22e-16).

Every compiler that uses a binary representation for floating point numbers has an epsilon value. The ANSI C standard defines the name of epsilon in a header file. In most situations, the "epsilon factor" is not a problem. If, however, a test on two floating point numbers seems to behave strangely, you may want to see whether an epsilon error is the cause.

Defining a Data Item in a C Program

Unlike BASIC (in which undefined data items default to a double-precision floating point value), C requires that you define a data item before you can use it. The formal syntax rule for defining a simple data item is

```
type-specifier variable_name;
```

That is, a data definition in C can be one of the type specifiers, shown in Table 3-1, followed by a variable name. Using this format, you might define an integer variable named num as

```
int num;
```

Now put this data definition in the context of a program. Start the QC compiler and type the program shown in Listing 3-1.

Listing 3-1. A C Program Using an Integer Value

```
#include <stdio.h>

main()
{
    int i;                 /* Data definition for i */

    i = 10;
    printf("i = %d\n", i);

}
```

Most of the program in Listing 3-1 looks familiar. Because a data definition must occur before you can use a data item, such definitions normally appear at the top of the function in which they are used. In Listing 3-1, the data definition for i appears near the top of main()'s function body.

After typing the program, press the F5 key to compile it. In a few moments, the program is compiled and the value of i is displayed on the screen. Now that the program is working, step back a moment and examine the program from the compiler's point of view.

The Compiler's View of Listing 3-1

The first thing that happens to your source code is that the preprocessor takes the contents of the stdio.h header file and stuffs it into the top of the program. Next, the compiler reads the variable name main() and, not seeing a semicolon at the end of main(), "knows" that there is more in this statement than just the name main(). When it sees the opening brace, it knows you are defining a function named main(). The compiler "breathes a sigh of relief" because it knows it had better find a main() somewhere or the program won't work.

The next thing the compiler sees is the line

```
int i;
```

The compiler must perform a number of things before it can go on. First, when the compiler sees the keyword int followed by a variable name and a semicolon, it knows that you want to define an integer variable named i. Once it knows this, it asks itself, "Can I do what is being asked?" The order in which it answers all of the parts of the question is not important, but you should be aware of all that it does.

First, the compiler checks to see whether you already have a variable named i defined in the program. The compiler performs this by checking an internal table (called a *symbol table*) that contains a list of previously-defined variables. If no other variable named i is defined, the compiler proceeds to the next step. If the search of the symbol table does find another i, QC displays an error message similar to

```
prog3-1.c : error C2086: 'i' : redefinition
```

This tells you that you have attempted to redefine the variable named i in the program named PROG3-1.C. Renaming one of the i variables should clear up the problem.

Assuming that you don't have multiple definitions for the variable i, the compiler now knows that it is safe to try to create a variable named i. It asks the MS-DOS operating system for enough storage space to hold an integer variable. As you learned earlier in this chapter, an int requires two bytes of storage. If QC cannot get enough storage space, it issues an out of memory message. You probably won't see such a message for most programs. Assuming some spare memory is available, MS-DOS gives QC a memory address where i can be stored.

So far, so good. The compiler creates an entry in the symbol table for variable i. To simplify things, view the symbol table entry as just two things: 1) the name of the variable (i); and 2) the memory address where the variable is stored. Now that i exists for use in the program, you can use it in your program.

The Proper Meaning of Data Definition

Now you are in a position to understand the proper use of the term *data definition*. The critical aspect that sets a data definition apart from a data declaration in C is

A data definition causes storage to be allocated for that data item.

Although we are not in a position to discuss fully the meaning of the term *data declaration*, the key distinction is

A declaration does not cause any storage to be allocated for the data item.

I flesh out the distinction between a data definition and data declaration in later chapters. It is important now, however, that you understand that data items must be defined (that is, have storage in memory for them) before you can use them in a program.

lvalues and *rvalues*

As we just saw, after the compiler finishes creating the storage allocation for variable i in Listing 3-1, a memory address is tied to variable i. Any time you use variable i in your program, the memory address of i is used to locate it. View this on the diagram shown in Figure 3-1. In Figure 3-1, I assume that the memory address for i is at location 50,000.

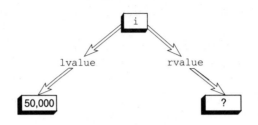

Figure 3-1. lvalue *and* rvalue *for* i

By the time the compiler finishes the line

```
int i;
```

the diagram in Figure 3-1 depicts the status of variable i as it looks in memory. Referring to Figure 3-1

An lvalue is the memory address for a data item.

The lvalue is considered the "left value" in Figure 3-1. On the other hand,

An rvalue is what is stored at an lvalue.

In other words, the rvalue (right value) is the contents of variable i as stored at memory location 50,000. However, because C does not initialize variables such as i in Listing 3-1, you have no idea what the value of i is. The rvalue of i is whatever random bit pattern happens to exist in memory at location 50,000 when the program starts to execute.

Now, consider what happens when the line

```
i = 10;
```

is executed. In this case, the diagram changes to that shown in Figure 3-2.

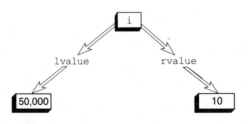

Figure 3-2. lvalue *and* rvalue *for* i

Note that, because we have assigned the value of 10 into i, the rvalue in Figure 3-2 has changed to the value of 10. Stated more formally, variable i still has an lvalue of 50,000 but has a known rvalue of 10.

Printing Numbers with *printf()*

The final line in the program

```
printf("i = %d\n", i);
```

looks a bit strange, perhaps, but it will all make sense in a moment. The percent sign (%) in a double-quoted string has special meaning to printf(). Specifically, the percent sign is a signal to the compiler that a *conversion character* follows the percent sign. The percent sign serves as an alert and tells printf(): "Get ready to print a data item on the screen." Table 3-2 presents a list of common conversion characters used in printf().

Table 3-2. printf() Conversion Characters (Partial List)

Conversion Character	Used to Print
Numeric Conversions:	
d, i	Signed decimal integer
ld	Signed long decimal integer
u	Unsigned decimal integer
o	Unsigned octal integer
x	Unsigned hexadecimal integer
e	Signed floating point numbers (scientific notation)
f	Signed decimal for floating point numbers
g	Signed floating point numbers (The shorter of %e or %f)
Character Conversions:	
c	Character
s	String

From Table 3-2, you can see that %d tells `printf()` to print a signed decimal integer. Table 3-2 also suggests that `printf()` can do much more than just print a string constant on the screen. Actually, there are two possible arguments in a `printf()` function call:

```
printf(control_string, data_items);
```

where the control string is a double-quoted string of characters that may include conversion characters. In Listing 2-1 in Chapter 2, only the control string was present (for example, "This is my first C program\n"). In Listing 3-1, we used one conversion character in the control string, so there is one data item in the data list. If we modified the call to `printf()` in Listing 3-1 to be

```
printf("i = %d, i = %x", i, i);
```

`printf()` would display

```
i = 10, i = a
```

showing the `rvalue` of `i` in both decimal and hexidecimal numbering systems. The conversion characters in the control string must match the list of data items that follow the control string, as seen in Figure 3-3.

Clearly, you can get into trouble with `printf()` if you have more conversion characters in the control string than there are data items in the data list.

Another possible mishap with `printf()` is to use the wrong conversion character with a data item. Try changing the x conversion character shown in Figure 3-3 to an s. Now `printf()` will try to print `i` as though it were a string of characters rather than a numeric variable. When I ran the program, the output was i = 10 for the first part of the `printf()` output, which is correct. However, the second conversion character produced a copyright message for the second "value" of `i`. Your results will likely be different, but still incorrect.

Type Qualifiers

In addition to the basic data types shown in Table 3-1, four type qualifiers exist and can be used to modify a basic data type. These type qualifiers are `long`, `short`, `signed`, and `unsigned`. Now you can fill in additional data types using the type qualifiers shown in Table 3-3.

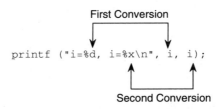

Figure 3-3. Conversion Character and Data List Matching

Table 3-3. QC Basic Data Types

Data Type	Permissible Range of Values
char, signed char	-127 – 127
unsigned char	0 – 255

int,
    short
    short int
    signed short int
	-32,767 – 32,767

long long int	2,147,483,647 – 2,147,483,647
unsigned long unsigned long int	0 – 4,294,967,295

unsigned
    unsigned int
    unsigned short
    unsigned short int
	0 – 65,535

float	1.175e-38 – 3.4e+38
double long double	2.225e-308 – 1.797e+308

When you read Table 3-3, notice that different keywords may be used to refer to the same data type. For example, the following data definitions

```
int i;
short i;
short int i;
signed short int i;
```

all create a variable named i that would take two bytes of storage and be capable of storing values between plus and minus 32,767. Likewise, a definition using char and signed char creates the same type of variable. Therefore, the indented type qualifiers and type specifiers are synonyms for each other. The only real exception is long double. A long double requires 10 bytes for storage versus eight for a "plain" double. However, precision rises from 15 to 19 digits when a long double is used.

char versus *unsigned char*

The American Standard Code for Information Interchange (ASCII) character set uses the values from 0 through 127. The ASCII characters between these limits include all of the normal printing characters you would expect to find on a standard Input/Output (I/O) device, such as a printer. Because an ASCII character must fall within these limits, only the lower seven bits of a byte are needed for an ASCII character. (See Appendix A for the ASCII character set.)

The IBM-PC, however, uses the remaining values (128 through 255) for special characters. These special characters form a combination of foreign characters, math symbols, and graphics characters and are often referred to as the *extended character set*. You may use the extended character set in your program in much the same way as you would the standard ASCII character set. At present, however, I limit the discussion to the ASCII character set.

One more comment: The extended character set most likely will not work in another environment. If your QC program uses the extended character set and you attempt to move that program to the Macintosh or to a UNIX machine, the probability that the extended characters will be the same for any other machine is virtually zero. In other words, the extended character set is not portable among machines. The ASCII character set is portable in most cases. (Character sets other than ASCII are used on mainframe machines and in foreign countries.)

If you wish to confirm the storage requirements and ranges for many of the data types shown in Table 3-3, you might inspect the `limits.h` and `float.h` header files that are supplied with the QC compiler. (If you have a standard installation on a hard disk, `limits.h` may be found in the INCLUDE subdirectory.)

Expressions, Operators, Operands, and Precedence

Before going too much deeper into C, I need to expand your understanding of how a C statement is constructed. I stated earlier that C statements end in a semicolon. I also stated that a statement was built up from C expressions. All right, so what is an expression?

An *expression* is any combination of operands and operators that yield a single value.

Hmmm, this seems to beg the question. What are operands and operators?

An *operand* is the value associated with a variable or a constant.

An *operator* is a symbol that causes some action to be performed on one or more operands. Common examples of operands are + for addition, – for subtraction, * for multiplication, and / for division.

Using the definitions presented previously, consider the following list of expressions.

```
a + b
i - 10
m + j / 5
a * b * i / 10
```

In the first line, variables `a` and `b` are the operands and + is the operator. Most operators in C are *binary operators*, so called because they require two operands to complete the expression. Other operators require only one operand (unary operators); one operator requires three operands (ternary operator). I discuss all of the operators in due course. For now, I concentrate on the binary operators.

If you take the list of expressions presented previously and add a semicolon at the end,

```
k / 5;
a + b;
i - 10;
m + j / 5;
a * b * i / 10;
```

they become C statements. Not very useful statements, but C statements nonetheless. To make such statements more useful (and more typical of what we would find in a C program), you might change them as follows:

```
m = k / 5;
c = a + b;
j = i - 10;
n = m + j / 5;
k = a * b * i / 10;
```

They become more useful because a new variable holds the final result of the expression. To see how operators and operands work, consider the example

```
n = m + j / 5;
```

Suppose that j equals 100 and m equals 10. Substituting the appropriate values, we find

```
n = 10 + 100 / 5;
```

The question now becomes, What is the value of n? If you add 10 and 100 to get 110 and then divide by 5, the result is 22. If you divide 100 by 5 first and then add 10, you get 30. Which answer is correct?

Precedence of Operators

To derive the correct result from your sample expression, you must know the order in which expressions are evaluated by the compiler. In C, the rules that determine this order of expression evaluation are called *precedence* rules for operators. I present the complete list here, although you are not yet ready for me to discuss all of them fully. In the table, the column marked "Associates" refers to the "direction" in which the compiler evaluates the expression. (I have also placed a short interpretation comment in parentheses after each of the operators.)

Table 3-4. Precedence Rules

Operators	Precedence Level	Associates
() (parentheses) [ ] (brackets) → (arrow) . (dot)	1	Left to right
! (NOT) ~ (one's complement) ++ (increment) -- (decrement) + (unary plus) – (unary minus) * (indirection) & (address of) (cast) sizeof (size)	2	Right to left
* (multiply) / (divide) % (modulus)	3	Left to right
+ (add) – (subtract)	4	Left to right
<< (shift left) >> (shift right)	5	Left to right
< (less than) <= (less than or equal to) > (greater than) >= (greater than or equal to)	6	Left to right
== (equal to) != (not equal to)	7	Left to right

Table 3-4 continues

Table 3-4. Precedence Rules (continued)

Operators	Precedence Level	Associates
& (bitwise AND)	8	Left to right
^ (bitwise exclusive OR)	9	Left to right
| (bitwise OR)	10	Left to right
&& (logical AND)	11	Left to right
|| (logical OR)	12	Left to right
?: (ternary)	13	Right to left
= (assignment) += (add-assign) −= (subtract-assign) *= (multiply-assign) /= (divide-assign) %= (modulus-assign) &= (AND-assign) ^= (EOR-assign) |= (OR-assign) <<= (shift-left-assign) >>= (shift-right-assign)	14	Right to left
, (comma)	15	Left to right

If you examine the list of precedence levels, you can see that parentheses have the highest level of precedence, whereas the comma operator has the lowest.

Looking back to our original sample expression

```
n = 10 + 100 / 5;
```

From the precedence table, you can see that the division operator (/) has a higher precedence than does the addition operator (+). We can also see that addition has a higher precedence than does the assignment operator (=). The compiler breaks the expression down in steps (that is, subexpressions) similar to the following sequence:

```
n = 10 + 100 / 5;
n = 10 + 20;
n = 30;
```

You can see that the precedence rules mean that the correct answer for n must be 30. If you wanted the answer to be 22, you would have to rewrite the expression as

```
n = (10 + 100) / 5;
```

Because parentheses have higher precedence than do the other operators, the steps now become

```
n = (10 + 100) / 5;
n = 110 / 5;
n = 22;
```

Take a few moments to review Table 3-4. In fact, you may want to dog-ear this page — you will probably be using it often later on.

A Program Using Three Variables

Now that you understand something about how the compiler evaluates expressions, you can expand the original program to include three variables rather than one. The program is presented in Listing 3-2.

Listing 3-2. Program Using Three Integer Variables

```
#include <stdio.h>

main()
{
    int i, j, k;

    i = 10;
    j = 15;
    k = i + j;
    printf("The sum of %d and %d is %d\n", i, j, k);

}
```

As simple as this program is, you can learn several things from it.

Comma Operator

The first thing you see in `main()` is the statement

```
int i, j, k;
```

In this statement, you define variables i, j, and k. Because the statement contains multiple data definitions, enough storage is allocated for each variable to hold one integer value. Note that you could accomplish the same result with the statements

```
int i;
int j;
int k;
```

However, C programmers rarely write such multiple definition statements for the same data type. Instead, the comma operator is used to separate each variable's data definition.

After the program finishes processing the data definitions for i, j, and k, each variable has its own entry in the compiler's symbol table. A diagram for this is shown in Figure 3-4.

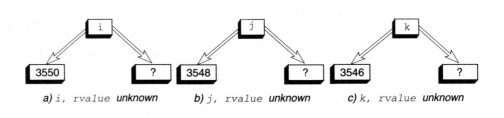

a) i, rvalue *unknown*   b) j, rvalue *unknown*   c) k, rvalue *unknown*

Figure 3-4. Diagram of Listing 3-2 After Data Definitions

Each variable has a memory address (`lvalue`) where it is stored. Because an integer takes two bytes of storage, each `lvalue` shows as two bytes less than the one defined before it. This "back-to-back" storage scheme may not always occur, but it reflects how QC goes about requesting storage for integer variables like those shown in Listing 3-2.

When the second line of the program in Listing 3-2 is processed by the compiler, the diagram changes to look like that shown in Figure 3-5.

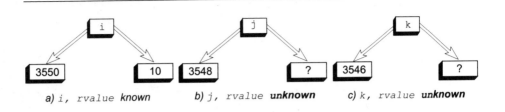

Figure 3-5. Diagram of Listing 3-2 After Assignment of i

Notice that the rvalue of i now has a known value. If you recall, question marks were used after the data definitions in Figure 3-4 because you did not know what was stored at each variable's rvalue. The rvalues were whatever random bit patterns existed at those memory locations when the program started. In Figure 3-5, i has been initialized so its rvalue is now known.

After the assignment statement for j, the diagram looks like that shown in Figure 3-6.

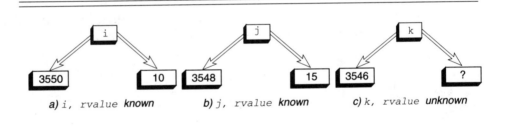

Figure 3-6. Diagram of Listing 3-2 After Assignment of j

Adding the values of i and j together and assigning the result into k produces the results shown in Figure 3-7.

Another thing to notice is that the assignment operator assumes that the operands are rvalues. That is, this operator takes the rvalue of i, adds it to the rvalue of j, and places the result into the rvalue for k. Therefore, you can conclude that

The default object manipulated with an operator is the rvalue of the operand(s).

As simple and obvious as this concept seems, understanding it makes the study of some of C's advanced topics a piece of cake. Study the step-by-step sequence shown in Figures 3-4 through 3-7 until you are confident that you understand them completely.

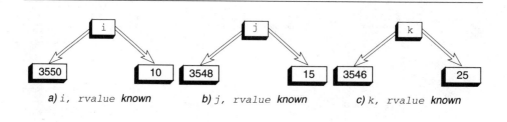

a) i, *rvalue* **known**   b) j, *rvalue* **known**   c) k, *rvalue* **known**

Figure 3-7. Diagram of Listing 3-2 After Assignment of k

Using the QC Debugger to Inspect *lvalues* and *rvalues*

In a moment, you will use the program presented in Listing 3-2 as part of your introduction to the QC debugger. But first, learn about the operator that allows access to the address of a variable.

Address-of Operator (*&*)

The *address-of* operator is a unary operator which acts on a variable as its operand. The symbol for the address-of operator is the ampersand (&). When using the address-of operator, the ampersand precedes the variable, as in

&i

When the compiler evaluates this expression, the result is the lvalue of i. Use this information to inspect the lvalues of the integer variables in Listing 3-2.

Suppose that you wish to observe variable i as the program executes. To do this, activate the Debug option from the Menu Bar (Alt-D). If you have the full menus option on (that is, from the Options menu), you see a submenu similar to that shown in Figure 3-8.

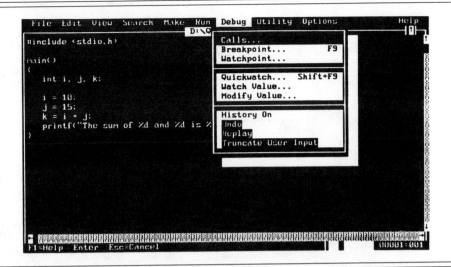

```
File  Edit  View  Search  Make  Run  Debug  Utility  Options           Help
                              D:\Q                                    ┤█├
#include <stdio.h>                    Calls...
                                      Breakpoint...         F9
main()                                Watchpoint...
{
    int i, j, k;                      Quickwatch...    Shift+F9
                                      Watch Value...
    i = 10;                           Modify Value...
    j = 15;
    k = i + j;                        History On
    printf("The sum of %d and %d is % Undo
}                                     Replay
                                      Truncate User Input




F1=Help  Enter  Esc=Cancel                                   00001:001
```

Figure 3-8. The Debug Submenu

To watch several values associated with i, select the Watch Value option from the submenu by using either the arrow keys to highlight and select it or by pressing the W key.

After you select the Watch Value option, a dialog box opens up and the cursor waits for you to type an expression. (See Figure 3-9.)

Now, type

```
&i
```

and press Enter. Notice that a new window, titled DEBUG, appears near the top of the screen. In the window, you see:

```
&i ' <Unknown identifier>
```

This is as it should be. After all, how can the compiler know about i when it has not even built its symbol table yet?

Now, select the Debug-Watch-Value option again and type

```
i
```

for the expression and press return. Now you see

```
&i ' <Unknown identifier>
i ' <Unknown identifier>
```

displayed in the DEBUG window. Again, this makes sense. If it does not know the lvalue of i (&i), how can we expect it to know its rvalue?

57

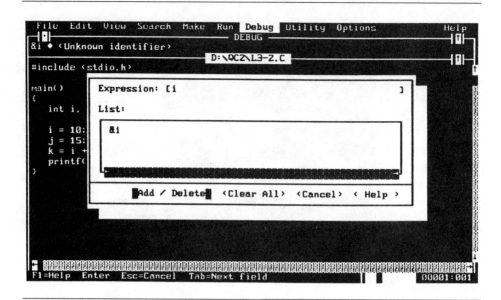

Figure 3-9. Setting a Watch Value

Single-Stepping the Program

After your watch values are set in the DEBUG window, you are ready to run the debugger. Because this is a very short program, things would happen too quickly for you to get a feel for what's going on if you let it run at full speed. Therefore, execute the program one line at a time, with a pause before the next line is executed. You can run a program in such a fashion by *single-stepping* the program.

To run a QC program in single-step mode, press the F10 key once. (I assume the program was compiled earlier.) Watch the screen closely to see QC flip quickly to the DOS window and then return immediately to the source code window. A highlight bar extends across the screen at the point of the opening brace for main().

Note that nothing in the DEBUG window has changed, except that the title of DEBUG now has the word main after it. This is because execution is taking place in the main() function.

Press F10 again. The highlight bar drops down to the assignment statement for i. Note that this also means that the compiler has processed the definitions for i, j, and k. How can you be sure that the definitions were processed? If you look back in the DEBUG window, you see something similar to

```
&i = 0x4d06:0x0dde
i = 41
```

Because the compiler has allocated storage for variable i, the compiler must have an address where i exists in memory. The (unary) address-of operator with i as its operand evaluates to memory segment 0x4d06, offset 0x0dde. (Hexadecimal numbers always begin with 0x in C.) The values you find for the segment:offset memory address will probably be different than those shown here.

Notice also that the rvalue of i automatically becomes known once the address of i is known. After all, address 0x4d06:0x0dde must have two bytes of memory. Therefore, whatever bit pattern existed when the allocation was made is the rvalue for i. When I ran the program, I just happened to get the value 41. The value you see will probably be different.

Now press F10 again. The highlight bar drops to the next line and the DEBUG window shows

```
&i = 0x4d06:0x0dde
i = 10
```

Because you just finished executing the assignment statement into i, it now has the proper value of 10. Continue pressing the F10 key to keep marching down through the program one line at a time. If you press the F10 key one more time after reaching the closing brace for main(), QC switches to the MS-DOS window and shows you the output of the program. Press any key, and control returns to the source code window.

Notice that what you see using the debugger agrees perfectly with the earlier discussion of Figure 3-5. That is, a data definition produces an lvalue, but an unknown (that is, garbage), rvalue.

Move Between Windows — F6

If you press the F6 key, the cursor moves from the source code window to the DEBUG window. If you press F6 again, the cursor moves back to the source code window. Try flipping between the two windows a few times. Big deal, right?

Format Conversions

Actually, being able to move between windows is quite useful. For example, move to the &i expression. Use the arrow keys to move just past the &i expression and touch the comma and D keys. Doing this correctly modifies the line to look like

```
&i,d = <Unknown identifier>
```

Now run the program using the F10 key. After the data definition statement was executed, my output looked like

```
&i,d = 3550
i = 41
```

The lvalue of i is now shown as 3550. Actually, 0xdde in hex is 3550 in decimal. In other words, you can use the F6 key to move the DEBUG window and modify things in it. In this case, you told the debugger to use the decimal mode for presenting the memory address (lvalue) of i. Note that QC shortens this address to just the offset for the variable. If you need segment information, stick to the (default) hex format for address-of information.

The d after the variable name and the comma is called a *format specifier*. The QC debugger recognizes most of the printf() conversion characters discussed in Chapter 2 as format specifiers (for example, d, o, x, u, f, e, g, c, and s plus others). These format specifiers let you examine the data in a manner that is most convenient for your needs without having to perform base conversions.

Closing the Debug Window

There are several ways to close the DEBUG window. One method is to select the Debug-Watch Value option and then use the Tab key to move to the <Clear All> field and press the Enter key. This removes the DEBUG window.

A second method uses the F6 key to move to the DEBUG window and the Alt-V keystroke combination to activate the View option from the Menu Bar. The last option in the View submenu is called Windows. Press the W key to select Windows. A dialog box appears with the following list, with the first entry in the list (Current) highlighted. If you press Enter, the dialog box and the DEBUG window disappear.

Perhaps the easiest way to close the DEBUG window is to use the F6 key to move to the DEBUG window and then press Ctrl-F4. This closes any window you might see except for the source window, which cannot be closed.

At this point, you might try adding the address-of operators for j and k and experiment using the debugger options explained in this section of the chapter. I cover some of its other features in later chapters.

Potential Problems with Integer Data

Now you can modify the values in Listing 3-2 to those shown in Listing 3-3.

Listing 3-3. Problem Area for Integer Data

```
#include <stdio.h>

main()
{
    int i, j, k;

    i = 250;
    j = 250;
    k = i * j;
    printf("The product of %d and %d is %d\n", i, j, k);
}
```

When this program is run, the output becomes

```
The product of 250 and 250 is -3036
```

Clearly, something is incorrect. When I square 250, the correct answer should be 62,500. Hmmm. Each integer takes two bytes, or 16 bits, of storage. If I raise 2 to the 16th power, the answer is 65,536. If I add –3036 to 65,536, I get 62,500, the correct answer for my problem. In an earlier discussion about integer numbers, I stated that the high bit was the sign bit. Because my answer is negative, the sign bit must be turned on (that is, a binary 1). However, because each integer variable is a signed quantity,

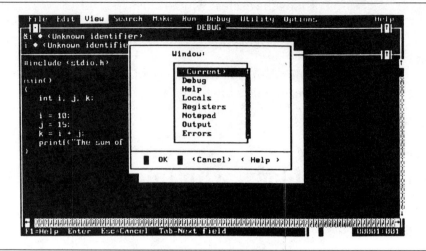

Figure 3-10. Setting Windows Using the View Option

only 15 bits are available for the answer. Therefore, my answer has overflowed the limits (a maximum of 32,767) that can be processed by an signed integer variable.

There are several ways to show that the compiler performed the proper math; I simply defined the variables incorrectly. To check things, change the last conversion character in the `printf()` function call to show the result as an unsigned number:

```
printf("The product of %d and %d is %u\n", i, j, k);
```

The `%u` serves to display an integer variable as an unsigned number. If you compile and run the program in Listing 3-3 with this modification to `printf()`, the proper answer is displayed.

Getting the correct answer, however, does not mean the problem is solved. The proper "bug" fix is to define the data types correctly:

```
unsigned i, j, k;
```

Note that, because the variables are unsigned data types, the conversion characters in `printf()` should be changed to

```
printf("The product of %u and %u is %u\n", i, j, k);
```

Any time you see integer data return negative values when you know the answer must be positive, the first thing to do is see whether the answer is too large for the data type to handle properly.

Character Data

The char is the basic data for character (ASCII) data. (See Appendix A for a list of the ASCII character set.) Consider the program shown in Listing 3-4.

Listing 3-4. Using Character Data

```
#include <stdio.h>

main()
{
    char c, d;

    c = 'A';
    d = c + 32;
    printf("The letter %c plus 32 is %c\n", c, d);

}
```

As with all variables in C, you must define the variable before you can use it. The first line in main()'s function body defines the two character variables c and d. The compiler allocates one byte (eight bits) for each variable and associates that memory location (lvalue) with the appropriate variable name.

The line

```
c = 'A';
```

shows how to use a character constant ('A') in an assignment statement. Any time you work with a single character in C, a pair of *single quote marks* surrounds the character constant being used. Therefore, examples of valid character constants might include

'A' 'c' '$' '\n' '\\'

Notice that the newline character ('\n') appears to be two characters, but the compiler treats it as though it is one. The reason is that the backslash character (\) is viewed by the compiler as a "lead in" character to an escape sequence and causes the compiler to process the next character in a special way. The last example '\\' would be used if you wanted to print a backslash as part of the message to the screen. Obviously, a double backslash is needed because the compiler always treats the first backslash as an escape sequence.

The line in Listing 3-4

```
d = c + 32;
```

adds decimal 32 to the character content of c. Look in Appendix A to see that an 'A' has the numeric equivalent of 65. Therefore, d holds the value 97 when the line is processed. Looking up the value 97 in Appendix A shows that 97 is the decimal number for the ASCII letter 'a'. You now know that the output of the program must be

```
The letter A plus 32 is a
```

This simple program reinforces an important fact about char variables in C:

char data types are an integer data type

This also means that you can add or subtract values from char data. Listing 3-5 shows how this information might prove useful in a program.

Listing 3-5. Using char Data

```
#include <stdio.h>

main()
{
    char c;
    int i;

    printf("Enter option number 1, 2, 3:");
    d = getch();
    i = d - '0';
    printf("\nThe choice was %d", i);

}
```

Now, inspect the program to see what's going on. The first call to printf() simply tells the user what to do — press the key for a 1, 2, or 3. Keep in mind that the keyboard sends an ASCII key code to the computer when you press one of these three keys. From Appendix A, you can see that the character 1 has the ASCII numeric value 49. The first four ASCII digit characters have the relationship

Digit Character	ASCII Numeric Value
'0'	48
'1'	49
'2'	50
'3'	51

The function `getch()` is a QC library function that reads one character from the keyboard. It has two special characteristics, however. First, you do not have to press the Enter key after touching the character to send the data from the keyboard to the computer. As soon as you touch a key, `getch()` has the ASCII value for the character. Second, the character touched on the keyboard does not show on the screen. (Most programmers would say that the character is "not echoed" to the screen. This invisibility is useful when you don't want the information displayed on the screen for others to see, such as when passwords are entered in a program.)

After `getch()` is called, d contains the ASCII value for the digit character pressed by the user. Now, consider the statement

```
i = d - '0';
```

What does it do? Well, suppose you run the program and touch the 2 key for your choice. Variable d holds the ASCII value 50. Substituting into the statement, we see

```
i = d - '0';
i = 50 - 48;    /* ASCII values substituted */
i = 2;
```

Note that I have converted the ASCII *representation* for the option ('2') as held in d to a pure *numeric* value (2) and assigned the value into i. Note that character digit '2' (that is, ASCII 50) is not the same as numeric value 2.

"Squished" Style

C programmers tend to combine statements when it makes sense to do so. For example, few C programmers write the lines

```
d = getch();
i = d - '0';
```

as two separate statements. Instead, they collapse them into the following single statement

```
i = getch() - '0';
```

We can do this because the program never uses the value of variable d other than to derive the value of i. The "squished" version allows you to remove variable d from the program.

Alas, squishing can get carried too far, as in

```
printf("\nThe choice was %d", getch() - '0');
```

This version also works perfectly, but now no variable holds the choice entered by the user; you could do away with variable i, too. Although such squishing works in this simple example, debugging the program becomes more difficult because you have no variables to examine.

Unfortunately, there are no hard and fast rules for the "proper" level of squishing C code. Perhaps it's best to say, squish only when the intermediate values are not needed (such as variable d in our example). As you gain experience debugging C programs and seeing code written by others, you will get a feel for workable levels of program squishing. Just keep in mind that over-squishing can make debugging more painful.

String Data

Quite often, you will want to work with a collection of characters, such as your name, an address, etc. In these cases, define an array of characters to hold the data. Listing 3-6 shows how to do this.

Listing 3-6. A Program Using String Data

```
#include <stdio.h>

main()
{
   char buff[ ] = "Jack";

   printf("The contents of buff is %s\n", buff);

}
```

The statement

```
char buff[ ] = "Jack";
```

accomplishes two tasks. First, the compiler creates storage for an array of characters named `buff[ ]`. Second, starting with the `lvalue` of `buff[0 ]`, it fills that storage with the string constant, `"Jack"`. Therefore, this is an example of initializing a variable as part of the variable's definition statement.

Note that double quotes (`"`) surround string constants, in contrast to the single quotes (`'`) associated with character constants.

How much storage was allocated for `buff[ ]`? Unlike other languages, string constants in C always end with a *null termination character*. The null termination character (that is, null character) is represented by '\0' in C. Therefore, if you assume that the compiler chose memory address 3000 for `buff[ ]`, the memory image looks like that shown in Figure 3-11.

```
              3001    3003
           | J | a | c | k | \0 |
             3000    3002    3004
```

Figure 3-11. Memory Image for the `buff[ ]` Character Array

As you can see, a string constant requires one more byte than the number of characters in the string constant. The reason is that any string variable (that is, character array) must always have enough room for the null termination character. In Listing 3-6, the compiler allocates 5 bytes of storage for the `buff[ ]` character array. The compiler knows this by counting the number of characters in the string constant and adding one to that total.

You could also define `buff[ ]` as

```
char buff[5 ] = "Jack";
```

Notice this specifies that you want enough storage space associated with `buff[ ]` to hold five characters — four letters plus the null character. What would happen if you tried

```
char buff[10 ] = "Jack";
```

thereby having "left-over" characters? No problem. The storage associated with `buff[ ]` is now 10 bytes, of which you are using only 5 now. The remaining bytes after the null character ('\0') are not used in the program.

In the call to `printf()`, the `%s` conversion character causes the `printf()` to march through the contents of the `buff[ ]` character array, displaying each character as it does. When it reads the null character ('\0'), `printf()` stops displaying characters — it has reached the end of the string.

(Other languages, such as BASIC and Pascal, accomplish this same task by using a length byte at the front of the string. That is, in Pascal, the first byte of the `buff[ ]` array would have the value 4 followed by the letters *J, a, c, k*. Because the length byte is often limited to one byte, you can understand why some dialects of PASCAL and BASIC limit a string to a maximum of 255 characters.)

Arrays Start with Element 0

Keep in mind, when using any type of array in C, that the first element is 0, not 1. Therefore, `buff[0 ]` in our program is the character `J` whereas `buff[1 ]` is `a`.

The fact that arrays start with element zero also means that the maximum element value is always one less than its defined value. For example, if you define `buff[ ]` as

```
char buff[5];
```

the maximum subscript value is `buff[4]`. Figure 3-12 shows why this is so.

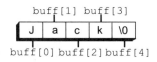

Figure 3-12. Memory Image for the `buff[ ]` *Character Array*

Notice that the definition of `buff[ ]` requests 5 units of storage, but the maximum subscript number using those 5 bytes is 4. If you ever have a situation where a variable's value seems to be changing for no apparent reason, it could be caused by overwriting the string storage space and clobbering whatever data item is stored "behind" it.

Array Bound Checking in C

C has no array bound checking! If you ask for a 5-byte array of characters and proceed to write the contents of *Gone With the Wind* into the array, that's fine with C. However, chances are pretty good that you're going to cause some problems somewhere. A bit of defensive advice: Always make character arrays larger than you think you'll need. Rarely are storage limitations such that a dozen extra bytes for an array make much difference in the program.

The *sizeof* Operator

You can check the size of a data item in C while the program is running (that is, at runtime) by using the `sizeof` operator. For example, if you add the line

```
printf("\nThe size of buff is %u\n", sizeof buff);
```

after the definition of `buff[ ]`, the program output shows

```
The size of buff is 5
```

The general syntax for the `sizeof` operator is

```
sizeof variable_name
```

If you want to find the size of a basic C data type, you must surround the data type specifier with parentheses. For example

```
sizeof(double)
sizeof(char)
```

yields the storage requirements (in bytes) for a `double` and `char` data type. In most real programs, C programmers use the parentheses, although they are not needed when used with variable names. Therefore, you will see

```
sizeof(buff)
```

more often than

```
sizeof buff
```

even though both forms are permitted. The parentheses are probably used because the parenthesized form works with variable names and C type specifiers (that is, C keywords for data types like `int`, `double`, etc.).

The program shown in Listing 3-7 is a modification of Listing 3-6, which makes the program more flexible.

Notice that buff[ ] has been defined to use 20 bytes of storage, but the contents of the character array are not initialized to any known values. The first printf() tells the user what to do. The function gets() is a standard C library function that reads characters from the keyboard into buff[ ] until the Enter key is pressed. When the Enter key is pressed, gets() replaces the Enter keystroke with the null termination character. Therefore, gets() is a standard library function for filling in string variables with keyboard input.

Listing 3-7. A Program Using String Data

```
#include <stdio.h>

main()
{
   char buff[20 ];

  printf("Enter your name:");
  gets(buff);
  printf("The contents of buff is %s\n", buff);

}
```

After the user presses the Enter key, the second call to printf() uses the %s conversion character to display the contents of buff[ ]. The gets() is a simple and efficient way to get character data into your programs; you will use it often throughout this book.

Looking at Character Arrays with Debug

Using the program presented in Listing 3-7, activate the Debug option (Alt-D) and select the Watch Value option. In the expression field, type

&buff

and press the Enter key. Now repeat the process and type a second expression

&buff[0]

You may recall that the address of operator (&) gives the lvalue of the data item that follows it. In this case, you are asking Debug to show the lvalue for buff and buff[0]. Now run the program using the F10 key and watch the values shown for &buff and &buff[0]. What did you find out? I will say more about this once you have a few more facts under your belt.

I urge you to try to write your own programs using data types other than those shown here. Write a program that squares two double data types and display the results. Then do the same type of program, this time using a long data type. Make a note of the problems you had displaying the anwsers. (Hint: Table 3-2 might help you with some potential problems.)

4

Using Operators to Control Your Programs

In this chapter, you learn about the following topics:

Arithmetic operators

Relational operators

Logical operators

Increment-decrement operators

Bitwise operators

Assignment operators

Control statements

One of the reasons C is such a powerful language is its rich set of operators. As you learn about these operators, you will see how they can implement decision-making to control program flow.

Arithmetic Operators

I touched on the arithmetic operators in Chapter 3; in this chapter, you use them more extensively. Table 4-1 presents a list of the arithmetic operators.

Table 4-1. Arithmetic Operators

Operator	Definition
+	Addition
–	Subtraction
*	Multiplication
/	Division
%	Modulus

All the arithmetic operators in Table 4-1 are binary operators. As explained in Chapter 3, this means that arithmetic operators require two operands, or expressions, to perform their task. Of the list presented in Table 4-1, only the modulus operator needs further explanation.

Modulus Operator (%)

The *modulus operator* yields the remainder of a division operation. Consider the following code fragment:

```
int i, j;

j = 17;
i = j % 5;
```

The value of `i` is 2, or the remainder of 17 divided by 5. As you will see later in this chapter, the modulus operator is very useful when you wish to trigger some event whenever a multiple of that event occurs. The one limitation of the modulus operator is that it can be used only with integral data types (that is, you cannot use `float` or `double` data types).

Relational Operators

A *relational operator* is used to compare one expression against another. Hence, relational operators are also binary operators. A list of relational operators is presented in Table 4-2.

Table 4-2. Relational Operators

Operator	Definition
>	Greater than
<	Less than
==	Equal to
>=	Greater than or equal to
<=	Less than or equal to
!=	Not equal to

Most of the operators presented in Table 4-2 are similar to those found in other languages, but there is one that will catch you from time to time. The equality operator uses *two* equal signs (==). It is easy to forget the second equal sign and end up performing an assigment operation rather than a relational test. (There is an example of the impact of this error later in the chapter.)

The inequality operator (!=) may also appear to be somewhat strange, but it is consistent with C's use of the exclamation point (!) for the word *not*. (You will see another example of a not operator below.)

The *if* Statement

Now that you know something about relational operators, we can discuss one of C's keywords that control the sequence of a program. Control statements give a program its ability to "decide" what to do next. The if keyword is the simplest of C's control statements.

There are several basic flavors of the if statement from which more complex combinations can be built:

1. An if controlling a single C statement
2. An if-else combination
3. An if or if-else controlling multiple C statements

Let's examine each of these basic combinations.
The basic if statement takes the form

```
if (expression)
    statement;
```

The expression has two possible outcomes. The expression is either logically True or logically False. Any nonzero expression is considered *logical True*. Any expression that evaluates to zero is considered *logical False*. If the expression evaluates to logical True, the statement is executed. You can, therefore, view the if statement in more verbose terms as

```
if (this expression is logical True)
    then execute this statement;
```

If the expression is not logically True, the statement is not executed.

The program in Listing 4-1 presents a simple program that shows how you can use in an if statement some of the material presented thus far.

Listing 4-1. Using an if Statement

```
/*
            A program to illustrate using a simple if statement.
*/

#include <stdio.h>

main()
{
    char buff[20];
    int i;

    printf("Enter a number: ");
    i = atoi(gets(buff));
    printf("\nThe number is ");
    if (i % 2 == 1)
        printf("odd.");
    if (i % 2 == 0)
        printf("even.");
}
```

The program begins by defining a character array named buff[] and an integer variable named i. The statement

```
i = atoi(gets(buff));
```

could have been written as two separate statements

```
gets(buff);
i = atoi(buff);
```

The function `gets()`, discussed in Chapter 3, is used to get a sequence of characters from the keyboard and place them into a character array (`buff[]`). When the user presses the Enter key, the null termination character ('\0') is added to the end of the characters, thus creating a string variable.

atoi() Function

The `atoi()` (ascii to integer) function is another standard library function that converts an ASCII string to an integer data type. The value that is returned from `atoi()`, therefore, is an integer data type. The assignment operator places the value returned from `atoi()` into `i`. Also, the `rvalue` of `i` is whatever number the user typed in response to the request, `Enter a number`:

Although you can break the statement into its two component statements, most C programmers "nest" the two function calls to `gets()` and `atoi()` into a single C statement, as shown in Listing 4-1.

The Result of a Relational Operation

The next statement in Listing 4-1

```
if (i % 2 == 1)
```

is used to see whether `i` divided by 2 yields a remainder. Recall that the modulus operator always yields the remainder of division. Therefore, if the number divided by 2 has a remainder, the number must be odd and you print the word *odd*.

If you've been paying attention, you've probably asked, "Which operation is performed first — the modulus operation or the test for equality?" Look in Chapter 3 at the list of precedence for operators to see that the modulus operator has higher precedence than does equality. Therefore, the compiler evaluates the `i % 2` expression before testing the result against 1 for equality.\

Clearly the second `if` statement is there to cover the situation when the number is even.

(By the way, C programmers rarely use the term *modulus.* More often, *modulus* is shortened to `mod`. Instead of verbalizing `i % 2` as *i modulus two,* you are likely to hear, *i mod two.*)

if-else Statement

The program presented in Listing 4-1 works just as you would expect, but few C programmers would write it that way. The program is perfectly suited for using the `if-else` statement combination. The general form is

```
if (expression)
    statement;
else
    statement;
```

Expanding the formal syntax above to more conventional English, you have

```
if (expression is logically True)
    then execute this statement;
else
    execute this statement;
```

You can simplify the statements from Listing 4-1

```
if (i % 2 == 1)
    printf("odd.");
if ( i % 2 == 0)
    printf("even.");
```

to

```
if (i % 2 == 1)
    printf("odd.");
else
    printf("even.");
```

The results are the same as before, but you have gained efficiency in some ways. First, you don't have to type as much. As a general rule, the less typing, the fewer errors. More important, however, the compiler does not generate code to perform the second `if` test. Finally, I think most would agree that the `if-else` version is easier to understand because its meaning is clear at a glance.

Still, there are other ways to simplify the program even more.

Evaluation of Relational Expressions

Earlier, I said that a relational expression is either logically True or logically False. These (True or False) are the only two possible states that can result from a relational test. In C, the result of a logically True statement is any nonzero value. The result of a logically False statement is always zero. With this in mind, you might view the if-else statement combination as

```
if (True)
   execute this statement;
else

   execute this statement;
```

Because you know that True is any nonzero value, you can also write

```
if (nonzero)
   execute this statement;
else
   execute this statement;
```

Therefore, any expression in an if statement that evaluates to a nonzero result is viewed as a logical True test to the program. Likewise, any expression that evaluates to zero is viewed as logically False. With this in mind, you can rewrite the if-else test as

```
if (i % 2)
   printf("odd.");
else
   printf("even.");
```

and the results will be the same as before. Why? If i equals 5, the modulus operator yields a remainder of 1. Because 1 is nonzero, the expression is viewed as a logical True condition and the word odd is displayed. If i equals 4, the remainder is zero, which is viewed as a logical False condition causing the else part of the statement to be executed.

Consider what happens if you write

```
if (1)
   printf("True");
else
   printf("False");
```

Clearly, the test expression has been replaced with the (nonzero) constant 1 in which case the if test is always logically True. The False condition could never occur.

To test your understanding of the material presented in this section, could you write the program without defining any integer variable? Does anything change if you write

```
if (atoi(gets(buff)) % 2)
    printf("odd.");
else
    printf("even.");
```

Think about it.

if with Multiple Statements

In the program shown in Listing 4-1, the if statement controls only a single C statment. The same condition holds in the if-else version of the same program; only one statement follows either the if or the else. Alas, life is usually not so simple. Many times you find that a single if must control dozens of statements. However, the syntax rules state that an if can control only one statement. What now?

Fortunately, an easy solution is available.

Braces in C

Any time you need to group two or more statements so that they are viewed as though they were a single statement, surround the statements with braces. In the case of an if statement, you can use the general form

```
if (expression) {
    statement1;
    .
    .
    statementn;

}
```

In an if-else, the same approach applies.

```
if (expression) {
    statement1;
    .
    .
```

```
   statementn;
} else {
   statement1;

        .

        .

   statementn;
}
```

The program shown in Listing 4-2 gives a more concrete example of how braces might be used.

Listing 4-2. Multiple Statements in `if`

```
/*
            A program to illustrate multiple statements with if.
*/

#include <stdio.h>

main()
{
   char buff[20];
   int even, num, odd;

   even = .odd = 0;
   printf("Enter a number: ");
   num = atoi(gets(buff));
   if (num % 2) {
      even = 1;
      printf("%d is odd", num);
   } else {
      odd = 1;
      printf("%d is even", num);
   }

}
```

The program is essentially the same as that in Listing 4-1, except that the new version shows how the `if` is used with multiple statements. Although the additional statements do nothing useful, they show how multiple statements are used with an `if` statement. Notice how an opening brace follows the expression evaluated by the `if`. A closing brace marks the end of the statements associated with the logical True condition. The opening-closing pairs of braces mark the start-end of what is called a *statement block*.

The same pairs of braces are used to delineate the statement block for the `else` part of the `if` statement. This statement block contains those statements you wish to execute if the `if` expression evaluates to logical False.

Programming Style and Statement Blocks with the *if* Statement

The style used for statement blocks in this text is that shown in Listing 4-2. The opening brace sits at the end of the line containing the C keyword (for example, `if` or `else`). The closing brace for the statement block aligns with the C keyword itself. Notice how the closing brace is tabbed in to align with the `if`. The closing brace for the `else` statement block also aligns with the `if`. It is easy to tell which statement block belongs to which keyword using this style.

Other styles do exist, however. One alternative is

```
if (num % 2)
    {
    even = 1;
    printf("%d is odd", num);
}
    else
    {
    odd = 1;
    printf("%d is even", num);
}
```

Some programmers prefer this style because it even more clearly defines which statements are associated with the `if` statement. The only disadvantage is that it takes more lines to hold the same amount of source code. You see fewer lines of source code on the screen at one time than with the previous style.

The style you select has no impact on the program itself. Select one you like and then stick to it. When you work on a project with others, you should collectively select one style. It makes maintaining the program easier if you all use the same programming style.

Logical Operators

In many programming situations, you need two (or more) test conditions present before some specific action can be taken. For example, to hold certain offices in this country, you must be a U.S. citizen and at least 30 years of age. Although you could handle such situations with multiple if statements, a more direct approach is to use the logical operators afforded by C. Table 4-3 presents a list of the available logical operators.

Table 4-3. Logical Operators

Operator	Definition
&&	Logical AND
||	Logical OR
!	Logical NOT

Now let's examine how these logical operators work.

Logical AND

The best way to explain the logical AND is by using a truth table, such as that shown in Table 4-4.

Table 4-4. Logical AND Truth Table

A	&& B	= C
True	True	True
True	False	False
False	True	False
False	False	False

As you can see from the table, if expression A is True and B is True, the combination of expressions A and B are True. If either or both statements are False, the result is False. Recalling that a logical True is nonzero (for example, 1) and logical False is zero, you can also view Table 4-4 in the form shown in Table 4-5.

Table 4-5. Logical AND Truth Table (Binary Version)

A	&& B	= C
1	1	1
1	0	0
0	1	0
0	0	0

The information in both tables is the same, but Table 4-5 emphasizes that zero and nonzero values determine the outcome as far as the computer is concerned.

When using a logical AND in an `if` statement, the formal syntax is

```
if (expressionA && expressionB)
    statement;
```

The result of these two expressions determines whether the result is logical True (1) or False (0).

The voting requirements test can illustrate a use for the logical AND. Suppose that you have a variable `uscit` that is 1 if the person is a citizen and 0 otherwise. You might perform the `if` statement this way:

```
if (uscit == 1 && age >= 30)
    printf("The person can run for office\n");
else
    printf("Throw the bum out\n");
```

If it is True that the person is a U.S. citizen (that is, `uscit == 1` is logical True) and the person is at least 30 years old (that is, `age >= 30` is logical True), the two expressions in the `if`

```
if (uscit == 1 && age >= 30)
```

are viewed by the compiler as though they were

```
if (1 && 1)
```

From Table 4-5 you can see that the result of the logical AND of these two (True) expressions is logical True. Therefore, the program displays the message, `The person can run for office`. Prove to yourself that any other combination of `uscit` and `age` results in a different message.

Logical OR

The logical OR operator is also used to evaluate two expressions and determine whether they form a logical True or False result. The logical OR truth table is shown in Table 4-6.

Table 4-6. Logical OR Truth Table (binary version)

A ¦¦ B		= C
1	1	1
1	0	1
0	1	1
0	0	0

Note that if either statement A or B is True, the result is also True. For example, suppose that you want to test whether a person is a problem drinker or drug user. Assuming that either variable is 1 if the person has a substance abuse problem, the if test might be

```
if (drinker == 1 || drug == 1)
    printf("Have person seek treatment\n");
else
    printf("No treatment necessary\n");
```

You should be able to convince yourself that if the person abuses either or both substances, he or she is told to get help. Only if the person is neither a drinker nor a drug user is no treatment necessary.

Logical Test Shortcuts

In both examples, you used the value 1 to represent the presence of a condition (for example, uscit, drinker, and drug) and 0 to mark its absence. Therefore, you may write the abuse test as

```
if (drinker || drug)
```

How about the earlier example

```
if (uscit && age >= 30)
```

Do these changes have any impact on the results of the program? No, they don't. The reason is that you used a nonzero value to represent the logical True condition in both examples. C programmers often use this expression form in "real" programs.

Logical NOT

The logical NOT operator is used to reverse the current logical state of an expression. The logical NOT operator is a unary operator and operates on just one expression. For example, you could use the logical NOT in the earlier example as follows:

```
if (!drinker && !drug)
    printf("No treatment necessary\n");
else
    printf("Have person seek treatment\n");
```

Notice that the messages are now reversed. The if expressions now read, "If the person is not a drinker and if the person is not a drug user, no treatment is necessary. Otherwise, get help for the person." The purpose of the logical NOT operator, therefore, is to reverse the current logical state of the expression. In some situations, the NOT operator can lead to economy of expression by testing for the absence of a condition rather than its presence.

Increment-Decrement Operators

If you have done much programming, you know that an operation such as

```
n = n + 1;
a = a - 1;
```

occurs very frequently. Because such increment-decrement operations are so common, C has special operators to do these operations. The operators are

```
++        /* increment -- Add 1 to the operand        */
--        /* decrement -- Subtract 1 from the operand */
```

These operators are unary operators because they require a single operand.

Each increment-decrement operator is further defined to have two flavors, depending on the placement of the operator relative to the variable name. The difference is best explained with an example. Consider the following code fragment:

```
int i, j;

i = 10;
j = ++i;                    /* Preincrement operation */
printf("j = %d", j);
```

If you used this fragment in a program, the value of j would be 11. Because the increment operator (++) appears before the variable being incremented (i), the rvalue of i is incremented by 1 *before* being assigned into j. This is an example of a *preincrement* operation. In this example, both i and j have the same value when the printf() call is executed.

Now consider a slight modification to the code fragment:

```
int i, j;
i = 10;
j = i++;                    /* Postincrement operation */
printf("j = %d", j);
```

Notice that the increment operator now appears *after* the name of the variable being incremented (i). So what is the value of j? Because the rvalue of i is assigned into j *before* the increment operation, the value of j is 10. This is called a *postincrement* operation because the increment on i occurs after the assignment takes place. Also note that the values of i and j are not the same after a postincrement operation on i.

The same behavior applies to the decrement operator. If the decrement operator appears before the variable name, it is called a *predecrement* operation. If the decrement operator appears after the variable name, it is a *postdecrement* operation. In the following code fragment, what are the values of i, j, and k?

```
int i, j, k;

i = 10;
j = i--;
k = ++j;
printf("i = %d j = %d k = %d", i, j, k);
```

The value of i is now 9; j and k both equal 11. The postdecrement of i means that 10 is assigned into j before i is decremented to 9. Because j is then preincremented before the assignment into k, both j and k equal 11 when their values are printed with the call to printf().

The increment-decrement operators are very convenient, especially when you start using loop constructs in your programs. Also, they may generate more efficient code than the alternative of adding or subtracting 1 from the variable.

Bitwise Operators

The creators of C wanted to develop a language that would allow them to be on intimate terms with the system's hardware. They wanted to be able to control data at the bit level. The result was a family of operators that can manipulate the bits within a data item.

Table 4-7. Bitwise Operators

Operator	Definition
&	Bitwise AND
¦	Bitwise OR
^	Bitwise Exclusive OR
>>	Bitwise right shift
<<	Bitwise left shift
~	Bitwise one's complement

Although you may not use these operators too often, they are there when you need them. You will also find them useful in a variety of I/O situations. The list is presented in Table 4-7.

Bitwise AND (&)

The bitwise AND operator is a binary operator that ANDs each bit of the two operands. For example, suppose that you AND the decimal values 14 and 3 (the binary equivalents for the numbers are also shown below):

$$14 = 00001110$$
$$3 = 00000011$$

$$2 = 00000010$$

In C, this operations would be written

`i = 14 & 3;`

and the value of `i` would be 2. Starting with the rightmost bit, the 0 in 14 is ANDed with the 1 in 3. From Table 4-5, we know that 0 AND 1 is zero, so the resulting (rightmost) bit is 0. In the next bit position, both bits are 1. Table 4-5 tells us that 1 AND 1 is 1, so a 1 is placed in the result. After all bits have been evaluated, you can see that the result is the binary equivalent for the decimal number 2.

Bitwise OR (¦)

The bitwise OR is also a binary operator. Using the same numbers as before

$$14 = 00001110$$
$$3 = 00000011$$

$$15 = 00001111$$

With the bitwise OR, if either operand's bit is a 1, the resultant bit is a 1. The result of the OR operation is consistent with the information in the truth table shown in Table 4-6.

Bitwise Exclusive OR (^)

The bitwise exclusive OR produces a 1 if either bit is a 1, but not both bits. If both bits are 1, the result is 0. Using the same example

$$14 = 00001110$$
$$3 = 00000011$$

$$2 = 00001101$$

Notice that the second bit position becomes 0 because the second bit position is 1 for both operands. Although the bitwise exclusive OR (EOR) is used less often than the other bitwise operators, you may find it useful in certain I/O, screen, and graphics applications.

Bitwise One's Complement

The one's complement operator is a unary operator that "flips" the bit values. For example, if the number initially is

```
00001010
```

and you perform a one's complement, the result becomes

```
11110101
```

Obiously, performing a one's complement on the same number twice leaves the value unchanged.

Bitwise Right Shift (>>)

The bitwise right shift operator causes the bits of the first operand to be shifted to the right by the number of bits specified in the second operand. Formally, the syntax is

```
value >> num_bits
```

where value is the number to be right-shifted and num_bits is the number of bit positions to be shifted. For example, if you write

```
i = 10;
i = i >> 1;
```

the bits in variable i are shifted to the right by one position. In binary form, decimal 10 looks like

```
10 (decimal) = 00001010 (binary)
```

Shifting i right one position yields

```
5 (decimal) = 00000101 (binary)
```

showing that the result is a value equal to (decimal) 5.

Bitwise Left Shift (<<)

The bitwise left shift has the same syntax as the right shift operator, except that the direction of the bit shifting changes to the left. The statement

```
i = 10;
i = i << 1;
```

produces a value for i of 20. Using binary representation

```
10 (decimal) = 00001010 (binary)
```

shifted left one bit position yields

```
20 (decimal) = 00010100 (binary)
```

You should remember that with either the right or left bitwise shift operators, bits shifted out of the data items are lost. That is, if a 1 is in the first bit position and we shift right one bit, the bit does not "flow back" into the high bit. Therefore

```
00000101 >> 1
```

becomes

```
00000010
```

after the bit shift. The low bit is lost.

You may think that you don't have much use for the bitwise operators, but it is surprising how often they can be used. If you have a good DOS book, take a look at how your PC stores the date and time values as single integers. Bit masking provides a quick and easy method to extract such "packed" data.

A Useful Fact

Because computers understand only two states (1 and 0), they are said to work with binary data. That is, everything takes place in base 2 arithmetic. Of the basic math operations, the two slowest operations are multiplication and division. In terms of speed, division by a computer is the pits.

Programmers often go to extremes to avoid multiplication and division in a program, especially if either occurs in a loop. For example, most programmers know that multiplying a number by 2 is slower than adding the number to itself. If floating point data are being divided by 2, it is quicker to multiply by .5.

Our bit shifting examples, however, show an even faster method of performing certain types of multiplication and division. Assuming that you are using integer data items

Right-shifting one bit position is equal to division by 2;

Left-shifting one bit position is equal to multiplication by 2.

Using our earlier binary examples

```
00000101 << 1        /* The value 5 */
```

yields

```
00001010             /* The value 10 */
```

Clearly

```
00001010 >> 1        /* The value 10 */
```

results in

```
00000101 >> 1        /* The value 5  */
```

What happens if you shift more than one bit position? Because everything operates in base 2 arithmetic, the result is affected by powers of 2. Therefore, a value of 16 that is right-shifted two bit positions is the same as dividing by four. The same value right-shifted three bit positions is equal to dividing by eight. Multiplication works the same way.

These shortcuts work only on integer data types (as do the bitwise operators). The integer must be positive, and you must take care when multiplying that you don't "overflow" the limits of the data item. Still, bit shifting can save significant time if you do the operation many times in a loop.

Assignment Operators

The last group of operators we examine in this chapter relates to the simple task of assignment. We have already used the basic assignment operator in many of our examples, such as

```
i = 10;
```

I have already shown that C's creators were clever enough to devise a special operator to cover the situation

```
j = j + 1;
```

That is, simply use the increment operator (++). However, there are hundreds of situations in which you have something like

```
j = j + k;
```

You can still use the increment operator if you know that k is 1 and never changes. Life is rarely that simple, however. Still, in an attempt to save you a little typing and give the compiler vendor some optimization clues, a class of special assignment operators was created. For example, instead of writing

```
j = j + k;
```

you can use

```
j += k;
```

These special operators collapse the two operators (addition and assignment) into one (+=). A list of these special operators appears in Table 4-8.

Table 4-8. Special Assignment Operators

Operator	Meaning	Alternate Form
+=	Addition	(i += j i = i + j)
−=	Subtraction	(i − = j i = i − j)
*=	Multiplication	(i *= j i = i * j)
/=	Division	(i /= j i = i / j)
%=	Modulus	(i %= j i = i % j)
&=	Bitwise AND	(i &= j i = i & j)
¦=	Bitwise OR	(i ¦= j i = i ¦ j)
^=	Bitwise EOR	(i ^= j i = i ^ j)
>>=	Right shift	(i >>= j i = i >> j)
<<=	Left shift	(i <<= j i = i << j)

The special assignment operators presented in Table 4-8 don't give us anything we didn't have before. However, QC optimizes such operations because it contends with only one expression. That is,

```
i = i + j;
```

is two expressions: First the compiler adds i to j and saves the intermediate result; second, the compiler assigns the intermediate result back into

i. This means fetching (finding lvalues) and storing (rvalues) quite a lot of data. The shortened form has but one expression to resolve, permitting the compiler to take certain shortcuts (optimizations) to produce the answer.

In general, use the special assignment operators whenever possible. It not only saves you some typing, but produces better code, too.

Believe it or not, there are still a few operators left to discuss. However, you have enough to chew on for now. Although there are a lot of operators to chose from, syntactically they are consistent in the way they are used. If you can remember the basic operator symbols (for example, &, |, =, !, etc.), their cousins are easily remembered. The QC compiler supports all of the operators presented in this chapter.

The *switch* Statement

Before ending this chapter, I discuss two more control statements. The first is called the switch statement, which has the following general form:

```
switch (expression) {     /* Brace is start of the switch body */
    case var1:
      statement;
    case var2:
      statement;

    case varN:
      statement:
}                          /* Close of switch body              */
```

The switch statement evaluates the expression in parentheses, which must resolve to an integral value. The switch then compares this integral value with the values in var1 through varN. If a match is found, program control is sent to the matching case. If no match is found, control passes to the first statement following the closing brace of the switch. Therefore, the value of expression determines where program control resumes.

Notice that each case variable is followed by a colon, not a semicolon.

The program in Listing 4-3 shows how the switch statement is used in a C program.

Listing 4-3. Using the switch Statement

```
/*
                Our first attempt to use the switch statement.
*/

#include <stdio.h>

main()
{
    char c;
    int i;

    printf("Enter an operator (+, -, *, /): ");
    c = getch();
    printf("The character is ");

    switch (c) {
       case '+':
          printf("addition");
       case '-':
          printf("subtraction");
       case '*':
          printf("multiplication");
       case '/':
          printf("division");
    }

}
```

The program asks the user to type a character that represents one of the four arithmetic operators. The call to getch() accepts a single keystroke without requiring the user to press the Enter key. (The key that is pressed is not displayed on the screen.) The character is then assigned in the char variable c.

The switch statement uses the value in c to decide which case statement to execute. The switch evaluates the character in c and looks for a case value that matches the value in c. If the character entered by the user is the division operator (/), the program displays

```
The character is division
```

If no match is found between the switch variable (c) and a case value, none of the cases is executed. (If you are familiar with BASIC, note that the switch-case combinations are similar to the ON-GOTO in BASIC.)

Now try running the program, but touch the plus (+) key this time. The output now becomes

```
The character is additionsubtractionmultiplicationdivision
```

Clearly, something is not working right. What happened? The switch found a match on the first case in the switch. Because each case is nothing more than a compiler-generated label, after printf() displays the word addition, program control falls into the next case. The second case statement displays subtraction and control falls into the third case, and so on. This behavior proves that the switch statement on variable c is nothing more than a conditional jump instruction to some memory location generated by the compiler. How useful can the switch be if all of the cases are executed in some situations?

Actually, I left out some useful details about using the switch statement.

Getting Out of a *switch* with the *break* Statement

C provides a means of transferring control out of the switch statement (and several loop structures). Listing 4-4 shows how to use the break statement.

Listing 4-4. Using the switch and break Statements

```
/*
              Our second attempt to use the switch statement.
*/

#include <stdio.h>

main()
{
    char c;
    int i;

    printf("Enter an operator (+, -, *, /): ");
    c = getch();
    printf("The character is ");
```

```
switch (c) {
   case '+':
      printf("addition");
      break;
   case '-':
      printf("subtraction");
      break;
   case '*':
      printf("multiplication");
      break;
   case '/':
      printf("division");
      break;
}

}
```

Notice how each `printf()` is now followed by the `break` statement. If the user enters a plus sign for the program shown in Listing 4-4, control is sent to the matching `case` statement. The `printf()` function is called and the word `addition` is displayed. When the `break` statement is executed, control is transferred to the first statement outside of the `switch` statement. You can trace the program flow when a plus sign is entered using Figure 4-1.

In Figure 4-1, control starts at the `switch` statement (1) and the program immediately evaluates the expression used to control the `switch` (2). Assuming the user entered a plus sign, control is sent to the matching `case` (3). (The QC compiler does this using a conditional jump instruction to the memory location that corresponds to the '+' `case`.) The program first executes the call to `printf()` (4) and then the `break` statement (5). The only function of the `break` is to transfer program control to the first statement following the close of the `switch` body (6). Now when the program is run with the `break` statements in their proper places, the results are as expected.

You will see the `break` statement used in Chapter 5, too. Its use is not limited to the `switch` statement. For a more precise picture of how program flow is controlled, try single-stepping the program using the F10 key to follow the program as it executes.

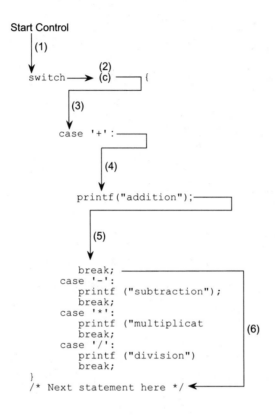

```
Start Control
    │(1)
    ▼             (2)
 switch ───────► (c) ───── {
          │(3)
          ▼
        case '+': ─────
                 │(4)
                 ▼
            printf("addition"); ─────
             │(5)
             ▼
            break; ─────
        case '-':
            printf ("subtraction");
            break;
        case '*':
            printf ("multiplicat          (6)
            break;
        case '/':
            printf ("division")
            break;
    }
    /* Next statement here */ ◄─────
```

Figure 4-1.Program Flow Using switch *and* break *(c* = '+')

default, the Catch-All Case

There will be situations in which you cannot expect to create a case
for all circumstances. Indeed, Listing 4-5 suffers when you enter something other than one of the (expected) arithmetic operators. If you do this,
it appears that nothing happens at all.

The C keyword default may be used to catch the unexpected events
in a switch statement. Listing 4-5 shows how this is done.

Listing 4-5. Using the `switch`, `break`, *and* `default` *Statements*

```
/*
            Our third attempt to use the switch statement.
*/

#include <stdio.h>

main()
{
    char c;
    int i;

    printf("Enter an operator (+, -, *, /): ");
    c = getch();
    printf("The character is ");

    switch (c) {
       case '+':
          printf("addition");
          break;
       case '-':
          printf("subtraction");
          break;
       case '*':
          printf("multiplication");
          break;
       case '/':
          printf("division");
          break;
       default:
          printf("\n *** Nobody reads prompts anymore ***\a");
          break;
    }

}
```

If the evaluation of `c` does not match any `case` value, control passes to `default`. In Listing 4-5, an error message (of sorts) prints and the program ends. Notice the `'\a'` escape sequence at the end of the string constant. The `'\a'` escape sequence causes the system's bell, or buzzer, to sound. This is called the *alarm* escape sequence.

It is good programming practice to always use a `default` statement in any `switch` statement. It can be very useful when something unexpected happens.

Falling Through Cases

Listing 4-3 showed what happens when program control "falls through" a series of `case` statements because no `break` statement was used. In some situations, however, falling through is not a bad thing. Suppose that you want to determine whether the user entered either an arithmetic or bitwise operator (excluding the shift operators). Consider Listing 4-6 for a moment.

Listing 4-6. Using the `switch` "Fall-Through" Feature

```
/*
                Our fourth attempt to use the switch statement.
*/

#include <stdio.h>

main()
{
    char c;
    int i;

    printf("Enter an arithmetic or bitwise operator: ");
    c = getch();
    printf("The character is a");

    switch (c) {
        case '+':
        case '-':
        case '*':
        case '/':
            printf("n arithmetic");
            break;
        case '&':
        case '|':
        case '^':
        case '~':
```

```
        printf(" bitwise");
        break;
    default:
        printf("\n *** Nobody reads prompts anymore ***\a");
        break;
    }
    printf(" operator");

}
```

In this program, use the `switch` to test for groups of responses (for example, arithmetic versus bitwise operators) and to display the appropriate messages. If an arithmetic operator is entered, program control is sent to the appropriate `case`, whereupon control falls through to the `printf()` function call. After the message is displayed, the `break` sends control to the final `printf()` call. Although you could write similar code using just `if` statements, the `switch` is a much cleaner approach.

Why leave the shift operators (`<<`and `>>`) out? Two reasons: First, `getch()` can read only one character at a time; second, and more important, a `case` expression must evaluate to a single integral value. The shift operators would require using string data because two characters are used for each operator. Although doing this would not be difficult, it would require me to introduce new concepts that are better postponed until later.

The *goto* Statement

The `goto` statement has received a lot of bad press in recent years because it violates structured programming techniques. Still, situations arise in which the lowly `goto` provides the easiest solution to a programming problem. Perhaps a more realistic approach is to view the `goto` statement as a tool that should be used sparingly in your coding.

The syntax for the `goto` statement is

```
goto labelname:
```

whereby `labelname` is whatever name you use to mark the point at which program control should resume after the `goto` statement is executed. Listing 4-7 presents an example of how the `goto` might be used.

Listing 4-7. The `goto` *Statement*

```
/*
                An example of using the goto statement
*/

#include <stdio.h>

main()
{
    char buff[20];
    int i;

    printf("Enter a number: ");
    i = atoi(gets(buff));
    if (i < 100)
        goto small;
    else
        goto big;

    small: printf("The value is less than 100");
        exit(0);

    big:
        printf("The value is larger than 100");

}
```

You can notice several things about the program: First, the label names `small` and `big` are not variables. (If they were, they would have been defined at the top of `main()`.) The labels used by the `goto` statement are simply points in a program that happen to have a name.

If you are familiar with how a compiler works, you may know that each label is nothing more than the `lvalue` of the statement that follows the label name. Prove this by using the F10 feature of QC to single-step the program. When you enter a value larger than 100, notice how control is not actually sent to the `big` label, but rather to the `printf()` call on the line below `big`. The statements following a label do not have to be on the same line as the label name. Control is sent to the first statement following the label regardless of any newline or space characters that follow the colon after the label name.

The *exit()* Function

The `printf()` associated with the `small` label is followed by a call to the `exit()` function. The `exit()` function is a standard library function that does some housekeeping chores before terminating the program. In other words, `exit()` provides a graceful means of ending a program before the closing brace of `main()` is reached.

Without the `exit()` function call, the program would simply continue to execute whatever statements happened to follow next in the program. The program's control flow would be similar to a `case` without a `break` statement. In Listing 4-7, a value less than 100 would cause both `printf()` calls to be executed if the `exit()` statement were not present.

A Restriction on the Use of a *goto*

Because I cannot provide a full explanation at this point in the book, suffice it to say that you cannot use the `goto` statement to transfer program control outside of the function body in which the `goto` appears. To illustrate, consider the following code fragment:

```
        /* You can't do this. */

main()
    {
    /* Some definitions and other statements here */
    .
    .
    goto nasty_error;
    .
}

func1()
{
    .
    .
    nasty_error:
        printf("Your hard disk blew up\n");
    .
}
```

In this example, you attempt to transfer program control from one function (`main()`) to a different function (`func1()`). You cannot accomplish a transfer of program control between functions using a `goto` statement.

For now, think of each function as a black box, the contents of which are invisible to any other function in the program.

Although you may view this "invisibility" as a limitation, it actually is a benefit because it means that the data defined within the black box is "private" to that black box. In some languages (for example, BASIC), there is no data privacy. If you have ever worked in such languages, you know that "fixing" a bug in one section of the program often triggers another bug somewhere else. The lack of data privacy is usually the cause of such "side effect" bugs.

This is the last time you see the `goto` statement in this book. Keep the `goto` in mind, however, because a situation might arise in which it provides the cleanest solution to a particular programming problem.

Create your own programs to experiment with the many operators and control statements presented in this chapter. They form the foundation for virtually any C program you write.

5

Loop Statements

In this chapter you learn about

while **loops**

do-while **loops**

for **loops**

Infinite loops

Controlled execution of infinite loops

Simply stated, loop constructs allow you to execute the same program statements more than one time. C gives you several different types of loops from which to choose. Each of these loop variations is covered in this chapter.

while Loops

The general form for the while loop is

```
while (expression) {
    statement(s);
}
```

Like the if statement discussed in Chapter 4, the while statement can control only one C statement unless braces are used to form a statement block. Because the braces forming the statement block cause no extra code to be generated, always use the braces from now on.

The reason for using the statement block braces, although they are not required when a single statement is controlled by the while loop, is due to debugging considerations. As you create your own programs, you invariably need to insert debugging statements into your loop constructs. Because the debugging statements must be controlled by the loop, you must add the statement block braces anyway. Therefore, there is little reason to not use them in the first place. Also, the presence of statement block braces makes seeing loop constructs in a program easier. I urge you to develop the habit of always using statement block braces with loop constructs.

The program shown in Listing 5-1 is a typical example of a while loop.

Listing 5-1. Using a while Loop

```
/*
        Program that uses a while loop
*/

#include <stdio.h>

main()
{
    int i;

    i = 0;
    while (i < 10) {
        printf("%4d\n", rand());
        i++;
    }
}
```

In this example, I initialize i to a value of 0 and enter the while loop. Notice that the expression that controls the while loop is a simple relational test to see whether i is less than 10. As long as i is less than 10, the expression is logical True and the while loop continues to execute the statements in the statement block.

The printf() statement prints out the integer value return from the call to rand(). As you might guess, rand() returns a (pseudo) random number. If you run the program a second time, notice that the same sequence of numbers is generated. This is why the value is called a pseudorandom number. If rand() returned numbers that were truly random, the sequence would not be repeated. Actually, repeating the same sequence of numbers can be useful when debugging a program. (See the `srand()` function in the *C For Yourself* manual if you need nonrepeating numbers.)

After the `printf()` function is called, variable `i` is incremented. Control returns to the top of the loop to test whether `i` is still less than 10. If it is, another iteration of the loop is performed. Otherwise, the test `i < 10` fails (becomes logical False), and the `while` loop terminates.

Common Elements of a Well-Behaved Loop

All loop structures, regardless of the C keyword used, have two elements in common:

1. A variable is initialized once to some starting value.
2. A test is performed to decide whether another iteration through the loop must be made.

In Listing 5-1, `i` is initialized to 0 before entering the loop. Note that Rule 1 states that a variable is initialized once. If you moved the initialization of `i` inside the `while` loop, would the program ever end? No, because `i` would never reach the value of 10.

What happens if you don't initialize `i` at all? That depends on the `rvalue` of `i` at the time the program starts. If the random bits at `i`'s memory location (that is, its `lvalue`) just happen to form a value less than 10, the program generates random numbers. If the value of `i` is greater than 10, no values are printed. You might try erasing the line

```
i = 0;
```

and see what happens when you try to run the program.

The second rule states that you must have some evaluation, or test, on an expression that enables you to end the loop at some point. In Listing 5-1, the relational test of `i` against 10 determines whether another pass through the loop must be made.

Finally, both conditions must be met. You can abide by Rule 1 or Rule 2 and still have a loop that can get out of control. For a well-behaved loop, both rules must be enforced and properly coded.

More is said in the rest of this chapter about how loops are properly written. Meanwhile, as you read the material that follows, ask yourself how the same programs conform (or don't conform) to the rule needed for a well-behaved loop.

do-while Loops

The do-while loop is similar to the simple while loop, except that the test to determine whether another iteration must be made is at the bottom of the loop. The general form of the do-while loop is

```
do {
    statement(s);
} while (expression);
```

Listing 5-2 shows Listing 5-1 modified to use a do-while loop. The output for Listing 5-2 is the same as that for Listing 5-1.

Listing 5-2. Using a do-while Loop

```
/*
        Program that uses a do-while loop
*/

#include <stdio.h>

main()
{
    int i;

    i = 0;
    do {
        printf("%4d\n", rand());
        i++;
    } while (i < 10);
}
```

Note that a do-while loop still obeys the two general rules:

1. Initialize i prior to entering the loop.
2. Test i at the bottom of the loop to see whether another iteration of the loop must be executed.

while Loops Versus *do-while* Loops

If the output is the same for both programs, does it matter whether you use a while or a do-while loop? Yes, because the two can produce different results. Because the do-while performs the test on i at the bottom of the loop, a do-while loop always executes at least one pass through the statement(s) contained in the loop's statement block. If the expression at the top of a while loop evaluates to logical False when the loop is started, none of the statements within the while statement block are executed.

It is likely that you will use the while loop more often than a do-while loop.

for Loops

The for loop in C is probably the most used of all looping constructs. The general form of the for loop is

```
for (expression1; expression2; expression3) {
    statement(s);
}
```

In the for loop, the three expressions normally have the following actions associated with them:

expression1	initializes one or more variables
expression2	tests to determine whether another pass through the loop is needed
expression3	increments the variable controlling the loop

The program in Listing 5-2 shows an example of a for loop's use.

Listing 5-3. Using a for Loop

```
/*
    Using a for loop to print the extended character set
*/

#include <stdio.h>

main()
```

Listing 5-3 continues

Listing 5-3 continued

```
{
   int i;

   printf("IBM Extended Character Set\n\n          ");

   for (i = 0; i < 10; i++) {
      printf("%5d", i);
   }
   for (i = 120; i < 256; i++) {
      if (i % 10 == 0) {
         printf("\n%-10d", i);
      }
      if (i < 128)
         printf("      ");
      else
         printf("%5c", i);
   }
}
```

The program in Listing 5-3 prints a table of characters comprising the extended character set for the IBM PC. Let's see how the `for` loops work in the program.

expression1 of the *for* Loop

Figure 5-1 displays the first `for` loop.

```
                        ┌──── expression1
                        ▼
            for (i = 0; i < 10; i++) {
```

Figure 5-1. Initialization expression in for *loop.*

`expression1` initializes to 0 the starting value of `i`. If necessary, you can also initialize other variables as part of `expression1`. For example,

```
for (j = i = 0; i < 10; i++)
```

In this case, both i and j are initialized to 0. If we need to initialize j to a value other than 0, that's fine, too. In that case, use the comma operator to separate the two subexpressions

```
for (j = 1, i = 0; i < 10; i++)
```

You can expand expression1 to whatever initialization sequence you need.

expression2 of the *for* Loop

The second expression in the for loop determines whether another iteration of the loop must be executed. Usually expression2 involves a relational operator as shown in both for loops in Listing 5-3.

expression2 is not limited to just the use of relational operators, however, as shown in Figure 5-2.

```
int j;
                /*          ┌─── expression2   */
                /*          │                  */
                /*          ▼                  */
    for (j = 10; j; j--)  {
        /* Some C statements here */
    }
```

Figure 5-2. Logical expression in for *loop.*

In this example, j is initialized to 10 at the start of the loop. After each pass through the loop, j is decremented by the decrement operator (that is, j--). After 10 passes through the loop, j becomes 0. Because 0 is a logical False condition, expression2 is False and the for loop terminates.

Finally, I need to cover one special case for expression2. If expression2 is missing, as in

```
for (i = 0; ; i++) {
```

expression2 is viewed as logically True (even though it may seem more logical for it to be logical False). I say a little bit more about this special case later in this chapter.

expression3 of the *for* Loop

expression3 forms the last expression in the for loop. In most cases, expression3 is either an increment or decrement operator on the variable that controls the loop. In Listing 5-3, the loop controlled by i

```
for (i = 0; i < 10; i++) {
```

uses an increment operator to advance i to its terminal value of 10. Once again, expression3 can be any valid C expression, but 95 percent of the time it involves either the ++ or -- operators.

Sequencing of the *for* Loop Expressions

It is important that you understand the sequence in which the expressions are executed by the compiler. It should be obvious that expression1 is executed first. After all, expression1 is typically used to set the starting value(s) for variables used within the loop.

After expression1 is evaluated, expression2 is immediately evaluated. Note that this evaluation comes before any statements in the body of the loop are executed. Therefore, if expression2 evaluates to logical False at the beginning of the loop, the statement block controlled by the for loop may not be executed at all.

If expression2 evaluates to a nonzero value (that is, logical True), the statements in the for loop statement block are executed.

After the statements in the for loop statement block are executed, expression3 is evaluated. In other words, expression3 behaves as though it were the last statement in the loop. For example, if you take the first for loop in Listing 5-3

```
for (i = 0; i < 10; i++) {
    printf("%5d", i);
}
```

and "stretch" it out, you can make it look like

```
for (i = 0;                /* Do expression1 first */
     i < 10; ) {           /* Do expression2 next  */
    printf("%5d", i);
    i++;                   /* Now expression3       */
}
```

Try changing the loop to look like this and see whether QC compiles it. If it compiles, does it execute as before? (Hint: Yes!)

The program in Listing 5-4 explicitly shows how the three expressions in a `for` loop are sequenced.

Listing 5-4. Sequencing in a `for` Loop

```
#include <stdio.h>

main()
{
   int i;

   for (printf("\nexpression1"), i = 0;
      printf("\n      expression2 (i = %d)", i), i < 10;
      printf("\n            expression3 (increment)"), i++)  {
      printf("%5d", i);
   }
}
```

Admittedly, the program in Listing 5-4 is a bit strange, but it is all perfectly valid C code. Also, when you run the program, you immediately see the sequence in which the loop expressions are executed. (Use the F10 key to single-step the program.)

To summarize, the execution sequence in a `for` loop is

1. `expression1` (initialization).
2. `expression2` (a logical True or False to start, continue, or stop the execution of the loop statement block).
3. `expression3` (increment or decrement).

Infinite Loops

If you have any previous programming experience and you're honest, you already have written a few infinite loops. Simply stated, an infinite loop is a loop that never stops executing. In most cases, infinite loops are the result of some oversight or other programming error. Still, programming situations exist in which an infinite loop is desirable.

For example, suppose that you have a computer system with three terminals, all of which network together. Further suppose that you have a short program which continually scans the terminals to see whether a mail request is made to one of the other two users. To keep things simple, assume that the number 999 means there is a pending message. The code might look like

```
while (1) {
    alert = scan_system();
    if (alert == 999) {
        send_mail();
    }
}
```

The `while` loop is an infinite loop because the expression is the integer constant 1 and means the expression always evaluates to a logical True state. Once inside the `while` loop, the function `scan_system()` is assumed to poll the three terminals looking for a mail message. If no mail is pending, `alert` is assumed to return some value other than 999. If a message is found waiting, `scan_system()` returns 999, which is then assigned into `alert`. The `if` statement tests `alert` and, on finding a value of 999, executes the `send_mail()` function.

After the `send_mail()` function processes the message, another pass is made through the `while` loop. Indeed, you stay in this loop forever. Therefore, although you have an infinite loop, it is a useful one.

Using *#define* To Make Things More Clear

The use of a constant 1 to keep the loop going is a bit obtuse until you recall what a 1 means in the expression of a `while` loop. That's why C programmers use a `#define` to give the 1 a slightly more obvious meaning in the program. You might rewrite the program as

```
#define TRUE    1



.
.
.

while (TRUE) {
    alert = scan_system();
    if (alert == 999) {
        send_mail();
    }
}
```

As mentioned in Chapter 2, the preprocessor reads the C source file, finds the `#define` for `TRUE`, and makes a note to itself (in something called the macro table) that the word `TRUE` is defined for this program to be a 1. When it finds the statement

```
while (TRUE) {
```

the compiler scans its macro table to see whether `TRUE` is defined. Because it is defined, it replaces the word `TRUE` with 1 in the program. Keep in mind that the replacement is a *textual* replacement. That is, it is as though you did a global "search-and-replace" of TRUE with 1 on your word processor. The ASCII characters for TRUE are replaced with the character 1.

Another popular infinite loop form is

```
for (;;) {
   alert = scan_system();
   if (alert == 999) {
     send_mail();
   }
}
```

In this `for` loop, all three expressions are empty. That is, there is no expression for any of the statements in the `for` loop — just two lonely semicolons. Such empty statements are called *null statements*, and they are perfectly legal in C. Because there is no expression to end the `for` loop, an infinite loop results.

Again, because this form of `for` loop is a bit strange, whimsy has led to a more popular form using the `#define`.

```
#define EVER    ;;

for (EVER) {
   alert = scan_system();
   if (alert == 999) {
     send_mail();
   }
}
```

Again, the textual substitution produces the same code as before, but the intention of the `for` loop is now more clear. It is a "forever" `for` loop.

The examples of the `#define` shown in this section represent *symbolic constants* that you may wish to use in the program. By convention, symbolic constants are one of the few instances in which uppercase letters are blessed by the C programming community. Using uppercase letters for symbolic constants has two advantages:

1. They are easy to spot in a source code file.
2. You know immediately that they are symbolic constants and not variables. (That is, a symbolic constant has no lvalue.)

You will see other uses for the #define preprocessor directive in later chapters. (In fact, a #define could have been created for the constant 999 above.)

break Statement in Loops

In Chapter 4, you saw how the break statement was used to transfer program control out of a switch statement. The same break statement can be used to transfer program control out of a loop. The code fragments in Figure 5-3 show how the break statement is used in the three types of loops.

All three loops perform the same task. The first assumption made in the program appears to be that there will never be more than MAXEMPLOYEES working at one time. The function get_employee_id() evidently returns a number that represents an employee's identification number.

The variable employed could be one of two things. First, employed might be a bogus number indicating that you have read the complete list of employees. Such special numbers are called *sentinel* values in that their values have special meaning in the program. If a company employs only 100 people, 9999 might be a sentinel value that marks the end of the employee data. A second interpretation is that employed will always have a value of one greater than the last valid employee number. In this situation, employed also marks the end of the data set. In either case, when num and employed have the same value, the break statement causes program control to be sent out of the loop to the call to forward_totals().

You should be able to convince yourself that all three examples behave in much the same manner. The break statement in the examples allows you to end the loop when the work is done, instead of hanging around until MAXEMPLOYEES makes its passes through the loop. Therefore, the break statement allows you to break out of a loop before it would otherwise terminate on its own.

a) **The** while **Version**

```
#define MAXEMPLOYEES      30000

     .
     .
i = 0;

while (i < MAXEMPLOYEES)  {
   num = get_employee_id();
   if (num == employed)  {
      break;
   }
   printf_paycheck(num);
   i++;
}
forward_totals();
```

b) **The** do-while **Version**

```
#define MAXEMPLOYEES      30000

     .
     .
i = 0;

do {
   num = get_employee_id();
   if (num == employed)  {
      break;
   }
   printf_paycheck(num);
   i++;
} while (i < MAXEMPLOYEES);
forward_totals():
```

c) **The** for **Version**

```
#define MAXEMPLOYEES      30000

     .
     .
for (i = 0; i < MAXEMPLOYEES; i++)  {
   num = get_employee_id();
   if (num == employed)  {
      break;
   }
   printf_paycheck(num);
}
forward_totals();
```

Figure 5-3. Various Loop Structures and the break *Statement*

The *continue* Statement in Loops

The continue statement provides a means to immediately go to the next iteration of the loop. For example, suppose that you are reading a data file filled with client numbers. Further suppose that the last digit in this client number represents the number of months that their account is past due. If the client is one month or less past due, you don't want to do anything. If the client is more than a month past due, you need to take certain action. Further assume that no client has an account more than 9 months past due (and still lives). The following code fragment shows how to handle something like this.

```
#define MAXCLIENTS  10000

int past, i;
 .
for (i = 0; i < MAXCLIENTS; i++) {    /* Start of for loop */
   past = get_last_digit();
   if (past <= 1)
      continue;
   switch (past) {                    /* Start of switch   */
      case 2:
         send_nastygram(i);
         break;
      case 3:
         send_very_nastygram(i);
         break;
      case 4:
         make_phone_call(i);
         break;
      case 5:
         call_attorney(i);
         break;
      case 6:
      case 7:
      case 8:
      case 9:
         process_suit(i);
         break;
      default:
         send_flowers();
         break;
   }                                  /* End of switch   */
}                                     /* End of for loop */
```

In this example, the `if` test determines whether to process any situation covered by the `switch` statement. If `past` is a month or less, there's no need to go through the `switch` code. Therefore, the `continue` statement transfers control to the next iteration of the `for` loop. This means that `expression3 (i++)` is executed after the `continue` statement is executed. It also means that you avoid executing a lot of code that should not be executed. In a `while` or `do-while` loop, the expression that controls the loop is the next statement executed.

The purpose of the `continue` statement, therefore, is to provide a simple and direct means of executing the next iteration of a loop. The `continue` allows you to bypass the rest of the statements in the loop statement block. Because the purpose of the `continue` statement is to bypass remaining loop statements, the `continue` statement cannot be used outside of a `for`, `do-while`, or `while` statement block. Any attempt to do so generates an error message.

A Little Practice on Your Own

Now that you are familiar with conditional (`if`) and loop statements, you are in a position to write some of your own examples. Of course, it is one thing to copy code from this text into the QC compiler and get it running. It is an entirely different matter to try to solve a programming problem without a framework to guide you. Therefore, try writing programs to solve some of your own problems. Given what you now know, write some nontrivial programs if you wish.

If you don't have anything in mind, how about trying to write a program to demonstrate the following method for squaring integer numbers.

A number of years ago, and quite by accident, I noticed that the sum of n odd integers starting with 1 equals the square of n. For example, if you want to find the square of 3, sum the first 3 odd integers starting with 1

```
1 + 3 + 5 = 9
```

If you want to find the square of 5, the answer is

```
1 + 3 + 5 + 7 + 9 = 25
```

Write a program that gets an integer number from the user and then displays the number squared using the algorithm I just stated. A classy program will recognize that some numbers will overflow a simple `int` data type. Give it a try.

6

More About Functions

In this chapter, I discuss

C functions and why they are used

The various parts of a C function

Function prototyping (ANSI versus K&R C)

Using header files with standard library functions

The material presented in this chapter helps you understand why the developers of C designed the language the way they did. I also flesh in some details about functions that I avoided until you could gain more knowledge of C. Functions form the foundation of all C programs. The material presented in this chapter helps you develop your own set of functions.

What Is a C Function?

A C function is a collection of one or more C statements designed to accomplish a single task. Multiple functions are used to build programs that ultimately solve the problem at hand. Each function, therefore, is a tool with which you craft an infinite variety of programs.

The ANSI X3J11 draft report not only addresses the C language and its syntax, but also specifies how more than 150 library functions work. The QC compiler, however, provides more than 400 library functions! Think of it. You already have 400 small tasks solved by drawing upon the treasures to be found in the QC library. Writing C programs reduces to connecting the proper functions in the right sequence to solve a programming problem.

If all of these functions already exist, why are they in a library rather than being part of the language? First, one of the original objectives of C was that it have a small language to "fit" on virtually any machine, large or small. Removing all the I/O tasks from the language helped to meet that objective.

Second, limiting the scope of the language kept those people who write compilers from being bound by C's syntax rules when implementing the I/O functions. This one fact made C flexible enough for the compiler vendor to implement the I/O functions in a manner suited to the compiler's hardware environment. Over the years, convention and good old "give-and-take" resulted in a core of common functions that form the nucleus of the ANSI C standard library. What you find in the ANSI standard library is the experience of thousands of programmers who continually improved those functions over the course of more than a decade.

Why So Many Functions?

If the ANSI standard library defines about 150 functions, why does the QC compiler add another 250 to the list? There are a number of reasons. First, because each function is designed to address some programming task, a large library reduces the programmer's work. Second, it also makes good marketing sense. Third, because the QC compiler runs in a known hardware environment, many of the additional functions were written to take advantage of that known environment. The graphics library and the special DOS functions are two examples of hardware-dependent library functions. Finally, the presence of some of the functions, although not part of the standard library, is expected for virtually all compilers. The low-level file I/O functions are not part of the standard library, but every compiler vendor makes them available.

Don't view the large numbers of library functions as an imposition of more work on you. True, you need to know what is available, but once you have mastered these functions, they save you work rather than adding to it.

With this view of library functions in mind, let's fill in some of the gaps I left open in earlier discussions about functions.

Filling in Some Missing Details About Functions

When we first discussed functions back in Chapter 1, we purposely left out some details. Now that you are more comfortable with C, especially the basic data types that are available to you, we can fill in some of the details that were omitted earlier.

In Chapter 3 you saw how to create an integer number from ASCII digits characters. The guts of the work was done with the statement

```
i = atoi(gets(buff));
```

Because integer numbers are used so often in C programs, you might elect to create a function that gets an integer number from the keyboard.

So, how to go about designing your function? First, you know that you want the function to return an integer value. Second, assume that the function is capable of displaying a prompt. Third, check the input to ensure that the value typed in fits within the range of an integer value. With this in mind, examine the formal syntax that is required for a function definition.

```
type_specifier    function_name(argument list)
{                             /* Opening brace for function body */

    statement(s);     /* Function body                      */

}                             /* Closing brace for function body */
```

This is similar to the format discussed in Chapter 2, with some missing details supplied.

Function Type Specifiers

The first thing that begins a function definition is the type specifier. The *type specifier* is the type of data that is returned from the function. In the function you are writing, the type specifier is an int data type because that is the type of data you want the function to return. For example, if you were writing a function that takes the square root of a number (which often requires decimal fractions), you would probably use a double type specifier. Later in this book, you will see functions that return many different types of data. In the final analysis, however, the type specifier will be dictated by the task the function is designed to fulfill.

Unless told otherwise, the rules of C state that every function returns an `int` data type. In other words, *the default type specifier for all functions is an* `int` *data type.* In all of the previous program examples, we wrote

```
main()
{
    /* main()'s function body */
}
```

Because you did not explicitly use a type specifier, QC said, "OK. The type specifier for `main()` is missing, so it must be an `int` by default." That is, omitting the function type specifier causes C to assume that the function returns an `int` data type. What you actually wrote, therefore, was

```
int main()
{
    /* main()'s function body */
}
```

Notice that an `int` type specifier was added to `main()`. From now on, always supply the type specifier for all function definitions. By explicitly writing the type specifier as part of the function definition (and not relying on the default type specifier of `int`) you are less likely to commit certain types of programming errors later on. (I cover some of these types of errors later in the chapter.)

The *return* Statement

Although you may not have known it, `main()` has returned an integer value for every program you have run in this book. In fact, you saw this integer value each time you ran a program using QC in the integrated environment. Whenever you compiled and ran a program, there was a line at the bottom of your screen that read something like

```
Elapsed time = 00:00:01. Program returned (23). Press any key
```

Perhaps you wondered what the "Program returned" was all about. (The value in the parentheses varies.) Actually, the number in parentheses was the integer value returned by `main()` after the program ran. Remember, all C functions return an `int` data type by default. Because you didn't tell QC otherwise, QC assumed `main()` returned an `int`.

Prove this by running the short program shown in Listing 6-1.

Listing 6-1. Experimenting with Return Values

```
#include <stdio.h>

int main(void)
{
    int i = 10;

    return i;
}
```

The `return` statement tells the compiler the *value* that the function should return. The type specifier tells the compiler the *type* of data to be returned. You have defined `main()` to return the value of `i` which is an `int` data type. The rules of C require that an `int` is the only data type that `main()` can return.

When you run the program in Listing 6-1, you see something like

```
Elapsed time = 00:00:01. Program returned (10). Press any key
```

Notice that the value returned is 10—the value of `i` in `main()`.

How Values Are Returned from a Function

When QC sees the `return` statement in a function, followed by either a variable name or a numeric constant, the compiler must do several things to process the `return` statement properly. For the purpose of discussion, I assume that the *return* statement looks like that shown in Listing 6-1. First, the compiler reads the name of the variable, finds its `lvalue`, and then fetches the `rvalue` of the variable. Next, the compiler looks at the type specifier for the function. Because `i` is an `int` and matches the type specifier for the function (also an `int`), QC reserves one integer-sized "chunk" of storage (i.e., two bytes) and shoves the `rvalue` of `i` into that storage.

So where is this storage? The storage used to return values from a function is called the *stack*, which is a section of memory that works like a stack of plates at a salad bar. The plates are piled on top of each other on a spring-loaded server. As a plate is removed, the pile shifts up. This also means that the first plate on the stack is the last one used. Conversely, the last plate on the stack is the first one used. (Ever notice how the last plates often tend to be hot? It's a good indication that people like the salad bar.)

The stack works much the same way in C. When QC sees the statement

```
return i;
```

QC checks the type specifier for the function (`main()` is an `int`) and reserves two bytes (plates?) for the return value. QC then places the `rvalue` of `i` into those two bytes on the stack. Figure 6-1 shows how this might look.

(I assume that X, Y, and Z represent other data that already might be on the stack.) The picture of the stack before the `return` statement is shown in Figure 6-1a. After QC processes the `return` statement, the stack looks like Figure 6-1b. Because `main()` returns an `int` data type (`main()`'s type specifier is an `int`), two bytes of stack space are used for returning the value of `i`. Figure 6-1c shows what the stack looks like after the value 10 has been "popped off" the stack. When QC displays its end-of-program message, it pops the value 10 off the stack and shows the value near the bottom of the screen.

(In reality, QC seems to take the return value from `main()` and display it as a signed `char` data type on the screen. If you try to return a value greater than 127, it is shown as a negative number. If the number is greater than 256, the number display is the result of that number modulo 256. This suggests that QC truncates the return value to a `char`.)

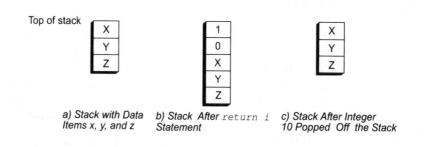

a) Stack with Data Items x, y, and z   b) Stack After `return i` Statement   c) Stack After Integer 10 Popped Off the Stack

Figure 6-1. The Stack Pictures Using a `return` Statement

The sequence shown in Figure 6-1 is a bit simplified, but understanding how values are passed back from a function call is important.

Values returned from a function are passed on the stack. The type specifier determines how much stack space will be used for the returned value.

Also keep in mind that any function definition that is missing its type specifier defaults to an `int`. However, I urge that you always write in the type specifier when defining a function, even when the function returns an !int.

Writing Your First Function

Now use what you've learned so far to write a function to return an integer data type. Listing 6-2 shows how the function can be written.

Listing 6-2. The `getint()` Function

```
/*****
                                 getint()

        This function is used to get an integer number from the
    keyboard. A prompt string is passed to the function and displayed
    on the screen. The value returned is the integer number.

    Argument list:        char prompt[]        the prompt string

    Return value          int                  the integer

*****/


int getint(char prompt[])
{
    char buff[20];

    printf("%s", prompt);
    gets(buff);
    return atoi(buff);
}
```

Whenever you define a function, including a comment about what the function does and what it returns is a good idea. I prefer the format shown in Listing 6-2, but feel free to use whatever style works best for you. You will, however, appreciate the long comments about the function and its arguments when you must debug it several weeks later.

The function definition begins with the type specifier `int`, followed by the name of the function—`getint()`. Next comes the argument list. In this case, the argument list is an array of `char`s that form a string. The function body defines some working storage for `buff[]` and then uses `printf()` to display the message that was passed to the function. The remainder of the function code should look familiar to you. The call to `gets()` stores your keystrokes in `buff[]`. Next, `atoi()` converts the contents of `buff[]` to an integer. The `return` statement then takes that value, shoves it onto the stack, and the function ends.

Now look at how to use it in a real program. The complete program is shown in Listing 6-3, including the code for the `getint()` function.

Listing 6-3. Program to Test `getint()`

```
#include <stdio.h>

int main()
{
    int i;

    i = getint("Enter an integer: ");
    printf("\ni = %d", i);
    return i;                           /* Looks weird if i > 127 */
}


/*****
                        getint()

      This function is used to get an integer number from the
   keyboard. A prompt string is passed to the function and displayed
   on the screen. The value returned is the integer number.

      Argument list:      char prompt[]        the prompt string

      Return value        int                  the integer

*****/



int getint(char prompt[])
{
    char buff[20];
```

```
    printf("%s", prompt);
    gets(buff);
    return atoi(buff);
}
```

In `main()`, call `getint()` with the prompt you wish to display on the screen. When `getint()` is finished, the integer value sits on the stack. The assignment statement

```
i = getint("Enter an integer: ");
```

causes QC to generate code that pops off the two bytes (i.e., an `int`) on the stack and place them at the `lvalue` of `i`. In other words, you replace the previous contents of `i` (the `rvalue` of `i`) with the two bytes that were placed on the stack by `getint()`. This also means that you have assigned the integer value entered into `i`—exactly what you want to do.

The remainder of the program displays the value and returns the value for QC to show after the program is run. (Don't forget: Values greater than 127 look strange because of the way QC displays the value returned from `main()`.)

(By the way, you have not checked the value entered to see if it is a valid integer. You're not ready to do this yet. However, if you wish to experiment with such error checking, you can look into the `limits.h` header file first to verify the valid ranges for an `int` data type.)

How to Mess Up Function Return Values

Suppose you now need a function that returns a `long` data type. You can modify the `getint()` to create the new function named `getlong()`. This is shown in Listing 6-4.

Listing 6-4. The `getlong()` *Function*

```
/*****

                            getlong()

        This function is used to get a long integer number from
    the keyboard. A prompt string is passed to the function and
```

Listing 6-4 continues

Listing 6-4 continued

```
displayed on the screen. The value returned is the long integer
number.

Argument list:        char prompt[]        the prompt string

Return value          long                 the long integer

*****/


long getlong(char prompt[])
{
   char buff[20];

   printf("%s", prompt);
   gets(buff);
   return atol(buff);
}
```

The code is identical to getint(), except you replaced atoi() with atol(). As you might guess, atol() is a standard library function that converts an ASCII string into a long data type. When QC processes the return statement in the getlong() function, the type specifier tells QC to use 4 bytes of stack space to hold the value. Figure 6-2 shows how this stack sequence might look, assuming the value 10 is again entered.

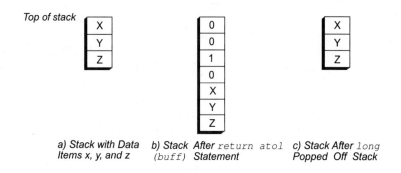

Top of stack

a) Stack with Data   b) Stack After return atol   c) Stack After long
Items x, y, and z   (buff) Statement   Popped Off Stack

Figure 6-2. The Stack Pictures for getlong()

Notice how 4 bytes of stack space are used. Figure 6-2a shows the stack before the `return` statement in `getlong()`. Figure 6-2b shows the stack after the value has been pushed onto the stack. Figure 6-2c shows how the stack should look after the `long` is popped off the stack; probably by assigning the value into a variable.

Listing 6-5 shows what you might try to do to test the `getlong()` function. (There is no reason to repeat the `getlong()` source code; I just assume that the code in Listing 6-4 is part of your program.)

Listing 6-5. Testing `getlong()`

```
#include <stdio.h>

int main()
{
    long i;

    i = getlong("Enter a long integer: ");
    printf("\ni = %ld", i);
    return i;
}
```

The program in Listing 6-5 won't work too well. Why? (There are several bugs in the program. I'll start with the most obvious bugs and fill in the details on some that are a bit more subtle later in the chapter.) First, when QC starts processing the function definition for `getlong()`, you get an error message similar to

```
error C2086: 'getlong' : redefinition
```

The problem is that, not knowing otherwise, QC assumes that `getlong()` (in `main()`) returns an `int` data type. After all, that is the default return data type from a function call and you didn't tell QC anything to the contrary. A few lines later in the program you define `getlong()` to return a `long` data type. QC now has conflicting information. In `main()`, `getlong()` appears (by default) to return an `int` but the type specifier in the function definition of `getlong()` says the return data type is a `long`. The result of this conflict is a QC "redefinition" error message. You attempted to redefine the (assumed) `int` return value in `main()` to be a `long` in the function definition of `getlong()`.

QC has called your attention to a very nasty type of bug—mismatched data types. Figure 6-3 shows what the stack would look like if QC didn't catch the mistake.

The stack picture in Figure 6-3 is the same as that in Figure 6-2, except for the last picture. Assuming that the getlong() function does indeed place the long on the stack as shown in Figure 6-3b, the stack is not cleared off properly in Figure 6-3c. Because main() thinks that getlong() returns an int, main() retrieves only two bytes from the stack. Because main() assumes that the return value from getlong() is an int, main() pops off only "half a long" from the stack! As a result, the wrong value is assigned into i if QC doesn't catch the mismatch between the (assumed int) return data type in main() and the actual (defined) long data type in the function definition for getlong().

Clearly, you need a way to tell main() that getlong() is returning some data type other than the default data type int.

There are two ways to let main() know that getlong() returns a long data type rather than an int. The first is to move the definition of the getlong() function before the definition of main(). That is, have the source code for getlong() appear in the program before main(). This approach explains why, in some programs, the source code for main() is near the end of the program.

Personally, I don't think this is the best approach because it forces you to have your function definitions appear before main(), which controls the program flow. A better way is to use a function declaration.

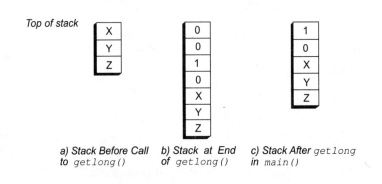

a) Stack Before Call to getlong() b) Stack at End of getlong() c) Stack After getlong in main()

Figure 6-3. The Stack Pictures for Mismatched Data Types

Function Declarations

A function declaration does nothing more than pass information to the compiler so that it can process subsequent function calls with a little more knowledge than otherwise. Listing 6-6 presents an example of a function declaration.

Listing 6-6. Function Declaration for `getlong()`

```
#include <stdio.h>

int main()
{
   long i;
   long getlong();                         /* Function declaration */

   i = getlong("Enter a long integer: ");
   printf("\ni = %ld", i);
   return i;
}
```

Notice the new statement

```
long getlong();
```

in `main()`. Whenever a statement includes a function's type specifier followed by its name, but is missing the function's source code, it is a *function declaration*. A function declaration, such as that shown in Listing 6-6, serves one purpose: To tell the compiler the return data type of the function. Because the return data type is now known, QC knows to pop off four bytes of data from the stack to retrieve the correct value returned by `getlong()`.

Define Versus Declare...Again

In Chapter 2, I said that data definitions cause storage to be allocated, but declarations do not. Clearly, in Listing 6-6 you have *defined* variable i and allocated storage for it. On the other hand, the next line *declares* what `getlong()` returns; no storage is allocated by this statement. The function declaration is a message with information about getlong() that the compiler stores in its symbol table during program compilation. The symbol table does not end up in the program itself.

The code shown in Listing 6-4 does allocate storage for the function. Listing 6-4 is an example of a *function definiton*, but Listing 6-6 is an example of a function declaration. As a general rule:

Function definition: the source code for the function body is given. Storage is allocated.

Function declaration: no source code present and no storage allocated.

It should be clear that function definitions cause the compiler to generate code to accomplish the function's task. On the other hand, a *function declaration* is in the program to pass information about the function to the compiler so that it can do its job properly. QC simply uses this information so that it can do its job correctly; the information does not cause QC to generate code that ends up in your program.

Function declarations must be used for any function that does not return an integer data type. Otherwise, the compiler does not know the proper number of bytes to pop off the stack for the return value from the function. Forgotten function declarations is a fruitful area for program bugs.

Always use function declarations when the function returns a data type other than int.

The *void* Data Type

What do you do when you write a function that does not return any type of data? The ANSI committee created a new data type—the void data type—specifically to cope with this situation. The void data type can be used 1) as a function type specifier in a function declaration or definition, or 2) to show that a function has no argument list. For example, for a program that uses the QC library function named qsort(), you can write

```
int main(void)
{
    void qsort();

    /* Whatever code main() needs */

}
```

Notice the two uses of the `void` keyword. First, `void` appears between the opening and closing parentheses of `main()`. This tells the compiler that there are no function arguments for `main()`. The next example tells QC that the `qsort()` library function does not return a value, so it shouldn't bother generating code to pop a value off the stack.

The use of the `void` keyword makes QC a lot smarter, too. For example, suppose you tried the statement

```
flag = qsort();
```

The function declaration that `qsort()` is a `void` function tells QC that no value can be returned from the `qsort()` function call. Armed with that information, QC flags the statement above as an error because you tried to assign a `void` data item (that is, a "nothing") into `flag`. It should be clear that the `void` data type is not a "wasted" data type. It prevents QC from generating unnecessary code (for example, popping data off the stack) and provides a means of checking for illegal assignments from certain types of (`void`) function calls. Both of these benefits, however, assume that you have told QC that a `void` function exists via a function declaration using the `void` type specifier.

Function Prototypes in C

As you saw in the section above, a function declaration provides a means for the compiler to check the data type returned from a function call, thereby catching potential errors in your program. ANSI C provides an additional means to detect potential errors through a mechanism called function prototyping. `Function prototyping` allows a compiler to perform type checking on the arguments that are passed to a function. For example, the second line of `main()`'s function body in Listing 6-6 is a function declaration for `getlong()`.

```
long getlong();
```

This function declaration tells the compiler (via the function type specifier) what data type is returned by the function. This is the standard pre-ANSI C (often called "K&R" C) form for a function declaration. You also know from the code shown in Listing 6-4 that the argument passed to `getlong()` should be an array of `char`s (i.e., a string). The problem is that QC doesn't know this. Because QC doesn't know about the argument list for getlong() when it is reading the code in main(), you can pass an int to getlong() and QC assumes that everything is fine. In other words, pre-ANSI C provides no means to check the data types in the argument list.

Function prototyping, however, provides QC with the ability to check the arguments that are passed to a function. Listing 6-7 shows how prototyping is used.

Listing 6-7. Using Function Prototyping

```
#include <stdio.h>


int main(void)
{
   long i;
   long getlong(char prompt[]);

   i = getlong("Enter a number: ");
   printf("\ni = %ld", i);
}
```

Note how the function declaration for getlong() in main() has been written. Not only do you tell QC that getlong() returns a long data type (via the long type specifier), but also that the function expects to be passed an array of characters. If you attempt to pass a different data type as the argument to getlong(), prototyping makes QC smart enough to flag the mismatched data types in the call to getlong() as an error. (As an experiment, edit Listing 6-7 to try to pass i as the argument and see what QC does. For now, pay special attention to the second error message.) Function prototyping provides a means by which type checking can be performed on arguments that are passed to a function.

Function prototyping can save you a lot of debugging time. Always use prototyping in function declarations.

An Abbreviated Form of Function Prototypes

Suppose you write a function that takes the square root of a number. The function declaration might be written as

```
double square_root(double number);
```

This function declaration tells QC that `square_root()` uses a `double` as an argument and that the return value is also a `double`. If you pass 25.0 to `square_root()` as a `double` data type, 5.0 (a `double`) is returned from the call to `square_root()`.

You can also write an equivalent function declaration as

```
double square_root(double);
```

Notice that you deleted the name of the variable. This form is perfectly valid C syntax. After all, the purpose of a function prototype is to tell QC the type of data being passed to the function. QC could not care less what the name of the variable is that is passed to the function; it cares only that the variable be a `double` data type.

Although both forms are valid, make it a habit to use the form that also gives an argument name. The reason is that properly selected names help document the purpose of the function. This is especially important for those functions that you write yourself. As your programs get larger and spread across multiple files, wisely chosen variable names help you remember the function argument's purpose.

In this book I always use the prototype form that uses the variable name along with the type specifier.

Function Declarations Don't Create Variables

The purpose of a variable name in a function declaration using prototyping is documentation only. The name is there to help you remember the purpose of the function's argument, not to create a variable. In other words, variable names in a function declaration cannot be used as variables in the program.

Listing 6-8 is almost identical to Listing 6-7 except that one new line is added.

Listing 6-8. A Function Prototyping Error

```
#include <stdio.h>


int main(void)
{
    long i;
    long getlong(char prompt[]);
```

Listing 6-8 continues

Listing 6-8 continued

```
    prompt[0] = 'E';
    i = getlong("Enter a number: ");
    printf("\ni = %ld", i);
}
```

The new statement

```
prompt[0] = 'E';
```

attempts to place the character `'E'` into the first element of `prompt[]` given in the function declaration. However, if it is true that function declarations do not create storage, there can be no `lvalue` for `prompt[]`. If there is no `lvalue`, you cannot assign something into it. If you try to compile the code in Listing 6-8, QC issues the error message

```
error C2065: 'prompt' : undefined
```

This exercise confirms that function declarations do not create storage for the variables that appear in the prototype of a function declaration.

Once again, the variable names found in the prototype of a function declaration are there for documentation purposes only; they don't exist as true variables.

Function Definitions Do Create Variables

Although declarations do not create storage, `definitions` do create storage. Therefore, the code in Listing 6-4 does define a function named `getlong()` and the function prototype does reflect a variable (`prompt[]`) that has been defined elsewhere in the program (that is, in `main()`). This is why you can use the variables that appear in the prototype of a function definition within the function body of that function.

Although all of this may seem confusing, the rules are simple:

1. Variable names that appear in the prototype of a function declaration cannot be used within that function.
2. Variable names that appear in the prototype of a function definition can be used within that function.

Just remember that declarations are for information only, but definitions are for use.

Define Versus Declare...Again and Again

When you saw the function definition of `getlong()` in Listing 6-4, did the following line bother you?

```
long getlong(char prompt[])
```

Many beginning C programmers find it a bit strange to have an array with no size specification given, as is the case for `prompt[]`. C allows this for two reasons. First, C does not perform boundary checking on array sizes. That is, C does not check to see if an array is large enough to hold the data you might be trying to shove into it.

Second and more important, the purpose of the argument list of a function is to tell the function what is being passed to it. Obviously, if the data are being passed to the function, that data must already "exist" (that is, have an `lvalue`. and `rvalue`) elsewhere in the program. The `getlong()` function, for example, does not have to know how large `prompt[]` is; it simply needs to know that the argument is an array of `char`s.

Referring to Listing 6-7, when QC sees the statement

```
i = getlong("Enter a number: ");
```

it allocates enough storage to hold the string constant `"Enter a number: "`. This also means that there is a memory location (`lvalue`) where the contents of the string (`rvalue`) are stored. All QC needs to do, therefore, is pass the `lvalue` of the string to `getlong()` and let `getlong()` do its thing.

Keep in mind that the storage for the string constant was defined by the compiler in `main()`; you simply use the contents of that storage in `getlong()`. Stated differently, you define the string constant in `main()` and declare what it is in `getlong()`'s function prototype. Because the prompt is already defined in `main()`, `getlong()` doesn't need to know how big it is; it only needs to know what it is so that it can be used as a string in the function.

If you can nail down the distinction between define and declare as they relate to functions, the rest of C is a snap! If things are still a bit fuzzy, look at Listing 6-4 again and ask yourself if there is anything in the function that needs to know how large `prompt[]` is. All `getlong()` needs to know is that it has been handed an unspecified array of characters. From a logical point of view, think how restrictive specifying the size of the array coming in would be. You would have to rewrite the function each time the size of the prompt changed!

Arguments in a function prototype have already been defined else-where in the program, so there is no need to worry about their size. (The only time a function cares about array sizes is when they have two or more dimensions. I discuss this little detour in Chapter 8.)

Cut and Paste with the QC Editor

It should be clear that, as you start writing your own programs and functions, you will want to provide function declarations for those functions that you write yourself. It is easy to use the QC editor to copy the first line of a function definition, move it to wherever it might be needed as a function declaration, and add a semicolon to make it a function declaration. For example, suppose you've typed in Listing 6-3 and now you want to write a function declaration for `getint()` in `main()`.

First, move the cursor to the first character of the line that starts the function definition for `getint()`

```
int getint(char prompt[])
```

Now hold the Shift key down and press the right arrow key until you reach the end of the line. As you press the right arrow key, the line is highlighted one character at a time. When you reach the end of the line, release the Shift and right arrow key and select the Edit option from the Menu Line (Alt-E). Now select the Copy option (the letter C is the hot key). The cursor once again appears in the source code window.

Use the up arrow key to move the cursor to the line just below the definition of variable `i`. Press the Alt-E keys to select the Edit menu again. Select the Paste option (the letter P is the hot key). Immediately the cursor returns to the source code window and copies the line from the function definition into the `main()` function.

The function definition does not require a semicolon at the end, but a function declaration does, so use the arrow keys to move to the end of the line and add the semicolon. You just used the Cut-and-Paste feature of the QC editor to copy text from one part of the program to another. Copying the function definition line is a fast and easy way to add function declarations to your programs.

Your Program Still Won't Work

Suppose that you've combined Listings 6-4 and 6-5 into a single program and, after correcting any errors discussed thus far, you find that the program still won't work properly. (It won't...yet.) Why not?

Clearly, the purpose of the atol() function is to convert the digit characters you entered at the keyboard into a long integer data type. However, have you done anything to tell QC that atol() returns a long? Bingo!

Getting Function Help

Assuming that the program is in the source code window, move the cursor to the atol() function and press the F1 key. The F1 key causes QC to supply context-sensitive help on the screen. The help message displayed is for the word under the cursor at the time the F1 key is pressed. Because the cursor sits on the atol() function, you are shown a help message similar to that shown in Figure 6-4.

```
 File  Edit  View  Search  Make  Run  Debug  Utility  Options          Help
                   HELP: atof, atoi, atol, _atold [138]
  ◄Description► ◄Example►                    ◄Up► ◄Contents► ◄Index► ◄Back►


   Include:   <stdlib.h> or <math.h>  (atof)
              <stdlib.h>              (atoi, atol)
              <math.h>                (_atold)

   Syntax:    double atof( char *string );
              int atoi( char *string );
              long atol( char *string );
              long double _atold( char *string );

   Returns:   the converted string, or 0 if the string cannot be
              converted.

   See also:  ecvt, fcvt, gcvt
                                    ──◆──
                         D:\QCZ\L6-6.C
     return atol(buff);
 }

 <F1=Help> <Esc=Close> <F6=Window> <Shift+F5=Restart>              00023:011
```

Figure 6-4. Example of Context-Sensitive Help

You have a problem because QC doesn't know that `atol()` returns a `long` data type. The solution is to provide a function declaration for the `atol()` function. The help message, however, says to `#include` the `stdlib.h` header file when using the `atol()` function. If you wish to view the `stdlib.h` header file, press Alt-V (for the View menu option) and then select the I option (for include files). Then type in the full path and file name of the header file to be viewed. (See Figure 6-5.) For my hard disk system, the QC header files are stored in the INCLUDE subdirectory, so I typed in

```
include\stdlib.h
```

Instantly the contents of the `stdlib.h` are displayed in the source window. Use the End cursor key to go to the bottom of the file, press PgUp a few times, and there it is—the function declaration for `atol()`.

When you finish viewing the `stdlib.h` header file, press Alt-F to get to the File menu option, followed by another F (that is, Alt-F-F). The original program source code immediately reappears in the source code window. This is really nice stuff, folks!

Before leaving the subject of function help, notice the line at the top of the help window in Figure 6-4 that reads

```
<Summary> <Description> <Example>
```

These fields give you even more information about the function. Activate these fields by pressing the F6 key to get to the top line of the help window, then use the Tab key to move among the three choices. By the time you read everything available, you will probably agree that there is little need to consult the written documentation for the function.

Header Files

If you spent some time browsing through the stdlib.h header file, you saw numerous symbolic constants (`#define`'s) and a bunch of function declarations. Clearly, header files contain function declarations that pertain to classes of functions. You are not ready for me to delve into all of the header files provided with the QC compiler, but Table 6-1 provides clues to several of the more frequently used header files.

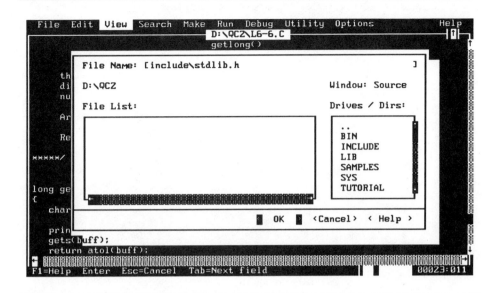

Figure 6-5. Using the View Option

Table 6-1. Common Header Files

File Name	Explanation
ctype.h	functions dealing with characters
limits.h	range limits for most data types
math.h	numeric, trig, and other math functions
stddef.h compiler	symbolic constants and variable names used by the
stdio.h	symbolic constants and function declarations for most I/O functions. Always #include this header file.
stdlib.h	declarations for many ANSI functions
string.h	string processing functions

I discuss additional header files throughout the rest of the book. The list in Table 6-1, however, gets you started in the right direction.

Now that you understand function prototypes, this is a good time to review Appendix B in the *C for Yourself* manual that came with the QC compiler. Appendix B helps you discover the wealth of library functions that are supplied with the QC compiler. Knowing what is available to you in the storehouse makes your programming tasks much simpler later on.

7

Privacy, Scope, and Storage Classes

In this chapter, I discuss the following related topics:

Data privacy

Scope

Storage classes

Reasons for using multiple program files

Using QC's Make facility

In this chapter, you learn another reason functions play such an important role in C. You also learn how you can restrict access to a data item by defining it in one of several different ways. Finally, you examine how multiple source files can be compiled to form a single program.

Data Privacy and Scope

A major reason that C won out over other languages I've experimented with is the privacy of a data item. If you've programmed in BASIC, you may have experienced how changing a variable in part of the program causes a new bug in a different part of the program. This problem exists in BASIC because all data items in C are available globally for use throughout the program. That is, each data item is "visible" to all parts of the program.

In C, you can restrict the visibility of a data item. Simply stated, the *scope* of a data item refers to the availability (or visibility) of a data item in a program. Listing 7-1 is an illustration of the scope of variable i.

Listing 7-1. Scope of a Variable

```
/*
     Program to show the scope of variable i
*/

#include <stdio.h>

int main(void)
{
    int i;
    void func(void);

    i = 10;
    func();
    printf("i = %d", i);
}

void func(void)
{
    printf("i = %d", i);
}
```

When you attempt to compile the program in Listing 7-1, QC issues the error message

```
error C2065: 'i':undefined
```

Obviously, the variable i defined in main() is not available for use in func(). In other words, the scope of i is local to main(). As an experiment, move the definition of i in main() so that it appears after the #include but before the beginning of main(). The relevant part of Listing 7-1 would be modified to look like

```
#include <stdio.h>

int i;        /* Note that we moved this definition of i. */

int main(void)
{
     /* The rest of Listing 7-1 */
```

Now try to compile the program. What happens? After making this change, QC offers no complaints and everything works just fine. Evidently, you changed the scope of i so that it is available to func(). Obviously, there are some rules about all of this that you need to understand.

Variables with Local Scope

There are two basic levels of scope:

1. Local
2. Global

I present the rules for local scope first. Once you understand the rules for local scope, the global scope rules become obvious.

There are three rules for local scope.

1. The scope of a variable is limited to the statement block or function block in which the variable is defined.
2. If two variables have the same name, the one defined at the current scope level takes precedence.
3. A scope level can only begin with a statement or function block.

Now you can see how each of these rules works.

In Listing 7-1, variable i was defined within the function block called main(). Therefore, the scope (visibility) of i extends from its definition in main() to the closing brace of main(). In practical terms, i is "dead" to anything that exists outside of main().

This also means that i is "private" to main(). No matter what you might try to do to i in some other part of the program, you cannot directly change i outside of main(). The advantage of local scope, or data privacy, is that you cannot inadvertently change i. This makes debugging much easier.

Listing 7-2 further illustrates the local scope rules.

Listing 7-2. Local Scoping Rules

```
/*
    Example of scope
*/

#include <stdio.h>

                                    /* Start scope level 0 */
int main(void)
{
    int i;                          /* Start scope level 1 */


    i = 10;
    if (i == 10) {                  /* Start scope level 2 */

        int i;

        i = 5;
        printf("i = %d\n", i);
    }                               /* End scope level 2   */

    printf("i = %d\n", i);
}                                   /* End scope level 1   */
                                    /* End scope level 0   */
```

The program in Listing 7-2 illustrates the first and second rules for local scope. Each time you enter a new statement block, you also enter a new scope level. For now, if you are not within a statement or function block, say you are in scope level 0. When you enter main(), you advance to a new scope level (that is, level 1). Notice that scope level 1 starts with the definition of i near the beginning of main().

Next you enter the if statement block. Because the if controls another statement block, you advance to another scope level (that is, level 2). Within scope level 2, you define a new i. Rule 2 states that any time two variables share the same name, the one defined at the current scope level takes precedence. In the example, the i defined at scope level 2 takes precedence. In other words, QC now has two variables named i, but they do not conflict because they are different variables. This also means that each i has its own lvalue and rvalue. The i defined at scope level 2 is the one that has the value 5 assigned into it, and that is the value displayed with the call to printf().

When program control leaves the if statement block, we leave scope level 2. This also means that the i defined within the if statement block is now "out of scope." In other words, the i defined at scope level 2 dies. Because the final printf() cannot see the "dead" i defined at scope level 2, only the i defined at scope level 1 is visible, or "in scope." This is why the final value displayed is 10.

To prove that Listing 7-2 does have two separate i variables, use the Debug option in QC to see the lvalues of the i variables. Use the Alt-D-W key sequence to set a watch value. The expression to type is

```
&i
```

because you want to see where the variable i is stored in memory; you want to see its lvalue.

When I ran the program in Listing 7-2 and used the F10 key to single-step through the program, the first memory address for i was at offset address 0x0dcc. After the definition of i in the if statement, the offset address was 0x0dca. QC has indeed created two i variables with different lvalues.

Do one more experiment to prove scope level. Listing 7-3 is just a modification of Listing 7-2, so it might be easier to use the Merge option in the File menu to create the program.

Listing 7-3. The Death of Local Scope

```
/*
     Another example of scope
*/

#include <stdio.h>

                              /* Start scope level 0 */
int main(void)
{
   int i;                     /* Start scope level 1 */


   i = 10;
   if (i == 10) {             /* Start scope level 2 */
      int j;
```

Listing 7-3 continues

Listing 7-3 continued

```
    j = 5;
        printf("j = %d\n", j);
    }                                           /* End scope level 2    */

    printf("i = %d, j = %d\n", i, j);
}                                               /* End scope level 1    */
                                                /* End scope level 0    */
```

Notice that you defined a variable j where i used to be in Listing 7-2. Now try to compile the program. Once again, QC says

```
error C2065: 'j' : undefined
```

when it tries to compile the final `printf()` statement. QC gives an error message because variable j has local scope. This means that j is in scope only at scope level 2. Because the final `printf()` is at scope level 1, j is out of scope and QC must issue the error message that j is undefined. After all, j died the instant you hit the closing brace of the `if` statement.

It should be clear that once you leave the scope level at which a data item is defined, that data item is no longer in scope. If a data item is not in scope, your program cannot have access to the data item.

An Implicit Assumption of Scope Rule 1

The first scope rule has a very subtle assumption associated with it. If you define a variable at a certain scope level, higher scope levels can access it subject to Rule 2. Listing 7-4 shows this nuance (and is a modification of Listing 7-3).

Listing 7-4. A Nuance of Scope Rules

```
/*
      Still more on scope
*/

#include <stdio.h>

                              /* Start scope level 0 */
```

```
int main(void)
{
   int i;                              /* Start scope level 1 */


   i = 10;
   if (i == 10) {                      /* Start scope level 2 */
      int j;

      j = 5;
      printf("j = %d, i = %d\n", j, i);
   }                                   /* End scope level 2   */

   printf("i = %d, j = %d\n", i, j);
}                                      /* End scope level 1   */
                                       /* End scope level 0   */
```

Notice that you now include variable i in the first printf() call within the if statement block. However, because you defined i before you entered this scope level, and there is no new variable i defined at the current scope level, you have full access to variable i at scope level 2 even though the definition of i was at scope level 1. You may want to reread this paragraph several times until you completely understand what it says.

Another way to view Listing 7-4 is in terms of statement blocks. A statement block has access to the data items defined at all lower scope levels, ending with the function block. That is, if you are in scope level 2 in Listing 7-4, you can use any data item defined at a lower level (scope level 1) down to the scope for the main() function block. The only exception is when a variable defined at the current scope uses the *same name* as one defined at a lower scope. In that instance, only the variable at the current scope can be accessed.

Another Reason Why Scope Is Important

Consider the sample program shown in Listing 7-5.

Listing 7-5. Data Privacy

```
/*
      Example of scope during function call
*/

#include <stdio.h>

int main(void)
{
    int i;
    void func(int);

    i = 10;
    func(i);

    printf("i = %d\n", i);
}


void func(int i)
{
    i *= i;
    printf("i = %d\n", i);
}
```

I urge you to type this program because its behavior is critical to understanding scope and the importance of data privacy. After you have typed the program, select the Debug option and set a Watch value (that is, Alt-D-W). The first expression to type is

&i

Then repeat the Alt-D-W sequence to add a second expression

i

These two expressions allow you to watch both the lvalue and rvalue of i as the program executes. Now compile the program (Alt-M-B).

The F8 Key

Rather than use the F10 key to single-step through the program, use the F8 key. The F8 key still single-steps the program, but it also traces the program flow through all function calls. (F10 executes the function calls, but does not single-step through them.)

When I ran the program in Listing 7-5, the lvalue of i in main() was at offset 0xdcc (the values you see may be different). As you press the F8 key, make a note of the offset address you see for the i in main(). Continue to single-step through the program until you've entered the func() function call.

Notice what happens to the lvalue of i when you are in func(). When I ran the program, the lvalue changed to 0xdc6. Clearly, the i in main() is not the same i that is seen in func(). If they were the same, they would have the same lvalue. Further evidence that they are not the same is the fact that the i in main() remains unchanged although func() squares the value passed to it.

Call by Value

The lvalues are different precisely because they are different variables. The behavior you see when Listing 7-5 executes happens because only a copy of i is sent to func(); not i itself. Think about it. If you were sending the i in main() to func(), their lvalues would have to be the same. Because the lvalues of i are different even though the rvalues are the same, func() actually receives only a copy of the rvalue of i in main(). Programmers refer to this behavior as *call by value.*

Unless you write certain types of function calls, any arguments passed to a function are only copies of the argument. This also means that a function cannot permanently change the value of the argument. (There are some exceptions, but I set them aside for the moment.) The benefit of call by value is that you cannot inadvertently change a variable that is not in scope. Stated another way, C lets your data have all the privacy you want it to have. You have fewer "side effect" bugs, and program maintenance becomes much easier.

The %p Conversion Character

You can see the lvalue of a variable without using the Debug watch window by using the %p conversion character with printf(). Listing 7-6 is identical to Listing 7-5, except that two printf()'s have been added using the %p conversion character.

The %p conversion character causes the variable to be displayed as a memory address, provided you place the address of operator (&) before the name of the variable being printed.

Listing 7-6. Using the %p Conversion Character

```
/*
      Example showing %p conversion character
*/

#include <stdio.h>

int main(void)
{
    int i;
    void func(int i);

    i = 10;
    printf("%p\n", &i);
    func(i);

    printf("i = %d\n", i);
}


void func(int i)
{
    printf("%p\n", &i);
    i *= i;
    printf("i = %d\n", i);
}
```

If you add the two printf() function calls to the program in Listing 7-5, you see that the memory addresses for i are displayed in much the same manner as they were when you used the Debug watch window to show the lvalues for i. The advantage of the debugger is that you do not have to get rid of the printf() statements when you no longer have use for them. Still, %p comes in handy when you need to see where something is located in memory.

Global Scope Rules

Situations arise from time to time when you would like to have a variable available to any and all parts of a program. *A variable has global scope if all parts of the program have access to the variable.* It follows that data with global scope have no privacy. The rules for global scope are simple:

1. The variable must be defined outside of a function block.
2. Global scope extends from its point of definition to the end of the source file in which it is defined.

Therefore, if you define a variable at the beginning of a source code file, it is available for use at any other scope level in that source file. If the definition of a global variable appears at the end of the source file, it doesn't do much good. The reason is that the variable is in scope only after it is defined. Listing 7-7 illustrates these points.

Listing 7-7. Global Scope

```
/*
      Two global variables -- one useful, one not.
*/

#include <stdio.h>

int i;                    /* Global scope -- useful      */

int main(void)
{
                          /* Source code for the program */
}
int j;                    /* Global scope -- not useful   */
```

Both i and j have global scope; both are defined outside of a function block. However, variable j is worthless in the program because its definition appears at the end of the source file. That is, because no code appears after the definition of j, no part of the program can make use of j. It should be clear that just because a variable has global scope, it is not necessarily available for use in all parts of the program. Always remember that *global scope only exists from the point of the definition of the variable to the end of the file* in which the definition appears.

Advantages and Disadvantages of Global Scope

If a variable is defined outside of a function block and has global scope, it can be used by any code that comes after its definition. This can be an advantage because all functions have access to the data without passing the data as a function argument. This means slightly smaller code size and slightly faster program execution because the data does not have to be placed on the stack and passed as a function argument.

The major disadvantage of variables with global scope is that they can cause some rather nasty bugs. A large number of such bugs occurs precisely because all parts of the program have access to the variable. Such bugs commonly occur when you call a series of functions in a particular sequence. Later during a debugging session, you change the sequence that uses the global data. Now all of the intermediate values are changed all the way to the end of the program.

Another problem with global variables happens when a global variable shares the same name with another variable with local scope. Recall that if two variables have the same name, the variable defined at the current scope level is the one that is visible. When this happens, you may forget that you are operating on the variable with local scope and expect the global variable to be changed. Some compilers issue an error message stating that `the current data definition masks a previously defined variable`. Unfortunately, QC doesn't catch this type of error.

When should you use global variables? There are no hard and fast rules about defining global data items. However, two situations seem to benefit from the use of global data.

1. Frequently used data: If a data item is needed by a large number of functions throughout the program, you can avoid passing it as an argument by making it a global variable. You might have a single data item (for example, the total amount of payroll deductions) that must be processed sequentially by a large number of functions (such as Federal, state, and local withholding taxes, social security, insurance, retirement or pension payments, union or professional dues, etc.) before the final value is determined. Global scope for such a variable can mean slightly smaller and faster programs plus a little less typing.

2. Infrequently changed data: Some programs use the same variable over and over but its content rarely changes. A common example is a file name in a program. As you will see in a later chapter, a file name rarely changes in a program, but many functions may need to have access to it. Another example is variables that set the foreground and background colors on the screen. Variables such as these are likely candidates for global scope.

A final thought about global data: Don't skimp on the length of a global variable name. Instead of using `td` as a variable name, use `total_deductions` or some other name to be very clear about the variable. Some programmers develop specific conventions to identify the variable as a global data item. Examples include appending a *g* to all global variable names (`g_total_deductions`), capitalizing the first letter of the variable name (`Total_deductions`), or other variations. If you adopt such a style convention, you must use it consistently for it to be of any value.

Because program maintenance and debugging are often complicated by global data, you should use them sparingly. Try to keep your data "private" (that is, use local scope) whenever possible.

Storage Classes and Scope

As you have seen in this chapter, variables can have one of two types of scope, local or global. In this section, I formalize the concept of scope into storage classes. Table 7-1 shows the four storage classes.

Table 7-1. C Storage Classes and Their Scope

C Keyword for Storage Class	Scope
auto	Local
register	Local
static	Local and Global
extern	Global

Each of these storage classes has an impact on the way the compiler views a data item. I discuss the items in the order in which they appear in Table 7-1.

The *auto* Storage Class

The auto storage class is the default storage class for all C variables. Almost all the examples you have seen in this book have used auto variables. For example, Listing 7-8 is the same as Listing 7-2 except that the missing (default) storage class for the variables has been supplied.

Listing 7-8. Listing 7-2 with Explicit Storage Class

```
/*
    Explicit storage class
*/

#include <stdio.h>

int main(void)
{
   auto int i;          /* Note the keyword auto here ... */

   i = 10;
   if (i == 10) {
      auto int i;       /* ... and here.                  */
```

```
    i = 5;
    printf("i = %d\n", i);
  }

  printf("i = %d\n", i);
}
```

Any variable defined within a statement block that does not have a storage class keyword before the type specifier is an auto storage class by default. As you saw earlier, auto storage variables come into scope in the statement block in which they are defined and "die" when control leaves that statement block.

The *register* Storage Class

Sometimes a data item must be processed as quickly as possible or some event may be missed. Interrupts, device drivers, and other time-sensitive programs are examples. The register storage class is used whenever you feel that a particular variable must be processed with the greatest possible speed. register variables are also useful when a variable will be used intensively, such as in a loop.

The register keyword is used to signal a request that the compiler place this variable in a central processing unit (CPU) register, if possible. Clearly, if the CPU has only eight registers and you attempt to define 20 register variables, some of them cannot be held in registers of their own. Therefore, using the register keyword does not guarantee that the data item actually ends up being allocated to a CPU register.

Listing 7-9 presents an example of how a register variable is defined. It also shows a restriction placed on register variables.

Listing 7-9. Defining a register *Variable*

```
#include <stdio.h>


int main(void)
{
    register int i;

    printf("%p   i = %d\n", &i, i);

}
```

To define a register variable, place the register keyword before the type specifier for the data item as shown in Listing 7-9.

If you attempt to compile the program in Listing 7-9, you will see the error message

```
error C2103: '&' on register variable
```

This makes sense. If a register variable does in fact end up in a CPU register, it does not have a memory address (lvalue) in the conventional sense. Because a CPU register resides inside the CPU chip, a register does not have a memory address. Therefore, you cannot use the address-of operator (&) when using register variables.

As an experiment, I defined 19 register variables in a test program. In part of the program, I also tried to use the address-of operator in a statement. When I compiled the program, the program issued 19 error messages stating that the variables did not have lvalues and that using the address-of operator was an error. In fact, the compiler could not have had all 19 variables in registers; the 8088 does not have that many registers available for use. It appears that QC is using the register keyword to rule out the use of the address-of operator on such data items, instead of basing the error message on where the data item is actually stored. (Some of those 19 variables had to be stored in regular memory and therefore, should not have generated the error message.)

This behavior on QC's part is not incorrect; the syntax rules for C do prevent using the address-of operator with variables that are defined with the register storage class. However, keep this anomaly in mind if you attempt to debug code in which you think a register variable is the culprit.

(As an aside, Release 2.5 of the QC compiler passes certain function arguments in registers. In releases prior to 2.5, all function arguments were passed on the stack. Using registers does permit better code generation and performance.)

The *static* Storage Class

Variables with the `static` storage class come in two flavors:

1. Internal static
2. External static

I discuss internal `static` variables first.

Internal *static* Storage

An *internal static* variable must be defined within a statement or function block. Listing 7-10 shows an internal `static` variable.

Listing 7-10. Internal `static` Data Item

```
int func(int count)
{
    static int i = 0;

    i += count;
    return i;
}
```

In this example, variable `i` is an internal `static` because it is defined within the function block named `func()`. As you have seen with the other storage classes, the `static` keyword must appear before the type specifier (for example, `int`) in the definition.

An internal `static` data item has a special property that makes it extremely useful at times. Unlike variables with the `auto` storage class, an internal `static` can retain its value after program control has left the function. In Listing 7-10, variable `i` is initialized to 0 when the program first starts running (that is, at "runtime"). When the function is called, `i` is increased by the function argument `count`, which is passed to the function. Suppose that `count` has the value of 5 the first time `func()` is called.

Now assume that you call `func()` a second time and `count` equals 2. The value returned from this second call to `func()` is 7 because `i` retains its previous value between calls. Note that this is not the type of behavior you saw with `auto` variables that die when you leave the statement block in which they are defined.

Internal `static` data items are very useful whenever you need to retain a value between function calls.

External *static* Storage

As you might guess, a variable defined as an external `static` must be defined outside of a function or statement block. An example appears in Listing 7-11.

Listing 7-11. External `static` Storage

```
#include <stdio.h>

static int i;

int main(void)
{

    /* Some program code */

}
```

Except for the keyword static, this looks very much like the previous definition of a variable with global scope. In a way, it does have global scope, *but only for the file within which it is defined*. The distinction is very important.

Suppose that you have a large program. Experienced C programmers divide the program into several smaller files. For the purpose of illustration, I assume that there are only two files, as shown in Figure 7-1.

In File 1, you made calls to `func()` and `func2()`. In File 2, you defined both functions, but notice that you made `func2()` a `static` function. This is perfectly acceptable C syntax and means that `func2()` is defined with external `static` storage class. Because you used the word `static` as the storage class for `func2()` in File 2, `func2()` is visible only in File 2.

```
                                                    File 1
#include <stdio.h>



int main(void)
{
    func();
    func2();
}
```

```
                                                    File 2
int func(void)
{
    printf("\nin func() in File 2");
}

static int func2(void)
{
    printf("\nin func2() in File 2");
}
```

Figure 7-1. Multiple Program Files

Now, suppose that you use QC to compile and link these two program files to form an executable program. (You will see how to use QC's Make facility to compile multiple files near the end of this chapter.) The compilation process goes smoothly, but the linker chokes and issues the message

```
error L2029: '_func2': unresolved external
```

The reason the linker issues the error message is that it cannot find func2(). Why not? After all, the code is sitting right there in File 2. Aha, but the keyword static at the beginning of the definition of func2() tells the compiler not to pass any information about func2() to anything outside of File 2. In other words, QC hides func2() from File 1. However, because you call func2() in File 1, the linker attempts to locate func2(). Because QC won't let the linker know about func2(), the linker gives up and issues the preceding error message.

It should be clear that whenever the keyword static is applied to a data item with global scope, that global scope is restricted to the file in which it is defined. This is a great way to avoid function and variable name conflicts across multiple files.

How can you fix things in Figure 7-1 so that QC can compile it? The solution is simple — just move the call to `func2()` into `func()`, as shown in Figure 7-2.

```
                                                    File 1
    #include <stdio.h>


    int main(void)
    {
        func();
    }
```

```
                                                    File 2
    static int func2(void);

    int func(void)
    {
        printf("\nin func() in File 2");
        func2();
    }

    static int func2(void)
    {
        printf("\nin func2() in File 2");
    }
```

Figure 7-2. Fixing the Problem in Figure 7-1

Now the program compiles and links properly because `func2()` is no longer called in File 1. The call to `func2()` in File 2 is okay because the definition of `func2()` occurs in the same source file (File 2). Note that you must place a function *declaration* for `func2()` at the top of File 2. If you don't do this, QC objects, stating that you have redefined `func2()`. The reason is that you changed the default storage class of `func2()` from global scope to external `static` scope.

The external `static` storage class is a good way to restrict program access to variables or functions. When writing a function that should be called only by another function, place both functions in the same file and make the supporting function a `static` function. Using Figure 2 as an example, if `func()` is the only function that should have access to `func2()`, make `func2()` a `static` function.

External `static` data items are beneficial in two important ways. First, they limit the data items' scope to the file in which they are needed. The `static` data items become invisible to all other program files. Second, because external `static` data items are private to the file in which they are defined, you don't have to worry about name collisions. In fact, in Figure 2 you could define another `func2()` in File 1 and it would not collide with the `static func2()` defined in File 2. (Try this yourself as an experiment.)

The Arguments for Multiple Source Files

As I stated earlier in this chapter, it's smart to break large programs into smaller source files for several reasons. First, most programming problems break down into a sequence that is natural for multiple files. For example, all but the most trivial programming tasks consist of five steps.

1. Initialization
2. Input
3. Processing
4. Output
5. Cleanup

The initialization (setup) step often involves initializing data items, opening data files, and presenting a data input screen. The input step gets the necessary information to solve the task at hand. It might involve reading information previously stored in a data file, reading data directly from a machine (such as specs from a milling machine in a robotics environment), or reading input from the keyboard. The processing step changes the data into a form that solves the program's task. The output step presents the solution to the task in a form that is desired by the user. The output might be to the screen, printer, disk file, or some other I/O device (for example, modem or FAX machine). The clean-up step may involve updating and closing data files, turning I/O devices off, switching from graphics back to text mode, as well as a host of other possibilities. The clean-up step includes those tasks that let you exit gracefully from a program.

For very simple programs, a single file handles all five steps very easily. However, when a program becomes fairly complex, splitting the program into multiple files along the logical lines of the program steps shown previously makes maintaining and debugging the programs later on easier.

A second advantage of multiple files is that you can avoid recompiling those files that are stable. If you lump everything into one big file, you end up recompiling a lot of source code that hasn't changed. This takes time and slows down the turn-around time between editing and compilation. On the other hand, if you split the program into multiple source files, you need only recompile those files that have changed since they were last compiled. The QC Make feature allows you to recompile only those files that actually need it. (I discuss the Make feature at the end of this chapter.) The Make feature saves a lot of time in the long run.

Now that you know that multiple source files for a single program make sense, I should discuss one more storage class. The `extern` storage class solves some potential problems that might arise when using multiple source files.

The *extern* Storage Class

The `extern` storage is used when a program is split among multiple source files. The *extern storage class is used to declare a data item in one file that has been defined in another file*. An example shows how the `extern` storage class is used.

In Figure 7-3, you have defined a variable named day in File 1. Assume, however, that `func()` and `func2()` in File 2 need to use day to accomplish their tasks. You cannot define day a second time in File 2; doing so results in a "multiply defined" error message from the linker. Because you place the C keyword `extern` at the start of the data declaration for day in File 2, QC knows that you are declaring what day is, not defining it.

When QC sees the keyword `extern`, it says to itself, "Oh! This variable has already been defined in some other file. I'll make a note of it here so that we can use it in File 2 and let the linker supply the actual `lvalue` where day is actually stored in memory." In other words, the `extern` storage class lets you use a variable in one file although it was defined in some other file.

The keyword `extern` can be used only with data items with global scope. To illustrate this limitation, consider Figure 7-4.

In Figure 7-4, day is defined with local scope and the `auto` storage class. As you saw earlier, day exists only for use within the function named `main()`. Once program control leaves `main()`, day ceases to exist.

In File 2, you have declared day to have `extern` storage class with global scope for use throughout File 2. When QC compiles File 1 and File 2, no error messages are generated. After all, QC sees valid syntax in both files. However, because day is compiled in File 2 with the `extern` storage class, QC leaves a message to the linker to find day's `lvalue` in some other file.

```
                                              File 1
#include <stdio.h>

int day;

int main(void)
{
    func();
}
```

```
                                              File 2

extern int day;

int func(void)
{

        /* Code that uses day */
}

int func2(void)
{
        /* Code that uses day */
}
```

Figure 7-3. Using the extern *Storage Class*

```
                                              File 1
#include <stdio.h>

int main(void)
{
    int day;
}
```

```
                                              File 2

extern int day;

int func(void)
{

        print("\nday = %d", day);
}

int func2(void)
{
        /* Code that uses day */
}
```

Figure 7-4. Limitation of the extern *Storage Class*

When the linker attempts to link File 1 and File 2, it finds the message in File 2 to use day's lvalue. However, because day cannot exist outside of main(), QC did not save day's lvalue after the main() function was compiled. After all, QC is smart enough to know when it no longer needs to retain a variable's lvalue in its symbol table. Once QC finished compiling main(), day's symbol table entry was discarded. All of this means the linker cannot find day when it tries to resolve day's lvalue in File 2. The linker has no choice but to issue the error message

```
error L2029: 'day' : unresolved external
```

to tell you that it cannot find day. The only way to solve the problem is to move the definition of day outside of main(). This gives day global scope and the linker can find day when it needs it to link File 2.

It should be clear that you can use the extern storage class only with data items that have global scope (that is, data defined outside of a function block). The situation depicted in Figure 7-4 prohibits using day in File 2 because of the link error. To correct the error, move the definition of day in File 1 so that it is outside of main(). With this correction, all the code in File 2 has access to day.

What if you want only func() to have access to day? To restrict the access of day to func(), move the extern declaration for day inside of func()

```
int func(void)
{
    extern int day;

    printf("\nday = %d", day);
}
```

Moving the declaration of day inside of func() makes day's scope in File 2 local to func(). This is a good way to restrict a data item with global scope in one file to local scope in another file. This approach helps keep day "private" in File 2.

An Easy Way to Define-Declare Data in Multiple Files

The extern keyword is designed to solve one particular type of problem: giving access to a data item for use in files other than the one where the data item is defined. Suppose that you have several variables that maintain the screen color (for example, foreground and background). Further assume that the program is split across multiple files, but each file must have access to the screen colors. The most direct way to accomplish the proper data definitions-declarations is to define the variables in the file that contains `main()` (often called the "main" file) and declare the variables in all of the other files using the `extern` storage class.

This approach works just fine, but it's a pain when you need to add, delete, or otherwise change such variables. Each change requires that you edit all the source files. There is an easier way.

You must do two things. First, create your own header file for the data items to be used. Second, you need to understand how to use two new preprocessor directives. I discuss the preprocessor directives first.

#ifdef and *#endif*

The preprocessor can be used for *conditional compilation*. That is, you can use the preprocessor to toggle program statements into or out of a program using an `if`-like preprocessor programming construct. Listing 7-12 shows an example of the preprocessor directives you need to know.

Listing 7-12. Using `#ifdef` and `#endif`

```
#ifdef SUPPORT
   extern
#endif

   int foreground, background;
```

Suppose that the source file contains only the information shown in Listing 7-12. The `#ifdef` preprocessor directive shown in Listing 7-12 says, "If the symbolic constant `SUPPORT` is defined, include the statement(s) up to the `#endif` in the program. If `SUPPORT` is not defined at this point in the program, omit the statement(s)." The `#ifdef`-`#endif` preprocessor directives allow you to toggle program statements into or out of a program based on the presence or absence of a symbolic constant.

In Listing 7-12, because `SUPPORT` is not defined, the preprocessor omits the keyword `extern` from the program. As a result, the only program statements seen by the compiler are

```
int foreground, background;
```

In other words, Listing 7-12 defines variables `foreground` and `background`.

Now suppose you modify Listing 7-12 as shown in Listing 7-13.

Listing 7-13. More on Using `#ifdef` and `#endif`

```
#define SUPPORT 1

#ifdef SUPPORT
    extern
#endif

    int foreground, background;
```

In this case, the symbolic constant SUPPORT is defined when the preprocessor sees the `#ifdef` directive. Because the "if-defined" test is logical True in this case, the preprocessor must include the keyword extern in the program. As a result, the compiler now sees the line

```
extern

    int foreground, background;
```

Because C doesn't care about white space (that is, newlines, tabs, blank spaces, etc.), the line looks like

```
extern int foreground, background;
```

Therefore, if SUPPORT is defined in the file, the foreground and background variables are declared in the file using the extern keyword. If you omit the SUPPORT symbolic constant from the file, the variables are defined in the file. This has possibilities!

Now, suppose that you place the contents of Listing 7-12 in your own header file called screen.h. Further assume that there are only two files, as shown in Figure 7-5.

Now see what happens when QC compiles these two files. When QC sees the preprocessor directive

```
#include "screen.h"
```

QC knows that it must include the contents of the file named screen.h in the program at this point.

```
                                              File 1
#include <stdio.h>
#include "screen.h"

int main(void)
{
    /* Our program code */

}
```

```
                                              File 2
#define SUPPORT 1
#include "screen.h"

int func(void)
{
    /* Whatever code we might need */
}
```

Figure 7-5. Using Your Own Header File

Header Files: Double Quotation Marks Versus Angle Brackets

Notice that double quotation marks are used around screen.h rather than the angle brackets (< and >) around the stdio.h header file. The double quotation marks tell QC to look in the *current working directory* for the header file named screen.h. On the other hand, the angle brackets tell QC to look somewhere other than the current working directory for the stdio.h header file.

When you installed the QC compiler, the installation program created a subdirectory named INCLUDE and placed stdio.h (plus all the other standard header files) in that directory. The angle brackets cause QC to look in the INCLUDE directory for the stdio.h header file. The double quotes cause QC to look in the directory in which you are writing the program (probably not the INCLUDE directory) for the screen.h header file. The use of double quotes and angle brackets lets you keep your own header files separate from the standard compiler header files.

After QC has read the screen.h header file into the program, the program source looks as though it were written

```
#include <stdio.h>

#ifdef SUPPORT
   extern
#endif

int foreground, background;

int main(void)
{
    /* Our program code */
}
```

However, because SUPPORT is not defined in File 1, the preprocessor simplifies the code so that it appears to be

```
#include <stdio.h>

int foreground, background;

int main(void)
{
    /* Our program code */
}
```

As a result, you define foreground and background in File 1. Now see what happens in File 2.

The first thing you see in File 2 is the definition of the SUPPORT symbolic constant. The preprocessor, on seeing the #define for SUPPORT, places SUPPORT in its own symbol table. Next, the preprocessor reads in the screen.h header file. The result is that File 2 looks like

```
#define SUPPORT 1

#ifdef SUPPORT
   extern
#endif

int foreground, background;

int func(void)
{
   /* Whatever code we might need */
}
```

Because the preprocessor has already defined SUPPORT, the resulting code looks like

```
#define SUPPORT 1

extern int foreground, background;

int func(void)
{
    /* Whatever code we might need */
}
```

when the preprocessor finishes processing the file. As a result, the foreground and background variables have the proper declaration for use in File 2. The advantage of using the screen.h header file and the #ifdef-#endif preprocessor directives is that you can add or delete data items from the program simply by editing the screen.h header file; you don't need to edit either File 1 or File 2. As a general rule, editing in one file is not only less work, but results in fewer mistakes. (Think what can happen if you forget to edit one of the files.) Keep in mind, however, that if you change a header file, you must recompile the program files that use that header file.

Consider creating a header file for a program any time you have global data that must be used in multiple program files.

What Is the QC Make Feature?

As you gain programming experience, your C programs will become larger and the advantages of splitting the program into multiple files will become obvious. When you do start writing multifile programs, take advantage of QC's Make facility. The Make feature allows you to treat multiple source code files as though they were one large program. There are several advantages to using Make with multiple program files.

First, moving around in smaller files is easier than in larger ones. Just moving from the top to the bottom of a 20,000-line program file gets old in a hurry. Second, if each file is limited to one of the five program steps presented in Table 7-2, identifying the file that needs work is easier during the debugging cycle. Third, if you are writing a program that might be ported to another type of machine later on (for example, moving from the PC to a Macintosh), isolating code that might be machine-specific is easier with multiple files. Fourth, multiple files make it easier for programming teams to work on a single program. Division of labor works in programming, too. Finally, program development is faster because compilation time can be reduced. This advantage is worthy of more explanation.

QC's Make module creates a list of source files that must be compiled and linked to form a complete program. However, QC is smart enough to know which files need to be recompiled. Suppose, for example, that you have divided your program into five files (one for each program step). Things have gone well and only the output step gives you trouble. It follows that this I/O file (for example, `pio.c`) will be edited and recompiled many times before you're done with it. On the other hand, however, the other four files are stable; they don't need to be recompiled each time the I/O file is compiled.

The QC Make module knows which files need to be recompiled. It knows this by looking at the date and time that each file was last compiled. When you edit a file, its date and time are changed. If the source file (for example, `pinput.c`) has a later date and time than the compiled file (for example, `pinput.obj`), QC knows to recompile `pinput.c`. On the other hand, if `pinput.obj` has a later date and time than `pinput.c`, recompiling the file is not needed. Think about it.

If all but `pio.c` are stable, only `pio.c` is recompiled. The linker simply links the other (stable) files into the revised version of `pio.obj` to form your latest version of the program. It should be clear that QC's Make facility reduces the amount of time it takes to compile and link a program. The result is faster program development.

How to Use the QC Make Facility

Suppose that you want to name your program "game" and it will consist of the files shown in Table 7-3.

Table 7-3. Source Files for make

File Name	Contents	
game.c	/* Contains main() and initialization step	*/
ginput.c	/* Contains the input functions	*/
gprocess.c	/* Contains the processing functions	*/
gout.c	/* Contains the output functions	*/
gclean.c	/* Contains the clean-up functions	*/

You want to create a Make file that compiles and links these source files into your game program. First, load and execute the QC compiler; then select the Make option from the program menu. Select the Set Program List option (the letter S is the hot key) from the Make menu. (See Figure 7-6.)

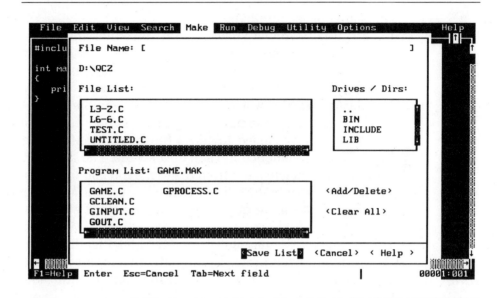

Figure 7-6. Setting the QC Make List

QC asks you to supply the name of the file that will contain the Make instructions. All Make files end in `mak`, so call it `games.mak`. Type the name and press Enter. QC asks you to enter the names of the source files that comprise the Make file. Type in the list of files shown in Table 7-3. QC keeps prompting for additional files after each file is entered.

After the last file name has been entered, press the Tab key and move to the <Save List> option near the bottom of the screen. Now press Enter to save the list of source files in the `game.mak` Make file. The disk drive activates and writes the `game.mak` file to disk. If the first file in the list (for example, `game.c`) does not already exist, QC asks whether it should create it. Answer Yes. QC creates the `game.c` file and places the cursor in the source window so that you can start entering the code for the `game.c` source file.

You proceed to create files for the other source files in Table 7-3. When you finish your first attempt at writing all the source files, press Alt-M-B to build a complete program. QC automatically compiles and links all the source files in the `game.mak` file.

Now, suppose that one of the files has an error, but the rest of the files compiled correctly. Correct the error and recompile the program (Alt-M-B). This time QC recompiles only the file that you just edited; the others are not recompiled.

Eventually you will have several Make files and you will be switching between different projects. If you want to change from the game program to a different project (for example, `hobby.mak`), activate a different Make file. To do this, press the Alt-M-S sequence to set a new program list. Type the name of the project's Make file (for example, `hobby.mak`) and press Enter. QC now uses the new Make file for subsequent development.

Whenever you need to add a file from the Make file list, use the Alt-M-S option sequence and add the new file. The same option sequence can be used to delete a file from the Make file list. Just press the Tab key to place the cursor in the File List Box. Then use the arrow keys (or mouse) to highlight the file to delete. Press the delete (Del) key and the file is removed.

Although you may not need QC's Make facilities right now, keep them in mind. Even programs of relatively modest length (that is, six or so pages of source code) can benefit from splitting the source code into multiple files.

8

Using Pointers in C

In this chapter, you learn

What a pointer is

How to define and initialize pointers

How to use pointer indirection

How to use pointers with functions

How pointers relate to arrays

Pointers and memory models

Pointers represent the "good news – bad news" aspects of C. Without a doubt, pointers are among the most powerful features of C. Pointers also provide a very efficient way of manipulating data in your programs. On the down side, pointers often are a trouble spot for beginners who have not yet had the opportunity to use pointers.

Actually, I have already laid the important groundwork for understanding pointers, so you should have no trouble understanding how to use them. Once you've mastered pointers, the sky's the limit!

What Is a Pointer?

A *pointer* is a variable that contains the memory location of another variable. Drawing on terms used throughout this text, a pointer is a variable whose `rvalue` is the `lvalue` of another variable. Think about these two sentences for a few moments before reading on.

How to Define a Pointer Variable

As with any other data item in C, you must define a pointer before you can use it. The general form for defining a pointer variable is

```
type_specifier   * variable_name;
     (3)            (1)        (2)
```

As you can see, three distinct elements are necessary to define a pointer. Suppose, for example, that you want to define a pointer variable named `ptr` that will be used to point to an `int`. The definition is

```
int *ptr;
```

This looks much like any other data definition, except for the asterisk. When used in a data definition, the *asterisk* (*) has special meaning to the compiler. The asterisk tells the compiler, "This is not an ordinary variable; you can use it as a pointer." The asterisk has no other purpose than to tell the compiler that you are defining a pointer variable. Therefore, the asterisk is the first element that you must understand about a pointer definition.

Next, the compiler needs to know the name of the pointer variable. This is the second element of the pointer definition (number 2 in the first example). The name of a pointer variable can be whatever you want it to be. (Many programmers use `ptr` in a pointer variable's name.)

Finally, the compiler needs to know what type of data the pointer will point to. This is extremely important, because it sets the scalar size of the pointer. This is number 3 in the first example, and it is our old friend, the type specifier.

Scalar Size and Pointers

The *scalar size* of a data item refers to the amount of storage used by that data item in memory. You already know that the QC compiler uses two bytes of memory to store an `int` in memory. Therefore, the scalar for an `int` pointer is two. You also know that a `char` only requires one byte of storage, so its scalar is one.

sizeof Operator: Finding the Scalar Size of a Data Item

If you are not sure of the scalar size of a data item, you can use the `sizeof` operator. Recall that the syntax for the `sizeof` operator is

```
sizeof(data)
```

Listing 8-1 shows how to use the `sizeof` operator.

Listing 8-1. Using the `sizeof` Operator

```
/*
        Example of the sizeof operator
*/

#include <stdio.h>

int main(void)
{
    int big;
    double value;
    big = sizeof(value);
    printf("The scalar size of a double is %d bytes\n", big);
}
```

The `sizeof` operator looks like a function call, but it's not. It is an operator in C. Remember that, if you are not using a type specifier as the operand for `sizeof`, you can change the line in Listing 8-1 from

```
big = sizeof(value);
```

to

```
big = sizeof value;
```

and the program functions the same. The parentheses are required only when the operand is a type specifier, as in

```
big = sizeof(double);
```

In this example, you do not use a variable name as the operand but a data type specifier instead. The version of the `sizeof` that uses the parentheses works with both variable names and type specifiers. For this reason, most programmers always parenthesize the operand for the `sizeof` operator.

Scalars and Pointers

As mentioned earlier, a pointer definition always includes a type specifier that can be used by QC to determine the scalar size for the pointer. It may be surprising that, although the scalar for a pointer varies according to the type of data being pointed to, the storage requirements for a pointer itself don't change. Listing 8-2 proves that the size of a pointer doesn't change regardless of the kind of pointer it is.

Listing 8-2. Pointer Storage Is Always the Same

```
/*
        Prove that pointers are always the same size
*/

#include <stdio.h>

int main(void)
{
    int *iptr;
    double *dptr;

    printf("The size of itpr is %d bytes\n", sizeof(iptr) );
    printf("The size of dtpr is %d bytes\n", sizeof(dptr) );

}
```

When you run this program, you can see that each pointer requires two bytes of storage. However, the scalar for iptr is 2, but the scalar for dptr is 8. The size of a pointer is always the same, but the scalar varies according to the type of data being pointed to.

Fortunately, QC keeps track of the scalar size of the pointer for us automatically. However, the concept of scalar size is important to understanding pointers.

Initializing a Pointer

A pointer is of little use unless it points to something useful. Therefore, the first thing to do after the pointer is defined is to make it point to something. Take this step by step before writing a program using pointers.

Suppose that you define a pointer as follows:

```
int *iptr;
```

This statement defines a pointer variable named iptr. You know it's a pointer variable because an asterisk appears in the definition of iptr. You also know that the scalar for iptr is set to that of an int variable. In other words, let iptr point only to integer data types.

Now define an integer variable to use with the pointer:

```
int num;
```

When QC picks an lvalue for each of these variables, the memory for each variable contains whatever random values happen to be in memory at the time the program is run. However, **the definition of a pointer says it contains the lvalue of some other variable.** In the example, you want iptr to contain the lvalue of num. Therefore, you must initialize iptr so that it holds the lvalue of where num exists in memory.

Look at an example to visualize the process thus far. Suppose that QC placed num at memory address 40,000. Further suppose that QC placed iptr at memory address 35,000. Figure 8-1 shows how this looks in memory.

In both cases, the rvalues are unknown at this point, so they are shown with a question mark.

How can you initialize iptr? Simple — use the address-of operator in an assignment statement. The statement

```
iptr = &num;         /* Initialize iptr to point to num */
```

tells QC, "Take the address of num (its lvalue) and assign it into (the rvalue of) iptr." Figure 8-2 shows the memory image after QC finishes this initialization statement.

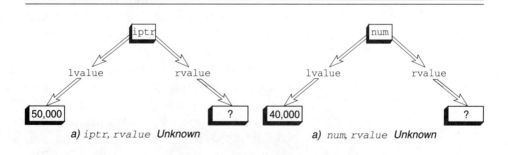

Figure 8-1. A Memory Image of iptr *and* num

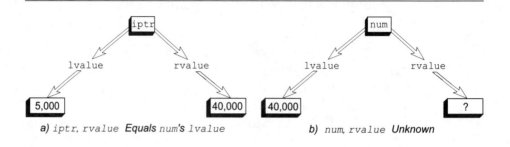

a) `iptr, rvalue` *Equals* `num`'s *lvalue*   *b)* `num, rvalue` *Unknown*

Figure 8-2. A Memory Image of `iptr` *and* `num` *After Initialization*

Notice that the `rvalue` of `iptr` is the `lvalue` of `num`. That is, you initialized `iptr` to point to `num`. Okay, now what?

Using Indirection on a Pointer

Obviously, there is a reason to have pointer variables. The reason is that you can change the value of one variable by using the process of indirection on the pointer variable. The term *indirection* means changing the `rvalue` of one variable by using a pointer variable. That is, you can use `iptr` to change the `rvalue` of `num`.

The Indirection Operator (*)

The indirection operator is also the asterisk (*). The asterisk is a busy operator in C. You have seen it used for multiplying, defining a pointer, and now indicating the process of indirection. This is what is called an "overloaded" operator; it has multiple uses depending on the context in which it is used.

Fortunately, determining the context of the asterisk is easy. In multiplication, the asterisk is a binary operator requiring two operands. When used with a pointer, the asterisk is a unary operator with only one operand. When the asterisk appears in a data definition, it tells QC to create a pointer variable; its single argument is the variable name. Any other time you see the asterisk used as a unary operator (that is, not part of a definition), it is indicating indirection.

To indicate indirection using `iptr`, write the statement

```
*iptr = 50;
```

Now see how QC views the statement. The statement says, "Use the `rvalue` of `iptr` as a memory address; go to that address and place the value 50 at that memory location."

Here is where the scalar becomes important. The value 50 is small enough to be represented in memory with only one byte. However, because you defined `iptr` to be an `int` pointer, QC knows that `iptr` points to an integer (`int`) variable. Therefore, QC knows that it can use two bytes (the `sizeof` of an `int`) of storage to hold the value 50.

Figure 8-3 shows how the memory image appears after you execute the indirection statement.

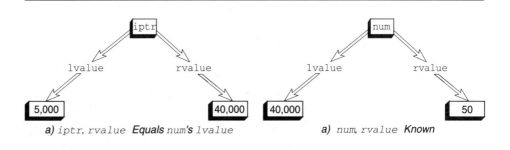

Figure 8-3. A Memory Image of `iptr` and num After Indirection

Note the steps that indirection causes to happen. First, you get the `rvalue` of the pointer. If you initialized the pointer correctly, this `rvalue` should be the `lvalue` of an appropriate variable. Second, you use the `rvalue` of the pointer to find the proper location in memory of the variable you wish to change. Third, place 50 into the scalar number of bytes using the `rvalue` of the pointer as the spot in memory where you should "deposit" the value 50.

Indirection, therefore, allows you to change the value of the variable without directly using the variable itself. Listing 8-3 puts all of this together into a program.

Listing 8-3. Program to Illustrate Indirection

```
/*
    Use indirection to change a value
*/

#include <stdio.h>

int main(void)
{
    int *iptr;                          /* Define the pointer */
    int num;

    iptr = &num;                        /* Initialize it       */
    *iptr = 50;                         /* Use indirection     */
    printf("num = %d\n", num);

}
```

To see all of this take place in a more understandable fashion, use the Debugger to single-step though the program. Before you run the program, set the following watch expressions using the Alt-D-W sequence

```
iptr
&iptr
num
&num
*iptr
```

Now press the F10 key to single-step through the program. When you run the program, you first see each expression with an <unknown identifier> message following it. This makes sense because the program has not executed the definitions of iptr or num yet. When I ran the program, after QC executed the definitions, my Debug window contained the following information (I've omitted the segment addresses):

```
iptr = 0x0029
&iptr = 0x0dcc
num = 16606
&num = 0xdca
*iptr = 10595
```

This information tells you that iptr is stored at offset address 0xdcc (lvalue) and it holds (the rvalue of) 0x0029. Variable num is stored at offset 0x0dca and contains (the random value) 16606. Notice that QC presents lvalues (memory addresses) in hexadecimal and rvalues in decimal.

After executing the statement that initialized iptr to point to num (iptr = &num), the Debug window reads

```
iptr = 0x0dca          /* Now has the lvalue of num */
&iptr = 0x0dcc
num = 16606
&num = 0xdca
*iptr = 10595
```

Notice that the rvalue of iptr now contains the lvalue of where num is stored in memory. You can see that iptr does point to num. Finally, after the indirection statement is executed, the contents of the Debug window reads

```
iptr = 0x0dca
&iptr = 0x0dcc
num = 50
&num = 0xdca
*iptr = 50
```

You can see that the contents of num have been changed to 50 using the process of indirection. Also notice that the rvalue of what iptr points to (*iptr) is also 50. After all, *iptr is the expression you used to change num's value.

Using Pointers with Functions

You might be saying to yourself, "Big deal! I can accomplish the same thing by simply assigning 50 into num." True, but can you do it in a function? Nope!

Recall from Chapter 7 that arguments passed to a function are "call by value"; only a copy of the argument is sent to the function. If that's the case, can you use a function to change the value of a variable defined in some other function? As you saw in Chapter 7, data defined within a function are in scope only within that function. I also presented a program demonstrating that you could not directly change the value defined in one function through a function call to another function. (See Listing 7-5 in Chapter 7.) Listing 8-4 presents a program that attempts to assign 50 into num using a function call.

Listing 8-4. Attempt to Change a Variable with a Function Call

```
/*
      Feeble attempt to change an auto with a function call
*/

#include <stdio.h>

int main(void)
{
   int num;
   void func(int num);

   printf("Before function call, num = %d\n", num);
   func(num);
   printf("After function call, num = %d\n", num);
}

void func(int num)
{
   num = 50;
   printf("In func(), num = %d\n", num);
}
```

When I ran the program, the first printf() printed num with a value of 41. The next printf() in func() showed the value as 50, which is to be expected. However, the final printf() shows the value of num as 41.

Again, the reason is that function calls receive copies of the data item, not the actual data item itself. This means that the lvalue of num in main() is not the same as the lvalue of num in func(). Because the lvalues are different, it is impossible for the program to change the num defined in main() in func(); they are not the same variable.

To prove this, use Debug to set watch values for num and &num. You can see that the two nums have different lvalues. It appears that there is no direct way to change num using a function call.

The word *direct* in the last sentence is the key limitation. You can use indirection to change values for variables that are not in scope. Rewrite the program in Listing 8-4 so that you can change the value of num using a function call.

Listing 8-5. Using Pointers as a Function Argument

```
/*
     Using a pointer to change a function value
*/

#include <stdio.h>

int main(void)
{
   int num;
   void func(int *iptr);

   printf("Before function call, num = %d\n", num);

   func(&num);                              /* Pay attention! */

   printf("After function call, num = %d\n", num);
}

void func(int *iptr)
{
   *iptr = 50;
   printf("In func(), num = %d\n", *iptr);
}
```

I urge you to type this program and set the Debug Watch values for

```
num
&num
iptr
&iptr
*iptr
```

I used the F8 key to single-step the program. When I reached the first
`printf()` call, the Debug window read (omitting the segment address)

```
num = 41
&num = 0x0e0c
iptr = <Unknown identifier>
&iptr = <Unknown identifier>
*iptr = <Unknown identifier>
```

This tells you that the (random) value of num is 41 when the program started and that value is stored in memory at offset address 0x0e0c. Because program control has not yet entered func(), iptr is unknown.

Now execute the function call to func(). Notice that you pass the address of num (&num, or its lvalue) to func(). This means QC places the memory address of num on the stack in preparation for the call to func().

Once program control reaches the assignment statement in func(), the values in the Debug window have changed to

```
num = 41
&num = 0x0e0c
iptr = 0x0e0c
&iptr = 0x0e06
*iptr = 41
```

Observe that you defined the argument to func() to be a pointer to int. Also notice that the address of iptr in func() is not the same as the address of num in main(). The iptr in func() resides at memory address 0x0e06 (not 0x0e0c). However, the rvalue of the iptr is the same as the address of num in main().

Hmmm. It looks as though you initialized iptr to point to num in main(). Look at a simplified version of QC's actions when func() was called in main(). The address-of (&) operator told QC to place the lvalue of num on the stack in preparation for the call to func(). QC now sets up the stack properly with the lvalue of num and calls func(). The function prototype for func() tells QC that it must create an integer pointer named iptr. QC also knows that, because this is a function argument, the value to be held in the pointer sits on the stack. Therefore, QC pops off the two bytes that contain the lvalue of num from the stack and stuffs them into iptr. As a result, you now have a pointer named iptr in func() that contains the lvalue of num in main(). You have initialized iptr to point to num using a function call!

Figure 8-4 shows how this was accomplished.

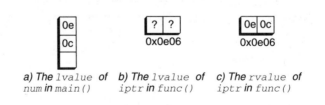

a) The *lvalue of* num *in* main()   b) The *lvalue of* iptr *in* func()   c) The *rvalue of* iptr *in* func()

Figure 8-4. Initializing a Function Argument

The call to func() in main() causes QC to do three things. First, QC places the address of num on the stack. This is shown in Figure 8-4(a). When program control reached func(), QC created an integer pointer variable named iptr in accordance with func()'s prototype. This step is shown as Figure 8-4(b). Finally, QC took the value on the stack and popped it off into iptr's memory location. Reviewing the steps shown in Figure 8-4, Figure 8-4(a) represents &num and Figure 8-4(c) is iptr. Because you know that QC popped the stack into iptr, the sequence in Figure 8-4 does not differ much from the statement

```
iptr = &iptr;
```

Therefore, the statement

```
*iptr = 50;
```

in func() assigns 50 into the memory locations used by num in main(). When program control returns from func() back to main(), num is once again in scope. However, num now finds that its rvalue was changed to 50 while it was out of scope.

The program in Listing 8-5 used the process of indirection to change a piece of data (num) that was out of scope at the time it was changed. One important advantage of pointers is that you can use indirection to change data that are private to some other part of the program. However, you can accomplish such a change only in a very deliberate manner. You must use pointers and indirection to change the data item. Because indirection forces you to set things up properly in several steps, the chances are small that you will contaminate data between functions when using pointers.

Why Scalars Are Important When Using Pointers

The simple program example in Listing 8-6 shows why scalars are important whenever you use a pointer variable.

Listing 8-6. Pointer and Scalar Mismatches

```
/*
    A mismatch on pointer types and scalars
*/

#include <stdio.h>
#include <string.h>
```

Listing 8-6 continues

Listing 8-6 continued

```
int main(void)
{
    int i, *iptr, len;
    char buff[128], *cptr;

    printf("Type in a sentence:\n");
    gets(buff);

    iptr = cptr = buff;
    len = strlen(buff);

    printf("\nThe string using a char pointer:\n");
    for (i = 0; i < len; i++) {
        putchar(*cptr++);
    }

    printf("\nThe string using an int pointer:\n");
    for (i = 0; i < len; i++) {
        putchar(*iptr++);
    }
}
```

In `main()`, you defined two pointers: an integer pointer (`iptr`) and a character pointer (`cptr`). You also defined a character array named `buff[]` to hold what you type via a call to `gets()`. After the string is entered, you initialize both pointers to point to `buff[]`.

Note: C allows you to use the name of an array (without a subscript) as the starting address of element 0 of the array.

This means that `buff` is equivalent to `&buff[0]` in the assignment statement

```
iptr = cptr = buff;
```

In other words, `buff` represents the `lvalue` where the character array `buff[]` starts in memory. Therefore, the statement initializes both pointers to point to the start of the `buff[]` array.

Using *strlen()*

The next statement in Listing 8-6 calls `strlen()`. `strlen()` is a standard library function used to determine the length of the string. In our example, strlen() determines the length of the string just entered. Recall that all strings in C end with the null termination character ('\0'). For example, if you type the word Test, it looks like Figure 8-5 in memory.

The argument to strlen() is the lvalue of where the string begins in memory. The strlen() function then spins through the string looking for the null termination character. The value returned from strlen() is the number of characters in the string, excluding the null termination character. Therefore, the value return for the string shown in Figure 8-5 would be 4.

If you need information on a function (for example, how it is used or its prototype), just move the cursor to the function name in the source window and press F1. A window will open up and present information about the function.

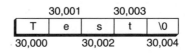

Figure 8-5. Memory Image of a String

Using *putchar()*

The program prints a message that you are displaying the string using the character pointer. The putchar() function is a standard library function designed to "put" a character on the standard output device (often referred to as stdout). The standard output device is the screen. Note the use of the increment operator in the statement

```
putchar(*cptr++);
```

Because of the precedence of operators, you first fetch the character pointed to by cptr, display it on the screen, and then increment cptr.

The Increment Operator...Again

What is being incremented? As before, the increment operator increments the rvalue of whatever is in the variable. Because cptr happens to have the memory address of buff[], increment the address of buff[] so that you end up looking at the next character. In terms of Figure 8-5, start at address 30,000. After the first increment operation, you have incremented the rvalue of cptr from 30,000 to 30,001. Note that this is exactly the same as moving from buff[0] to buff[1].

On each pass through the loop, you increment the address held in cptr. You stop incrementing when len characters are displayed.

Incrementing Through the String with *iptr*

Now the program tries to do the same thing, using iptr this time. Here is where the output falls apart, but the concepts of the chapter begin to fall together.

Suppose that you type the string, "Wherever you go, there you are." The output of the program is "Weee o o hr o r," plus some additional garbage. What went wrong?

Recall that when you define a pointer, QC must keep track of the scalar associated with the pointer. Because the for loop now is using an int pointer, the scalar is 2. However, the data the pointer operates on is an array of char data, which has a scalar of 1. Therefore, doing an increment operation advances iptr by 2 bytes because its scalar is 2. What you see is every other letter in the string because the scalars don't match!

If you tried to compile the program presented in Listing 8-6, you saw the error message

```
Warning C4049: '=': Indirection to Different Type
```

QC warns you that you are mismatching data types. That is, you are trying to initialize an integer pointer (iptr) to point to character data (buff). Note that this is a warning, not a fatal error. C allows you to initialize a pointer to a nonmatching data type. However, if this is not done properly, it usually produces weird results.

What caused all the rest of the garbage on the screen? Because the increment operator moves through memory two bytes at a time, you end up "viewing" twice as many bytes as were in the string. Each pass through the for loop increments the memory address in iptr by 2. If the string entered was 20 bytes long, you look at every other byte for the next 40 bytes of memory! The last half of what you see on the screen is whatever byte values happen to be stored in memory after the string ends.

Perhaps the reason that scalars are important is clearer now. QC does a good job of telling you when you don't match the data types correctly. Still, keep the scalar concept in the back of your mind. Knowing how QC automatically manipulates scalars in a program is often useful for tracking down pernicious bugs.

Writing Your Own *strlen( )* Function

You use the `strlen()` function shown in Listing 8-6 often in your programs. Although `strlen()` is a simple function, try to write your own versions of standard library functions for some good practice. There are two reasons for rewriting existing functions from the standard C library. First, those functions are there for a reason; you will use them often in your programs. Rewriting them helps you better understand how the functions are used. Second, you have a standard frame of reference to test whether your version of a function works properly. Reading the documentation on a function is not the same as actually using it.

With these reasons in mind, write your own version of `strlen()`. An example is shown in Listing 8-7.

Listing 8-7. A First Attempt at `strlen()`

```
/*****
strlen()

        This function determines the length of a character
    string, excluding the null.

        Argument list:      char buff[]      the array that holds the
                                             string

        Return value:       int              the length of the string
*****/

int strlen(char buff[])
{
    int i;
```

Listing 8-7 continues

Listing 8-7 continued

```
    i = 0;
    while (buff[i] != '\0') {
        i++;
    }
    return i;
}
```

Note that you defined the argument to strlen() as a character array. You don't have to specify a length because the array itself was defined in main(). All QC must know is what type of data it is, not how big it is.

Next initialize i to 0 and enter the while loop. Check each character for the null termination character. As long as you have not read the null, continue incrementing i. When you do read the null, you end the while loop and return the length of the string.

Function Style and Function Names

Whenever I write a function that might be reused later, I try to write a comment for it using the style shown in Listing 8-7. The style shown contains enough information to jog your memory, but it isn't tedious to write. Develop a function comment style of your own and use it consistently.

Also remember that any time you write a function using the same name as an existing standard library function (as you did with strlen()), your code — not the standard library version — is used in the program. QC leaves messages to the linker only for those functions whose source code is not part of the program. Because you wrote your own version of strlen(), QC leaves no message for the linker about strlen(). Its location is already known by QC.

Simplifying the *while* Loop in *strlen()*

The code presented in Listing 8-7 works, but it is not the best way to write the function. You can make some improvements. First, test the string for the null termination character. The statement

```
while (buff[i] != '\0') {
```

can be simplified. Realize that you are marching through the string in a straightforward fashion instead of skipping around in the string. Start at the beginning of the string and continue to examine consecutive characters until you find the null termination character.

Second, note that the null termination character (`'\0'`) has a binary representation of 00000000. It is an eight-bit number with each bit set to zero. Not only is the null termination character zero in ASCII, it is also zero in the binary, decimal, and octal. Because a `while` loop executes only as long as the test expression is nonzero (that is, logical True), a null character causes a logical False condition when it is read. This information provides a clue to simplifying the expression a bit.

You can write the new version of the test as

```
while (buff[i]) {
```

Why does this still work? Suppose that the string contains the word `Test`. (Its representation in memory was shown in Figure 8-5.) Instead of showing the memory image in ASCII, show it in its decimal equivalence. (See Figure 8-6.)

If you look up the decimal equivalent for the letter *T* in Appendix A, you see that its value is 84, a lowercase *e*'s value is 101, and so on. The word *Test* is shown in Figure 8-6, using the decimal numbers in place of the letters.

Now consider what happens in the `while` loop if you examine the letter *T*. What QC actually sees is

```
while (84) {
```

because `buff[0]` equals *T*. However, the letter *T* is represented in memory as the number 84. Because 84 is nonzero, the `while` test is logical True and you look at the next character.

Eventually you look at the null character, which has a numeric value of 0. The `while` expression for `buff[4]` is seen by QC as

```
while (0) {
```

Because 0 equates to logical False, the `while` loop terminates. Therefore, simplify the `while` loop to

```
while (buff[i]) {
```

You see this construct used many times in C programs, and you should understand what the test is doing. In the example, you are testing `buff[i]` until a null character is read.

```
          30,001          30,003
    ┌──────┬──────┬──────┬──────┬──────┐
    │  84  │ 101  │ 115  │ 116  │  0   │
    └──────┴──────┴──────┴──────┴──────┘
   30,000          30,002          30,004
```

Figure 8-6. Memory Image of a String in Decimal

Using Pointers Instead of Arrays

You simplified the test expression in the `while` loop to

```
while (buff[i]) {
```

and the code still behaves as before. Now look at what QC does on each pass through the `while` loop. To evaluate the test on `buff[i]`, QC must perform a number of steps to find the appropriate element in the `buff[]` array.

First, QC locates the `lvalue` of where `i` is stored in memory. Second, QC loads the `rvalue` of `i` from memory into a CPU register. Third, QC calculates an offset to find the proper element of the `buff[]` array. If you wish to examine the third element of the array (for example, `buff[2]` when `i` equals 2), QC must multiply the `rvalue` of `i` (for example, 2) by the scalar of `buff[]`. Because the scalar of a `char` is 1, QC multiplies the `i` times 1 (that is, offset = 2 * 1). If `buff[]` were an integer, the offset would be `i` times the scalar size of an `int`, or 2 * 2. Fourth, QC adds the offset just calculated to the starting address of `buff[]`. If `buff[]` starts at memory address 30,000, as shown in Figure 8-6, the proper memory address becomes 30,000 plus the offset, or 30,000 + 2. Finally, QC goes to the calculated memory address (30,002) and fetches the `rvalue` found at that address. QC finds the letter `s` stored at memory address 30,002. Therefore, `buff[2]` is the letter `s`.

It should be clear that the trivial C expression

```
buff[i]
```

involves a lot of code. Most of the work centers around getting variable `i` so that you can calculate the proper offset. Keep in mind that QC must execute all these steps each time it passes through the `while` loop. There has to be a better way . . . and there is.

Clearly, you speed things up a bunch if you can do away with all the code that uses `i` to calculate the offset into the `buff[]` array. Do that by using `buff[]` as a pointer.

Suppose that you write the `while` loop as

```
ptr = buff;
while (*ptr) {
    ptr++;
}
```

What does QC do now? As you saw earlier in the chapter, `buff` and `&buff[0]` both equate to the `lvalue` of where the `buff[]` character array is stored in memory. Therefore, the statement

```
ptr = buff;
```

initializes `ptr` to point to `buff[]`. Also, `*ptr` gets the `rvalue` of what it stored at `buff[0]`. In terms of Figure 8-5, `buff` is the `lvalue` of `buff[0]`, or 30,000. It follows that `*ptr` is what is stored at memory address 30,000. From Figure 8-5, you also know that `*ptr` returns the letter *T*.

The statement controlled by the `while` loop (`ptr++`) increments the value of `ptr`. However, because the `rvalue` of `ptr` is the `lvalue` of `buff[0]`, you increment the value 30,000. Because `ptr` is a pointer to `char` which has a scalar of 1, the increment causes `ptr` to point to 30,001. Now you process the next iteration of the `while` loop.

On the second pass through the `while` loop, `*ptr` points to address 30,001. Therefore, the expression

```
while (*ptr) {
```

is seen by QC as

```
while ('e') {
```

which is the second character in the string.

Keep passing through the loop and incrementing the address until you read the null character. When the null is read, the `while` loop becomes

```
while (0) {
```

and the loop ends. How can you determine the length of the string? buff is still set to 30,000. On the other hand, ptr now equals 30,004. (See Figure 8-6.) My oh my! If you subtract buff from ptr you get the length of the string! That is

```
string length = ptr - buff
              = 30,004 - 30,000
              = 4
```

The modified code is presented in Listing 8-8.

Listing 8-8. A First Attempt at `strlen()`

```
/*****
strlen()

        This function determines the length of a character
    string, excluding the null.

    Argument list:       char buff[]     the array that holds the
                                         string

    Return value:        int             the length of the string

*****/

int strlen(char buff[])
{
    char *ptr;

    ptr = buff;
    while (*ptr) {
        ptr++;
    }
    return ptr - buff;
}
```

This version of `strlen()` is slightly faster than the earlier versions primarily because you do not have to use variable `i` to index into the `buff[]` array. As a general rule, any time you are processing an array in a linear fashion (that is, no skipping around within the array), pointers are faster than using index numbers into the array.

Would defining the function argument in `strlen()` as

```
int strlen(char *buff)
```

make any difference? When an array is passed to a function, the `lvalue` of the array is passed. Also, pointers are designed to hold `lvalue`s of other variables. Therefore, changing `buff[]` to a pointer has no impact on how the function behaves.

The *const* Keyword

The ANSI standard added a new keyword named const that should be used in your strlen() function. Change the first line of Listing 8-8 to read

```
int strlen(const char buff[])
```

The keyword const tells the compiler that nothing should change the value of the variable as long as this variable is in scope. Because the purpose of strlen() is only to read the character array (not change it), using const in the function prototype is appropriate. Likewise, any time you write a function in which a variable should not be changed, use the const keyword in your prototypes and function definitions. It might prevent a bug or two from creeping in.

Multidimensional Arrays

Suppose that you want to write a list of prompt messages in a program. Further suppose that the messages are

```
"Enter your name:"
"Enter your street address:"
"Enter your age:"
```

One way to tackle the problem is to create a double-dimensioned array of chars, as in

```
char prompts[][27] = {
    "Enter your name:",
    "Enter your street address:",
    "Enter your age:"
};
```

Notice that the second size of the array must be specified, but QC fills in the first dimension (for example, 3) by counting the number of string constants. Although there are only 26 characters in the longest prompt message, 27 characters must be allocated for it because QC must add the null termination character to the end of each prompt. (The second dimension must be added because that is the scalar size for the array.)

Also remember that you must allocate the same amount of storage space for each message as that of the longest prompt message. Although the last two prompts are shorter, you must allocate 27 bytes of storage for them.

ANSI and Initializing *auto* Arrays

Finally, this example shows how to initialize a multidimensioned array. The initializer list must start and end with an opening-closing pair of braces. Within the braces, a comma separates each string from the next. The exception is the last element, which has no comma after it.

Prior to the ANSI standard, array variables with the auto storage class could not be initialized. Although QC supports initialization of auto arrays, other compilers do not. Keep this in mind if you plan to port your programs to other environments.

If you use a compiler that does not allow you to initialize auto arrays, change the storage class from auto to static. Pre-ANSI compilers allow you to initialize local variables using the static storage class.

Listing 8-9 presents a program that prints out the contents of the prompt array.

Listing 8-9. Printing a Two-Dimensional Array

```
#include <stdio.h>

int main(void)
{
    char prompts[][27] = {
        "Enter your name:",
        "Enter your street address:",
        "Enter your age:"
    };
    int i, j;

    for (i = 0; i < 3; i++) {
        printf("\n");
        for (j = 0; prompts[i][j]; j++) {
        printf("%c", prompts[i][j]);
        }
    }
}
```

After you define and initialize the array, two for loops print each character in the array. The call to printf() uses the %c conversion character to display the string prompts one character at a time using the two nested for loops.

Improving Performance by Eliminating Unnecessary Array Indexes

Although Listing 8-9 works, it is not the best way to display the prompt messages. Indexing into an array with one index is slow, but indexing with two variables is worse. Listing 8-10 shows a simple modification that builds on your knowledge of string variables and scalars.

Listing 8-10. A Better Way to Print a Two-Dimensional Array

```
#include <stdio.h>

int main(void)
{
    char prompts[][27] = {
      "Enter your name:",
      "Enter your street address:",
      "Enter your age:"
    };
    int i;

    for (i = 0; i < 3; i++) {
        printf("\n%s", prompts[i]);
    }
}
```

This version does away with one index variable and one pass through a for loop. You can do this for two reasons. First, once you realize that the data is in string form, you know that the %s conversion of printf() is perfect for displaying the prompts. The second factor is a bit more subtle.

Using *sizeof* with Two-Dimensional Arrays

If you use the sizeof() command on the prompt[][] array

```
len = sizeof(prompt[0]);
```

the statement returns a value of 27. Also then, the scalar for the prompt[][] array is 27 bytes per element. Therefore, moving from element 0 to element 1 (that is, moving from the first to the second prompt) increases the lvalue by 27 bytes. In fact, sizeof tells you a lot about the prompt[][] array using the variations shown in Table 8-1.

Table 8-1. Using sizeof *with Arrays*

(Assumed Basic Definition Size prompts[3][27])

Statement	Value Returned
sizeof(prompt[0][0])	1
sizeof(prompt[0])	27
sizeof(prompt)	81

Observe the first line in Table 8-1 to see that the scalar for one element of the array is 1. This makes sense because each character in C requires one byte of memory. The second line shows what happens when you want to view one complete row of the two-dimensional array. This variation yields a value that is equal to the second size dimension in the data definition (that is, 27). Finally, the third line tells you the size of the entire array. The prompt[][] array requires 81 bytes of storage (81 = 3 * 27).

Hmmm. There might be something useful here. Given the sizeof variations in Table 8-1, a portable way of knowing the number of elements in a two-dimensional array is

```
element = sizeof(prompt) / sizeof(prompt[0]);

 (3)    =     (81)      /     (27)
```

This also makes sense. The total size divided by the number of items in the row yields that number of elements in the array (3).

Arrays of Pointers

Although Listing 8-10 is an improvement on Listing 8-9, you can still do better. Yet another refinement is shown in Listing 8-11.

Listing 8-11. An Even Better Way to Process Two-dimensional Arrays of chars

```
#include <stdio.h>

int main(void)
{
    char *prompts[] = {
```

```
    "Enter your name:",
    "Enter your street address:",
    "Enter your age:"
};
int i, number;


number = sizeof(prompts) / sizeof(prompts[0]);
for (i = 0; i < number; i++) {
    printf("\n%s", prompts[i]);
}
}
```

The program functions the same as before, but you have made one small improvement. Notice that you changed the definition of prompts[][] to be an array of pointers to char. The version of the program shown in Listing 8-11 uses less memory than earlier versions. Why?

The easiest way to understand how pointers can save memory is with a memory image of what QC does with the code in Listing 8-11. This is shown in Figure 8-7. I assume that the array of pointers starts at memory location 40,000. I also assume that QC places the prompts (that is, the string constants) starting with memory location 5,000.

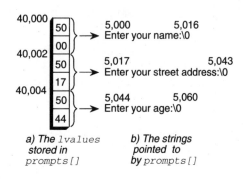

Figure 8-7. Array of Pointers Memory Image

Because QC uses 2 bytes for each pointer, the `prompts[]` array of pointers requires 6 bytes of storage. In part (a) of Figure 8-7, you can see that each array of pointers contains the `lvalue` of where the prompt messages are stored. If you add up the storage requirements for the prompt messages plus the six bytes for the array of pointers, you find that 66 bytes are needed. Recall that the storage requirements for the version in Listing 8-10 was 81 bytes; almost 20 percent less with the pointer version.

The reason the pointer version uses less storage is that each prompt message is allocated only the exact number of bytes it needs. With the array version, you must make all elements as long as the longest prompt message, wasting storage for the shorter prompts.

Two good reasons for using pointers rather than indexed arrays are

1. Pointers process information faster than indexed arrays.

2. Pointers may use less storage than arrays.

One small change in Listing 8-11 allows you to use a pointer version to access `prompts[]`. The only line you need to change is the `printf()` call.

```
printf("\n%s", *(prompts + i) );
```

How does this statement work? It is no different than the array version in Listing 8-11. Because `prompts` equates to the `lvalue` of `prompts[0]`, `i` becomes an offset that is added to `prompts`. Once again, `i` is adjusted by the scalar size of `prompts`. Even though `i` is an `int` data type, it is adjusted automatically by QC to the scalar size of a `pointer`.

On the first pass through the `for` loop, `i` is 0, so you access the first pointer in `prompts[]` array. The indirection operator (*) on the outside of the parentheses tells you to use the address stored at `prompts[0]` to find the string you wish to print. (The parentheses are necessary because of the hierarchy of operators. Add the offset `i` to `prompts` before you use indirection.) Table 8-2 shows the `lvalue` found on each pass through the `for` loop.

Table 8-2. `lvalues` Found When Executing the `for` Loop

(Scalar for pointers is 2)

i	prompts + i	=	pointer address	rvalue
0	40,000 + 0 * 2	=	40,000	5,000
1	40,000 + 1 * 2	=	40,002	5,017
2	40,000 + 2 * 2	=	40,004	5,044

As you can see from Table 8-2, each pass through the `for` loop causes you to examine the next pointer in the array. Each pointer contains the address of where the next string is stored in memory. Therefore, `prompts[1]` has an `lvalue` of 40,002 with an `rvalue` of 5,017. `*(prompts[1])` uses indirection to go to memory address 5,017 and print the string at that address. A comparison of the contents of Table 8-2 with Figure 8-7 shows that they are two ways to view the same information.

Dynamic Storage Allocation

In many programs, you do not know the amount of storage needed for a data item before the program is run. In these situations, you must get the necessary storage to complete the task at hand. Any time your program needs storage for data, the amount of which is unknown at compile time, use the technique of *dynamic memory allocation*. Dynamic memory allocation allows you to request storage from the operating system at run time.

For example, suppose that you want users to tell you how many random numbers they would like to have generated by the program. Further suppose that you want to save the random numbers in an array for subsequent use in the program. Listing 8-12 shows how this can be done.

Listing 8-12. Dynamic Memory Allocation

```
#include <stdio.h>
#include <stdlib.h>
#include <malloc.h>

int main(void)
{
   char buff[20];
   int i, j, *iptr, *get_storage(int num);
   void fill_storage(int *ptr, int num);

   printf("How many random numbers: ");   /* How many numbers */
   i = atoi(gets(buff));
   iptr = get_storage(i);                  /* Enough memory    */
   if (!iptr) {                            /* If not, tell them */
     printf("Not enough memory.");
     exit(0);
```

Listing 8-12 continues

Listing 8-12 continued

```
    }
    fill_storage(iptr, i);              /* Fill 'em in      */
    for (j = 0; j < i; j++) {           /* Show 'em         */
        if (j % 10 == 0) {
            printf("\n");
        }
        printf("%6d", *iptr++);
    }
    free(iptr);
}

/*****
get_storage()

     Function attempts to get enough storage to store num
     integer data types.

     Argument list:    int num      the number of integers to store

     Return value:     int *        a pointer to the storage

*****/

int *get_storage(int num)
{
    return (int *) calloc(num, sizeof(int));
}


/*****
fill_storage()

     Function fill in the storage pointed to by the pointer
     with a series of random numbers.

     Argument list:    int *ptr     pointer to storage for numbers
                       int num      the number of random integers

     Return value:     void

*****/

void fill_storage(int *ptr, int num)
```

```
{
    int i;

    for (i = 0; i < num; i++) {
        *ptr++ = rand();
    }
}
```

This program is a bit longer than most you have seen, but it is not complicated. First, you enter the number of random numbers to be generated. Next, the program calls `get_storage()` to see whether enough free memory exists to store all the random numbers you want.

The `get_storage()` function calls `calloc()`, a standard library function that gets free storage from the operating system (that is, MS-DOS). The function prototype for `calloc()` is normally found in the `malloc.h` header file. If you look at the prototype, you see that there are two arguments. The first argument is the number of items you want to store. In the example, this is the value that was typed when the program started.

The second argument is the number of bytes (the scalar size) required to store one of the data items. Although you can use the constant 2, it is not a portable way to write code. If for example, you move the program to the Macintosh, you must change the 2 to a 4 because integers take 4 bytes of storage on the Mac. However, by using the `sizeof` operator, the compiler always fills in the proper integer storage requirement regardless of the computer on which the program is compiled. With few exceptions, the second argument for `calloc()` should always use in it a `sizeof` operator.

Note how you defined the `get_storage()` function:

```
int *get_storage(int num)
```

In this case, the type specifier for the function is

```
int *
```

The type specifier for a function tells you the type of data returned from the function. Therefore, you tell QC that `get_storage()` returns a pointer to `int` data type. That is, you want `get_storage()` to return an integer pointer to the free memory where you can store your random numbers. Observe that you declared that `get_storage()` does return a pointer to `int` in `main()` so that QC knows the type of data being returned by the function call.

Using the Cast Operator

You used a new operator in the `get_storage()` function. In the statement

```
return (int *) calloc(num, sizeof(int));
```

pay particular attention to the

```
(int *)
```

expression between the `return` keyword and `calloc()`. This is an example of the *cast operator*. The cast operator converts (casts) the data type returned by `calloc()` into the data type between the two parentheses. In the example, you tell QC to take the value returned by `calloc()` and convert it to an integer pointer.

Another example may help you understand how a cast works. Suppose that you have an integer you want to stuff into a `double`. If x is a `double` and i is an integer, the statement

```
x = (double) i;
```

takes the value of i, converts its value from the two-byte representation of an `int` to the eight-byte representation of a `double`, and then assigns it into x. Casts, therefore, are a means of coercing one data type to match a different data type.

In the `get_storage()` function, `calloc()` is defined to return a `void` pointer. Although ANSI defines a `void` pointer so that it can match any other type of pointer (making the cast unnecessary), not all compilers meet this ANSI specification. It does no harm to use the cast, so make a habit of casting the return value from `calloc()` to match whatever data type you will use with the pointer.

The Null Pointer

After program control returns from `get_storage()`, the integer pointer created by `calloc()` is assigned into `iptr`. The `if` statement

```
if (!iptr) {
   printf("Not enough memory.");
    exit(0);
}
```

checks the pointer to see whether the call to `calloc()` in `get_storage()` was successful. If the operating system could not provide enough storage, the value returned by `calloc()` is a *null pointer*. A null pointer assumes the value zero. Therefore, the test on `!iptr` is logical True only if a null pointer was assigned into `iptr`. (To see this check in operation, run the program and enter 32,000 for the number of random numbers to create.) A null pointer causes the error message to display. The call to `exit()` does some housekeeping and the program ends.

Assuming that `iptr` is not a null pointer, the call to `fill_storage()` fills the storage area with the proper number of random integer values. The statement

```
*ptr++ = rand();
```

takes the pseudo-random number produced by `rand()` and assigns it to the memory location pointed to by `ptr`. After the random number is stored, the postincrement operator (++) increments the pointer to point to the next location in memory. Keep in mind that the increment is scaled to fit an integer data type because that's the way you defined `ptr` in the function prototype for `fill_storage()`.

When control returns from `fill_storage()`, print the random numbers using a `for` loop. The modulo operator allows you to print a newline after each set of 10 numbers are displayed on the screen.

Note that the statement:

```
if (!iptr)
```

discussed earlier in this section could also be written

```
if (iptr==NULL)
```

The symbolic constant for NULL is defined in the `stdio.h` header file. Either form works, and the choice is more a matter of style than substance. Over the years, I've opted for the shorter version, although the NULL version may appear more clear.

The *free()* Function

The last thing to do in the program is call the `free()` standard library function with `iptr` as its argument. This is important, because `free()` releases the storage obtained from the call to `calloc()` for subsequent use. As a general rule, always call `free()` as soon as you finish using the storage that was obtained by the call to `calloc()`.

By the way, use the `free()` function call only for pointers obtained by calling `calloc()` or one of its related functions. Using `free()` under any other circumstance can cause all kinds of mischief.

Practice Using Pointers

Pointers are one of the most powerful features of C, but they are also the most troublesome for beginning C programmers. It may take some time for the light to turn on, but when it does, you will see immediately the potential for these little programming gems. I use them in many programs throughout the remainder of this text. However, trying to use them in some programs of your own is a good idea. It's the best way to learn.

Try something simple. Write a program that asks the user to enter a number and then call a function to square the number. The function should replace the original number with its square. That is, the call to the function should look like

```
square(&num);
```

This gives you practice changing variables with `auto` storage class via a function call.

Another exercise is to write your own version of the standard library function `strncpy()`. The purpose of `strncpy()` is to copy (at most) `n` characters from one string into another string. The function prototype is

```
char *strncpy(char *dest, const char *source, int n);
```

The function should copy no more than `n` character from `source` into `dest`. The return value is a pointer to the first character in `dest`.

Pointers and Memory Models

As I mentioned earlier in the chapter, memory addresses for the Intel 8088, 80x86 CPU chips consist of a segment and offset address. If only one code and data segments are used in a program, two-byte pointers are used by default. This means that you can have 64K of code space and 64K of data space for a program without having to worry about segment addresses. This configuration is called the *small memory model*. QC, however, gives you several memory models from which to choose. These are shown in Table 8-3.

Table 8-3. QC Memory Models

Memory Model	Code Segments	Data Segments
Tiny	*	
Small	1	1
Medium	1 per module	1
Compact	1	Multiple
Large	1 per module	Multiple
Huge	1 per module	Multiple**

* The Tiny memory model requires the code and data to fit in one segment. The result is a .COM file rather than an .EXE file. This feature is not available prior to Release 2.5.

** Except for the Huge memory model, no single data item can exceed 64K. The Huge memory model allows a data item to span a segment.

As you write more complex programs, you may need to use a different memory model. As a rule, the linker tells you when your present program exceeds the code or data limitations. For example, if you have a large program with relatively modest data requirements, use the Medium memory model. If a program uses large code and data space, use the Large memory model. If you have a large program in which a single data item exceeds 64K (for example, a large array), you must use the Huge memory model.

To change the default memory model, select Options from the main menu, then the Make option, followed by Compiler flags (Alt-O-M-C). Then use the cursor keys to move the radio button to the memory model you wish to see.

For now, all the programs you have written can use the small memory model, so there is no need to change memory models. Later you may need to change the default memory model as your programs get more complex.

Review the QC library documentation now to see the various types of functions available to you. If you've followed things this far, you should know enough to understand almost all the function prototypes. (File I/O is a possible exception.)

Take the time to understand pointers fully . . . they're worth the effort!

9

Structures, *unions*, *enums*, and *typedefs*

In this chapter, you learn about

Structures

unions

typedefs

Enumerated data types

Bit fields

The ternary operator

With the exception of enumerated data types, the other data types covered in this chapter are extensions of those you have already studied. Learning about these extensions allows you to arrange your data in a much more convenient way.

Structures

My favorite definition of a *structure* is "an array for adults." A common array is a group of identical data items that can be referenced by a single name. You saw several program examples that used arrays of chars, ints, and pointers. The common element of such arrays is that the group of data is a homogenous unit. That is, the arrays consisted of all chars, ints, or pointers.

Structures, by contrast, may consist of different data types, yet they are referenced through a single variable name. In other languages, a structure is similar to a record or a field. An example will help you understand how all this fits together.

Suppose that you teach a class and must keep track of each student's name, social security number, major, attendance, and exam grades. Even though the data items you must maintain are very different, you want to treat them as a single, cohesive unit. A structure variable is a perfect means for organizing such data.

Declaring a Structure

The first thing to do is tell QC what the structure contains; in other words, declare the structure. An example of a structure for students is shown in Figure 9-1.

```
struct student {
    char name[20];       /* Name                     */
    char socsec[12];     /* Social Security number   */
    char major;          /* Major                    */
    int days_missed;     /* Days absent from class   */
    int scores[20];      /* Exam scores              */
};
```

Figure 9-1. Declaring a Structure

The C keyword struct tells QC that you are declaring a structure data type. The identifier student is called a *structure tag* and lets QC identify which structure is being declared. A program can have as many structures as needed, and the structure tag lets you apply a name to the type of structure being declared.

The opening brace starts the list of the variables that are contained in the structure. The variables between the opening and closing brace of the structure declaration are called the *members of the structure*. The structure members can be any C data type, including other structures or *unions*. (I cover unions later in this chapter.)

Note that the declaration shown in Figure 9-1 does not define a structure variable. Rather, a structure declaration describes the members of the structure. Think of a structure declaration as a cookie cutter. The purpose of a structure declaration is to tell QC the shape of the cookie cutter.

Defining a Structure Variable

To use a structure in a program, you must define the structure variable. Figure 9-2 shows how to define a structure variable of type student.

```
struct student {
    char name[20];      /* Name                      */
    char socsec[12];    /* Social Security number    */
    char major;         /* Major                     */
    int days_missed;    /* Days absent from class    */
    int scores[20];     /* Exam scores               */
} class;
```

Figure 9-2. Defining a Structure Variable

In Figure 9-2, a structure variable of type student and named class has been defined.

If you want an array of student structures, use the definition shown in Figure 9-3.

```
struct student {
    char name[20];      /* Name                      */
    char socsec[12];    /* Social Security number    */
    char major;         /* Major                     */
    int days_missed;    /* Days absent from class    */
    int scores[20];     /* Exam scores               */
} class, entire_class[MAXSIZE];
```

Figure 9-3. Defining an Array of Structures

In Figure 9-3, you have defined a single variable of type struct student named class plus an array of such structures named entire_class[]. If MAXSIZE is #defined to be 100, you have defined an array of 100 structures of type student.

Accessing a Structure Member — the Dot Operator

Suppose that you want to enter a student's name. You need to know how to access a specific member of the structure. Do this with the *dot operator*. The following code fragment shows how to use the dot operator.

```
printf("Enter the student's major: ");
m = (char) atoi(gets(buff));
class.major = m;
```

Whenever the dot operator is used, it appears between the structure variable name (class) and the member of the structure that is to be accessed. In the example, you enter a number that represents the student's major. I'm assuming that there are no more than 127 majors — the range of a signed char. (A more robust example would check the number entered.)

Because you know that there are no more than 127 majors, you have no reason to use more than one byte of storage for this structure member. Although the major is a numeric value, store it as a char to save a byte. The call to atoi() converts the number you entered to an int, and you use the cast operator to force the int back to the size of a char. If you type the number 65, that is the numeric value of m stored as a one-byte quantity.

The statement

```
class.major = m;
```

says to QC, "Find the structure variable named class. Now find a member of that structure variable named major. Go to the memory location of major (its lvalue) and stuff m into that memory address." The purpose of the dot operator is to give QC a way to determine which structure to access (class) as well as which member of that structure variable to use (major). The dot operator separates the variable name for the structure from the member name within that structure.

If you want to assign the contents of the major structure member into some other variable named uc, the statement is

```
uc = class.major;
```

The process is reversed. QC locates the class structure variable, finds the lvalue of the major structure member and stuffs its rvalue into uc.

Structures Without Tags

If you need only one structure variable, you can also define a structure variable without using a structure tag. This is shown in Figure 9-4.

In this example, you have a structure variable named `class`, but have no name (that is, no structure tag) for the "cookie cutter." This form of structure definition is used mainly when your program needs only a single variable of this structure type. For example, suppose that you have a disk file containing `student` structures, as shown in Figure 9-2. To read the data file and print out the students' names, you need only one `student` structure. The program reads a student's structure data from the file into `class` and prints the name. The statement

```
printf("\n%s", class.name);
```

then displays the name on the screen. The program reads the next student into `class` and displays that student's name, and so on until all of the names are read.

```
struct {
    char name[20];        /* Name                     */
    char socsec[12];      /* Social Security number   */
    char major;           /* Major                    */
    int days_missed       /* Days absent from class   */
    int scores[20];       /* Exam scores              */
} class;
```

Figure 9-4. Defining a Structure Variable Without a Tag

Initializing a Structure

Suppose that you wish to initialize the first element of an array of `student` structures. One way to do this is shown in Figure 9-5.

In Figure 9-5, you have declared the `student` structure and then used the statement

```
struct student my_class[MAXSIZE] = {
```

to define a variable named `my_class[]` of structure type `student`. Any time you wish to define a variable for a structure that has already been declared, the syntax is

```
struct structure_tag variable_name;
```

```
struct Student {
    char name[20];          /* Name                    */
    char socsec[12];        /* Social Security number  */
    char major;             /* Major                   */
    int days_missed         /* Days absent from class  */
    int scores[MAXGRADES];  /* Exam scores             */
};

struct student my_class[MAXSIZE] = {
    {"Dave Cooper",  "231-54-7608", 68,3,79,88,91,93},
    {"Don Dudine",   "123-45-6789", 68,20,75,82,72,70},
    {"Chuck Lieske", "301-22-3341", 65,0,89,81,90,93},
    {"Jim Rheude",   "435-24-1182", 54,0,71,73,80,81},
    {"Regina Ridley", "234-27-3508", 70,0,87,88,94,92}
};
```

Figure 9-5. Initializing a Structure

You must use a structure tag in the declaration of the structure if you wish to define structure variables this way. In the example, you follow the structure definition of `my_class[]` with a partial list of each student's information. The initialization list begins and ends with a set of opening-closing braces. In addition, each element of the `my_class[]` structure array must also be contained within braces, separated from one another by a comma. Only the last element initialized is not followed by a comma.

What happens to the other MAXSIZE minus 5 elements of the `my_class[]` array? Any data items not present in the initializer list are set to zero. Therefore, if MAXSIZE is 100, 95 elements of `my_class[]` are initialized to zero for all members' values. Also note that you specified only 4 of the exam scores. The remaining 16 values are set to 0 by QC.

Listing 9-1 presents a small program to test the structure declarations-definitions from Figure 9-5. If you copy the contents of Figure 9-5 before `main()` in Listing 9-1, you can see how everything fits together.

Listing 9-1. Program to Test Structure Initializiation

```
#include <stdio.h>

#define MAXSIZE   100
#define MAXGRADES 20

int main(void)
{
    int i, j;

    for (i = 0; i < MAXSIZE; i++) {
        if (my_class[i].name[0] == '\0')
            break;
        printf("\n\nName: %s\n", my_class[i].name);
        printf("SS#: %s\n", my_class[i].socsec);
        printf("Major: %d\n", (int) my_class[i].major);
        printf("Days missed: %d\n", (int) my_class[i].days_missed);
        printf("Grades: ");
        for (j = 0; j < MAXGRADES; j++)
            printf("%4d", my_class[i].scores[j]);
    }
}
```

Notice how the `my_class[].major` is cast to an `int` before being displayed. This ensures that it prints as an integer value. (You could use a `%c` conversion character, but the number would appear as its ASCII equivalent rather than a number.)

A `for` loop is used to display the exam grades. In the statement

```
printf("%4d", my_class[i].scores[j]);
```

variable `i` is used as an index to the proper element of the `my_class[]` structure array. Variable `j` is used as an index to the proper exam score for the current student. Because you have initialized only the first four exam scores, the remaining 16 values are displayed with their (QC-initialized) values of zero.

Pointers to Structures

Suppose that you want to write a function that fills in the number of days the student is absent from class. Further assume that the student structure has local scope. This means you must pass a student structure pointer to the function. The function to accomplish the task is shown in Listing 9-2.

Listing 9-2. Passing a Pointer to a Structure

```
/*****
get_absent()

        This function is used to fill in the number of days
      the student is absent from the class.

      Argument list:        struct student *d    pointer to the
                             student structure

      Return value:         void

*****/

void get_absent(struct student *d)
{
   char buff[20];

   printf("Enter days absent: ");
   (*d).days_missed = atoi(gets(buff));
}
```

Because you are using a pointer to the structure, you must use indirection to "fill in" the number of days absent. What does the statement

```
(*d).days_missed = atoi(gets(buff));
```

do? The expression on the right side of the equal sign should be familiar by now. It takes the input you entered and converts it into an int. Now for the weird part. The expression

```
(*d).days_missed
```

requires some study. Because the dot operator has precedence over the indirection operator, you must parenthesize the name of the student

structure that is passed to the function. Because d is a pointer to the student
structure from main(), the expression

(*d)

causes QC to use the the rvalue of d as the memory address (lvalue) of the
structure's memory location. The dot operator makes QC fetch the address
of where days_missed is located within the d structure space. In other words,
you can view days_missed as an offset from the starting lvalue of d. Figure
9-6 shows how this looks from the first element of the student structure
(assuming that the first element of the structure is located at memory
address 1000).

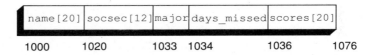

Figure 9-6. Memory Image of the student Structure

The subexpression

(*d)

generates the address 1000. The second part of the expression

days_missed

causes QC to add an offset of 34 to the base address of 1000. As a result,
the statement

(*d).days_missed = atoi(gets(buff));

causes QC to shove the integer value you entered into the two memory
locations starting at address 1034. You just used indirection to fill in the
number of days the student is absent!

Indirection When Using Pointers — A Shorthand Method

Programmers — especially C programmers — don't like to type any more
than they have to. "Economy of expression" is a phrase often used to

decribe C. At every turn, the designers of C sought ways to reduce the number of keystrokes necessary to accomplish a given task. The increment-decrement operators (++ and --) and the complex assignment operators (+=, *=, -=, etc.) are clear examples of operators that reduce keystrokes.

It is only logical that an operator exists to replace the clumsy expression

```
(*d).days_missed
```

The shorthand expression for structure indirection is

```
d->days_missed
```

Note that the dot operator is replaced with the *arrow operator*. The interpretation is exactly as it was with the parentheses and the indirection operator. An easy way to remember when to use the indirection operator is that the arrow "points" from the structure to the member being referenced. (Often you will hear other C programmers verbalize the expression, "D sub days_missed.")

Now that you understand how the get_absent() function works, and how to use the arrow operator, you can replace the statement in Listing 9-2

```
(*d).days_missed = atoi(gets(buff));
```

with its equivalent statement

```
d->days_missed = atoi(gets(buff));
```

and the function behaves in exactly the same manner.

If you want to enter the number of days that the twentieth student has missed, how do you call get_absent()? Because arrays start with 0 in C, the twentieth student is found when the index number is 19. Therefore, the call

```
get_absent(&my_class[19]);
```

in main() would pass the lvalue of the twentieth student to the get_absent() function.

Structure Passing and Assignment

In the days before ANSI C, it was illegal to pass a structure to a function. The only option was to use a pointer to the structure. Likewise, to assign the contents of one structure variable into a different variable (of the same type of structure), you had to assign each individual member of the structure. In other words, structure assignment was illegal.

These limitations of pre-ANSI C were a real pain. For example, consider how you would copy the members from one structure into another using pre-ANSI C.

```
int i;
struct student mine, yours;

/* Some code that fills in the mine structure   */
/* Now comes the code to copy mine into yours   */

strcpy(yours.name, mine.name);
strcpy(yours.socsec, mine.name);
yours.major = mine.major;
yours.days_missed = mine.days_missed;
for (i = 0; i < MAXGRADES; i++)
   yours.scores[i] = mine.scores[i];
```

You can see that a lot of source code was needed to copy the contents of large, complex structures. Fortunately, ANSI C allows you to assign structure variables just like any other type of variable. With QC, the statement

```
yours = mine;
```

copies the `mine` structure contents into `yours`. One statement, nice and simple!

Likewise, you can pass a copy of a structure to a function with an ANSI C compiler. Be aware, however, that you are working with a copy of the structure if you are not using a pointer to the structure. For example, to change the structure `mine` without using a pointer, use code similar to that shown in Listing 9-3.

Listing 9-3. Passing a Structure to a Function

```
int main(void)
{
   struct student mine;
   struct student func1(struct student m);

   mine = func1(mine);
}
```

Listing 9-3 continues

Listing 9-3 continued

```
struct student func1(struct student m)
{
    /* Code that fills in the m structure */
    return m;
}
```

Several things in Listing 9-3 warrant further study. First, you must declare that `func1()` returns a data type of `struct student`. Second, the statement

```
mine = func1(mine);
```

takes the `m` structure returned from the call to `func1()` and assigns it into `mine`. The structure `m` in `func1()` is a copy of the `mine` structure defined in `main()`. Therefore, the entire copy of the structure, including any changes made to `m` in `func1()`, is pushed on the stack by the `return m` statement at the end of `func1()`. When program control returns to `main()`, the structure data sitting on the stack is assigned into `mine`.

Prior to the ANSI enhancements to C, the technique of passing a copy of a structure to a function and then assigning the copy back into the variable on return from the function was not possible. Structure passing and assignment have made things a lot simpler for the programmer.

Structures may seem a bit strange at first, but once you've mastered them, they are extremely useful data structures that lend themselves to a wide variety of programming tasks.

Unions

A `union` is a piece of memory capable of holding different types of data at any given moment. A `union` is not much different from a general purpose buffer that can hold any specified data type. For example, suppose that you are reading numbers from a data file. Assuming that the numbers represent

1. Years of service with the company (`service`)
2. A company identification number (`id`)
3. Your present salary (`wage`)

you can organize the data as a structure

```
struct employee {
    int service;
    long id;
    double wage;
} worker;
```

If you evaluate the expression

```
i = sizeof(worker);
```

what is the answer? The answer is the sum of the number of bytes for an int (2), plus a long (4), plus a double (8). The total storage requirement for the employee structure is 14 bytes.

However, if you are reading data from a disk file, you may not need to preserve the entire record. Rather, you might read one number from the disk, process it, read the next number, process it, and then read and process the last number. A union is perfect when you need a place to put a data item while it is being processed. A union for the same type of data would be

```
union employee {
    int service;
    long id;
    double wage;
} worker;
```

The syntax rules are virtually identical to that of a structure. There is one major difference, however. If you evaluate the statement

```
sizeof(worker);
```

using the union definition of worker, the size is 8, not 14. The reason is that QC scans the list of members in the union, determines the largest member in the union, and allocates that number of bytes for the union. Therefore, a union has a byte size equal to the largest member of the union. In this case, worker now occupies only 8 bytes of storage space instead of the 14 bytes used for a structure. Note, however, that the union is large enough to hold any one member of the union.

The employee *union tag* serves the same purpose as a structure tag; it allows QC to keep track of multiple unions in a program.

Putting a *union* to Work

Suppose that you want to write a function that returns the number of columns available on the screen. MS-DOS provides certain routines, or *interrupts,* that allow you access to such information. Specifically, function 0x0f of the video interrupt (number 0x10) allows you to determine the number of columns available on the screen.

The QC compiler provides a header file named dos.h containing certain definitions that can be used when working with interrupts. Figure 9-7 shows one part of dos.h that is of interest.

First, a structure named WORDREGS is declared. WORDREGS mirrors the word-length (two-byte) registers of the 80x86 family of CPU's. A second structure declaration represents the byte-length registers found in the CPU. Note that both structures have members that are unsigned int's and char's because the high bit may be important when processing an interrupt.

```
/* word registers */

struct WORDREGS {
     unsigned int ax;
     unsigned int bx;
     unsigned int cx;
     unsigned int dx;
     unsigned int si;
     unsigned int di;
     unsigned int cflag;
};

/* byte registers */

struct BYTEREGS {
     unsigned char al, ah;
     unsigned char bl, bh;
     unsigned char cl, ch;
     unsigned char dl, dh;
};

/* general purpose registers union -
 * overlays the corresponding word
    and byte registers
 */

union REGS {
     struct WORDREGS x;
     struct BYTEREGS h;
};
```

Figure 9-7. Partial Listing of dos.h

Finally, you see a union declaration (REGS) that contains a WORDREGS and BYTEREGS structure definition (that is, variables x and h). Because REGS is a union, QC first examines the size requirements for a WORDREGS (that is, seven int's would be 14 bytes) and BYTEREGS (eight char's would be 8 bytes) structure. Realizing that WORDREGS is the larger of the two structures, QC allocates 14 bytes for the REGS union.

Note that the storage allocated for REGS is large enough to hold either a WORDREGS or BYTEREGS data structure. With that in mind, write a program that tells you the number of video columns currently available on the screen.

Listing 9-4. Number of Screen Columns

```
#include <stdio.h>
#include <dos.h>

int vcol(void);

int main(void)
{
   printf("Your screen has %d columns.\n", vcol());
}



/*****
                        vcol()

   This function determines the number of video columns
presently being displayed on the screen. The function
uses interrupt 0x10, function 0x0f.

   Argument list:    void

   Return value:     int     the number of columns on the screen

*****/

int vcol(void)
{
   union REGS ireg;
```

Listing 9-4 continues

Listing 9-4 continued

```
   ireg.h.ah = 0x0f;                  /* Function number of interrupt */
   int86(0x10, &ireg, &ireg);
   if (ireg.h.al < 2)
      return 40;

   if (ireg.h.al > 3 && ireg.h.al != 7)
      return 0;
   else
      return 80;
}
```

All the work takes place in `vcol()`. First, define a `union` of type REGS named `ireg`. The `ireg union` can hold either a WORDREGS or BYTEREGS structure at any given moment. The MS-DOS documentation for the video interrupt routines tells you to load the `ah` register with the function number 0x0f when you call the video interrupt routine to find out the number of screen columns. Therefore, the statement

```
ireg.h.ah = 0x0f;
```

says, "Find the `union` named `ireg`, assume that you are using the BYTEREGS structure named `h`, and stuff 0x0f into the `ah` member of that structure." QC keeps track of all the details for you.

Next, call the `int86()` library function with three arguments. The first argument is the interrupt routine you wish to invoke (the video interrupt, 0x10). The second argument is a pointer to the `ireg union` that contains the setup information required by the interrupt (that is, the function number in `ireg.h.ah`). The third argument is a pointer to a union that holds the return information after the interrupt is called. Because you do not need to "reuse" the information passed to the `int86()` function, `ireg` can do double duty by being used as both the input and return values.

The MS-DOS documentation also tells you that if the value returned in `ireg.h.al` is less than 2, you are in the 40-column mode. If the return value is greater than 3, but not equal to 7, the screen is in graphics mode. All other combinations are 80-column screens. Therefore, `ireg.h.al` contains the number of screen columns after the call to `int86()` is completed.

Although in this example, you used the BYTEREGS structure in the REGS `union`, other interrupts require the WORDREGS structure. Note, however, that because `ireg` is a union, either structure is accessible from the same storage space. The `ireg` union is a "flexible" storage space capable of holding different data types.

One final point about Listing 9-4: Some purists complain that it uses poor coding style because it has multiple return points. Indeed, three of them are in the function. You could set a variable according to each `if` test and have a single `return` statement at the bottom of the program to return the variable. For several reasons, this seems like wearing a bulletproof vest in a snowball fight.

First, the function is small enough for all the `return` statements to be visible at one time. Second, you avoid creating a variable whose existence is questionable in the first place. Third, you avoid executing unnecessary code. If the value is 40 columns, why test for a graphics screen and 80 columns before returning from the function? Finally, this is the way I write code in "real life." If using multiple `return` statements bothers you, by all means follow your own preference.

If you wish to test the program presented in Listing 9-4, type the MS-DOS command

```
mode co40
```

and press the Enter key. The screen uses this command to switch to 40-column mode. Now run the program a second time. The program in Listing 9-4 should display the value 40. Type

```
mode co80
```

at the MS-DOS prompt and press Enter. If you run the program again, the number of columns will be 80.

Your Responsibilities When Using *Unions*

You must remember that a `union` is capable of holding the data you defined as being a member of the `union`. For example, if you define a `union`

```
union value {
    char c;
    int i;
    long big;
    double x;
} number;
```

`number` is large enough to hold any one of the four different data types. If you put a `long` value into the union, as in

```
number.big = 5L;
```

the `union` properly stores the `long` value in the union. (Recall that the `L` following a numeric constant tells QC that 5 is a `long` numeric constant, not an `int`.) Just for the sake of argument, suppose that the `union` named `number` is stored at memory address 50,000. The memory image might look like that shown in Figure 9-8.

Now suppose that for some reason you think the `union` holds a `double` rather than a `long`. That is, if you perform the statement

```
interest = number.x;
```

QC takes the contents of the full eight bytes in the `union` named `number` and assigns them into `interest`. Unfortunately, the value shown in the memory image depicted in Figure 9-8 is a `long` and is probably not even close to the QC floating point `double` you thought was in the `union`. It is your responsibility to keep track of what is actually in the `union`. C has no way to protect you from assigning an improper data type to or from a `union`.

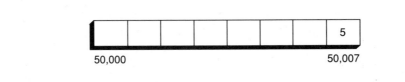

50,000   50,007

Figure 9-8. Storing a Value in a Union

Complex Data Definitions and Attribute Lists

You have seen a wide variety of data types that you can use in your programs. Another nice feature of C is that you can build complex data types from the basic data types. Structures and unions are but two examples of such data types. You can also build complex data types without using structures or unions.

Right-Left Rule for Complex Data Types

Some data definitions can be less than obvious at first glance. Consider the following example of a complex data definition:

```
int *many_num[10]:
```

What type of data is this? To understand `many_num[]`, you need to construct an attribute list for the variable. An *attribute* refers to the context in which the data item can be used in a C expression. An *attribute list* is all the attributes of the data item collected into a list.

In the example, you can construct an attribute list for `many_num[]` by starting at the name of the variable (that is, its identifier) and spiraling out from that point in a right-left manner. Step 1 in creating the attribute list (see Figure 9-9) is the statement, "`many_num` is"

```
          (1)
int *many_num[10];
```

Figure 9-9. Step 1 in Constructing an Attribute List

The second step requires looking to the right of `many_num` for the next attribute. There you see the brackets for an array of 10 "somethings." Step 2 is depicted in Figure 9-10.

The verbal attribute list says, "`many_num` is an array of 10." After looking at the attribute to the right of the identifier (`many_num`), you must look to the left for the next attribute. The third step is shown in Figure 9-11.

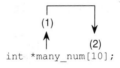

```
(1)
             (2)
int *many_num[10];
```

Figure 9-10. Step 2 in Constructing an Attribute List

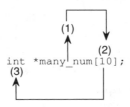

Figure 9-11. Step 3 in Constructing an Attribute List

The next attribute is the asterisk, so you know it is a pointer. You can now verbalize the attribute list as, "many_num is an array of 10 pointers to." If you spiral back to the right for the next unused attribute, you find none. (Don't count the semicolon in an attribute list.) Therefore, you must spiral back to the left to find the int keyword. The attribute list is now described as, "many_num is an array of 10 pointers to int." Because there are no further unused attributes, this is the full attribute list.

Attribute lists are important because they tell QC the type of data operations that can be performed on a variable. Without an attribute list, QC would be severely restricted in many of the error messages that it produces. For example, if you define an int and then try to perform indirection on it, QC knows that "pointer" is not one of the variable's attributes, so indirection should not be done using this variable. An error message occurs.

*typedef*s and Attribute Lists

A typedef is a convenient way to abbreviate a complex attribute list with a single word. Suppose that you need three variables similar to many_num[ ], shown in the previous example. Using a typedef simplifies the task.

```
typedef int *ARRAY_PTR[10];
    .
    .
    .
ARRAY_PTR table1, table2, table3;
```

The final preceding statement defines three variables that have the attribute list, "array of 10 pointers to int." (Note that C style conventions normally have typedef names written in uppercase letters.) The typedef for `ARRAY_PTR` shown previously is an abbreviated form for the data definitions

```
int *table1[10], *table2[20], *table3[10];
```

Contrary to what some might say, a `typedef` does not create a new data type. Rather, a `typedef` is a way to simplify a complex data definition by making it a single word. Verbalizing the attribute list, you can say, "`ARRAY_PTR` is an array of 10 pointers to `int`." Likewise, you can also say, "`table1` is an array of 10 pointers to `int`." Therefore, a `typedef` allows you to "tack on" a previously defined attribute list to a newly defined variable.

If you choose your `typedef`s carefully, you gain three benefits. First, you don't have to type as much, which means fewer errors. Second, the `typedef` name can make the intent of the variable(s) clearer. Finally, if you need to alter the attribute list at some time in the future, you need change only the `typedef` itself, not all variables that use the `typedef`. This saves a considerable amount of editing time.

Certain *typedef*s Found in the ANSI Standard

In Chapter 10, you discover a `typedef` named `FILE` that is used with most disk file operations. Two other `typedef`s that are defined in the ANSI standard are `size_t` and `ptrdiff_t`. The `size_t typedef` is used most often as the data type returned when using the `sizeof` operator. By using a `typedef` for this value, ANSI avoids certain problems when code is compiled by different compilers and different machines. For example, some MS-DOS compilers return an `int` for the `sizeof` operator. Other compilers return an `unsigned int`. Using a standard `typedef` minimizes the problems caused by such differences if both compilers have defined a `typedef` named `size_t`.

The `ptrdiff_t typedef` is used for data that perform pointer arithmetic. Again, pointers for one compiler might be 2 bytes long, whereas pointers for another compiler may be 4 bytes long. Using a standard pointer `typedef` reduces problems associated with moving source code between machines. Also, the name `ptrdiff_t` identifies the purpose of any variables defined using this `typedef`.

Although this may be obvious, redefining a `typedef` that is part of the ANSI standard is not a good idea. You will find various `typedef`s in the header files provided with the QC compiler.

To see several examples, browse through `stdio.h`, `stddef.h`, and `time.h`.

The *enum* Data Type

Although in use prior to the ANSI standard, the enum data type is formalized with the ANSI standard. An enum data type is an integer constant that is tied to a name. The formal syntax for an enum declaration is

```
enum_type_specifier identifier {enumerated list};
```

For example, suppose that you want to rank from poor to excellent the responses on a questionnaire. Do this with an enumerated data type as follows:

```
enum response {POOR, GOOD, EXCELLENT};
```

These three enumerated variables are also associated with the values 0 (POOR), 1 (GOOD), and 2 (EXCELLENT). Unless told to do otherwise, the enumerated list of variables begins with 0 and increases by one for each variable in the list thereafter.

Note: There is a slowly emerging trend to write the members of the enumerated list in uppercase letters. I'm not sure I agree with the trend, because it tends to encroach on the style for symbolic constants using the #define preprocessor directive. Whichever style you select, use it consistently.

Using some other values for the members of the enumerated list is easily done. For example, suppose that you want to identify the age groups *driver, voter, retiree*. The enum declaration is

```
enum people {DRIVER = 16, VOTER = 21, RETIREE = 65};
```

Note that the automatic numbering system picks up with the last defined value. Therefore, if you add a fourth type of person, as in

```
enum people {DRIVER = 16, VOTER = 21, RETIREE = 65, POST_RETIRE};
```

where no value is explicitly assigned to POST_RETIRE, its value is 66 — one greater than the variable that appears before it in the enumerated list.

Keep in mind that the examples above are enumerated declarations; you have not defined an enum variable yet. To define an enum variable, you can use

```
num response low_income, hi_income;
enum people male, female;
```

These statements define the variables `low_income`, `hi_income`, `male`, and `female`. In theory, the enumerated variables should not be allowed to assume any value other than those in the enumerated list. That is, `low_income` should be allowed only the values 0, 1, and 2. This also means that the compiler could perform certain kinds of type checking on the data. However, ANSI does not require compiler vendors to check that the values assigned into `enum` variables are in the enumerate list of values. (QC does not check enumerated values.)

To assign a value to an enumerated variable, you can say

```
male = DRIVER;
```

which assigns the numeric value 16 into `male`.

When you give some thought to the `enum` data type and the name given in the enumerated list, the program can be made much easier to read and understand.

enum Versus *#define*

Perhaps you've noticed that the `enum` data type does not seem to give you much more than can be accomplished with a `#define`. For example, you can write a program with

```
#define DRIVER    16
#define VOTER     21
#define RETIREE   65
```

and use this the same way as you would the `people` enumerated data type discussed earlier. Because QC (and most other compilers) don't check for enumerated-only values being assigned to enumerated variables, many of the type-checking benefits of the `enum` data type are lost. Still, when compilers begin to perform type checking, `enum` data types will be much more advantageous than an equivalent list of `#define`s. Until that time, because the `enum`'s at least have potential for improvement in the future, they are preferred over a `#define`. Also, because `enum` variables have `lvalues` and `rvalues` and `#define`'s do not, the `enum` does offer some advantages when it comes time to debug a program.

Bit Fields

Some writers have referred to C as a "high-level assembly language." One reason people view C this way is that it lets you get down to the bit level if needed. You have already seen how the bitwise operators allow you to manipulate bits. Bit fields offer a convenient way to treat individual bits of an integer as a cohesive unit.

The formal syntax for a bit field is

```
struct structure_tag {
    type_specifier identifier : constant_expression;
};
```

The only valid type specifiers for a bit field are signed or unsigned `int`s. The identifier is the name that you wish to associate with the bit field. The `constant_expression` is the number of bits needed for the bit field. The size of the bit field is dictated by the range of values you expect to "fit" in the bit field. If the type specifier is simply `int`, the top bit is taken to be the sign bit. Therefore, if you had a bit field that was declared as `int` with a width of 2, the binary number 11 is not 3 as you might exprect, but rather –1. The reason is that the high bit is used as the sign bit. If the field should hold the values 0 through 3, the bit field should be declared an `unsigned int`.

An example might help show how things fit together. Each character you see on a PC screen is comprised of two bytes. The first byte is the ASCII character itself. The second byte is the attribute byte. The interpretation of the attribute byte varies according to whether you have a color or monochrome monitor. The interpretation of the bits for each monitor type is shown in Table 9-1.

Table 9-1. Interpretation of Screen Attribute Byte

Monochrome

Bit Number	Interpretation
7	If on (1), character blinks. If 0, no blink
6, 5, 4	If on (111), white background. If 0, black background
3	If on (1), high intensity. If 0, normal
2, 1, 0	000 is inverse (black foreground), 001 underline with white foreground, 111 is normal (white foreground)

Color

Bit Number	Interpretation
7	If on (1), character blinks. If 0, no blink
6, 5, 4	Background colors
3, 2, 1, 0	Foreground colors

Suppose that you want to manipulate data for a color monitor. You can define a bit field similar to

```
struct screen {
    unsigned blink      :1;
    unsigned backcolor  :3;
    unsigned forecolor  :4;
} color;
```

Now use an `enum` to present a list of colors.

```
enum shades {black, blue, green, cyan, red, magenta, brown,
             white, gray, ltblue, ltgreen, ltcyan, ltred,
             ltmagenta, yellow, iwhite} colors;
```

It is now possible to set the foreground and background bit fields with the statements

```
color.background = red;
color.foreground = white;
```

You could argue that the bitwise operators can accomplish the same type of tasks as bit fields. For example, if you wish to examine only the lowest two bits of an `int`, you can use

```
low_bits = word & 0x03;
```

The constant 0x03 (often called a *bit mask*) is ANDed with the variable `word`. This statement "masks off" all but the lowest two bits.

Even though the bitwise operators can perform tasks similar to bit fields, there are reasons for using bit fields. Bit fields help document the variables in a program. They are useful for minimizing storage requirements for flags, status variables, and other small numeric values. For example, if a record in a data base includes 6 status flags that are either

0 or 1 (for example, male-female, in school-graduated, college-high school, etc.), you can store the status flags in a bit field using only one `int` rather than 6 `char`s.

Although bit fields are not used often, you may find a situation in which they present the perfect solution. Bit fields are but another tool in your programming arsenal, and a good programmer never throws away a useful tool!

Writing to Video Memory

The final section of this chapter brings together several data types and shows how to write directly to video memory. As you may know, there are two basic ways to write something on the screen. The first is to use the resources provided by the operating system (MS-DOS). Although this method is the most portable because the operating system must cope with any hardware variances, it is also the slowest. MS-DOS must execute a lot of code just to put one character on the screen.

The second method takes advantage of the fact that you can access video memory directly, bypassing MS-DOS. On the down side, writing directly to video memory is not completely portable because some MS-DOS machines locate video memory at "nonstandard" memory addresses. Examples are the Z100 and the Tandy 2000 systems. In most cases, however, IBM compatibles place video memory at the expected locations in memory. I assume that you are using a true IBM-compatible machine.

Your first task is to determine what kind of monitor is being used when the program is run. Fortunately, QC provides a (non-ANSI) library function named `getvideoconfig()` that gives you the needed information. The argument to `getvideoconfig()` is a structure that looks like that shown in Listing 9-5.

Listing 9-5. The `videoconfig` *Structure from* `graph.h`

```
struct videoconfig {
    short numxpixels;
    short numypixels;
    short numtextcols;
    short numtextrows;
    short numcolors;
    short bitsperpixel;
    short numvideopages;
```

```
short mode;
short adapter;
short monitor;
short memory;

};
```

The `videoconfig` structure contains information determining the type of video display the program is using when it is run. Of particular interest is whether you are facing a color or monochrome monitor. You can tell which type by inspecting the `mode` member of the `videoconfig` structure after a call to `_getvideoconfig()`. `mode` tells you that you are running with a monochrome monitor if the base address for the video memory starts at memory location 0xb000:0000. That is, the segment address is 0xb000 and the offset is 0x0000. If the monitor supports color, the base address starts at 0xb800:0000. Once you know the starting address, you know where to start writing to video memory. The program is presented in Listing 9-6.

Listing 9-6. Writing Directly to Video Memory

```
#include <stdio.h>
#include <graph.h>          /* Contains videoconfig structure */
#include <dos.h>

#define OFFSET 600
#define MONOTEXT 0xb0000000L
#define COLORTEXT 0xb8000000L

int main(void)
{
   unsigned far *base;
   char message[] = "This is a test";
   unsigned attribute;
   unsigned char *ptr;
   struct videoconfig my_screen;
   enum shades {black, blue, green, cyan, red, magenta, brown,
                white, gray, ltblue, ltgreen, ltcyan, ltred,
                ltmagenta, yellow, iwhite} colors;

   _getvideoconfig(&my_screen);
   printf("My screen is in mode %d\n", my_screen.mode);
```

Listing 9-6 continued

```
base = (my_screen.mode == 7) ? (unsigned far *) MONOTEXT:
                               (unsigned far *) COLORTEXT;
base += OFFSET;
ptr = message;
attribute = ((red << 4) + iwhite) << 8;

while (*ptr) {
   *base++ = attribute + *ptr++;
}

}
```

Using a *far* Pointer

The statement

```
unsigned far *base;
```

defines a far pointer for the QC compiler. The default pointer type for QC is a near pointer. If you are familiar with the 80X86 family of CPU chips, you know they use a segmented architecture. Each memory address is divided into two component parts:

1. A segment address
2. An offset address.

Each component requires two bytes of memory. If you access only data that resides in the current data segment, only the offset address is needed by the pointer (that is, a standard two-byte pointer). On the other hand, if you access data outside of the current data segment, the pointer must contain both the segment and offset addresses (a four-byte pointer).

By using the QC keyword far, you tell QC that you will access data residing outside the current data segment. Therefore, you must use a far pointer because the video memory resides outside the current data segment. Keep in mind that far and near are not actually C keywords, but are reserved for use by QC.

Why make base an unsigned int rather than an unsigned char? With each screen location using one byte for the character and a second byte for that character's screen attributes, each character on the screen requires two bytes of storage in the text mode. If you combine the two bytes and treat them as a single unit, you need to access the pointer only once. This approach is very easy to use, especially when the character attributes don't change.

Notice how an `enum` was used to list the possible colors for the screen. Because you have not initialized any of the members in the enumerated list, `black` corresponds to 0, `blue` to 1, and so on. The program in Listing 9-6 "hard codes" the color for the character attributes, but you can use the information in Table 9-1 to change `attribute` for use with a monochrome screen.

A number of variables are then defined including a `my_screen` structure. The call to `_getvideoconfig(&my_screen)` passes a pointer to `my_screen` to the function and fills in the information about the video display device. On return from the call, the program displays the current display mode being used.

The Ternary Operator

The statement

```
base = (my_screen.mode == 7) ? (unsigned far *) MONOTEXT:
                              (unsigned far *) COLORTEXT;
```

makes use of the *ternary operator*. As the name implies, there are three operands for the ternary operator. The general form is

```
(expression1) ? expression2 : expression3
```

`expression1` is usually some form of logical test. Notice that a question mark separates `expression1` and `expression2`. A colon separates `expression2` from `expression3`. If `expression1` is logical True, `expression2` is evaluated. If `expression1` is logical False, `expression3` is evaluated.

Actually, the ternary is shorthand for the following `if` statement:

```
if (expression1)
   expression2;
     else
   expression3;
```

Using the code in Listing 9-6, the equivalent statement is

```
if (my_screen.mode == 7)
 base = (unsigned far *) 0xb000000L;
   else
     base = (unsigned far *) 0xb8000000L;
```

The interpretation is that if the `my_screen.mode` returns the value of 7, you are facing a monochrome screen. Otherwise assume that you face an 80-column color text screen. You probably should check `mode` to make sure that the mode is 3, which is the 80-column color text screen. A problem may arise if the screen is in a graphics mode, for example. However, I contrived things a bit so that I could introduce you to the ternary operator.

After the ternary operation is performed, `base` points to the start of video memory. Next you add an offset to `base` so that the message to be printed doesn't scroll off the top of the screen. You also initialize `ptr` to point to the message you want to display on the screen.

Setting the Foreground and Background Colors

The statement

```
attribute = ((red << 4) + iwhite) << 8;
```

is used to form the two bytes of information needed by the character and its attribute byte. As you saw in Table 9-1, the lowest four bits set the foreground color, and the next three bits set the background color. The color red has been selected for the background color. The decimal number for `red` in the `enum` list is 4, so the binary image in an eight-bit space is

```
00000100
```

To have a red background, you must shift the value for `red` four bit positions to the left. Doing this bit shift places `red` into bits 4, 5, and 6, which are the bit positions for the background color. This looks like

```
01000000
```

Next add `iwhite` (intense white) for the foreground color. From the `enum` list, you know that the decimal value for `iwhite` is 15. In binary, 15 is represented as

```
00001111
```

The next step adds the two colors together, which produces the binary representation of

```
01001111
```

This binary repesentation has a decimal value of 79.

Finally, bit shift the resulting binary pattern eight positions further to the left. Why? Keep in mind that QC stores things in a low-byte, high-byte pattern. Therefore, if you want to treat the attribute as an `unsigned int`, and the attribute follows the character in video memory, the attribute byte must sit in the low-byte position in the `unsigned int`. The resulting binary image for the `unsigned int` is

```
01001111 00000000
```

All the attribute information appears in the proper position for writing it to the screen.

The `while` loop is used to write the message directly to the video screen. Because `ptr` points to the message, `*ptr++` fetches a character from the message string and then (post) increments the pointer in preparation for the next character. The first letter of the message is T, which has a binary representation of

```
01010100
```

which is 84 in decimal. Therefore, the expression

```
attribute + *ptr++;
```

adds the attribute value and the first letter of the message and produces the following binary image

```
01001111 01010100
```

In decimal, this looks like

```
79 84
```

You then write these two bytes to the location pointed to by `base`. Because of the way QC stores integer numbers, the letter T appears on the screen followed by the attribute byte. The result is that the T appears in intense white on a red background.

Because `base` is a pointer to an `unsigned int`, the increment operator increases `base` by two bytes (its scalar value) in preparation for the next character. You should be able to convince yourself that you will spin around in the `while` loop until `ptr` points to the null termination character.

Although the program is simple, it provides for rapid writing of string data to the screen and draws on several of the data types covered in this chapter. (A function that can write directly to video memory but with `printf()` flexibility can be found on page 53 of my book, *The C Programmer's Toolkit*, available from Que Corporation. A shameless plug, but a worthwhile function.)

10

Working with Disk Files

In this chapter, you learn about

High- and low-level disk file functions

File functions provided by the ANSI library

Standard output devices

Sequential and random access files

Using command line arguments

Although you can write a lot of interesting programs without using disk data files, most large applications require that data be stored on disk. Read on to learn about using the standard library functions that let you use disk files.

Fundamental Types of File I/O

C provides two types of file input and output (I/O):

1. Low-level
2. High-level

When *low-level file I/O* is used, data are read from the disk in blocks that are convenient for the host operating system. MS-DOS typically uses 512 bytes as the size of the block when reading from or writing to the disk. The actual size of the data block that is used depends on the hardware and operating system constraints of the machine.

High-level file I/O is geared to process the data in a convenient manner for the programmer. If you work with a data base for which each record takes 144 bytes of data, high-level file I/O makes working with such "nonstandard" data block sizes easy. The high-level file I/O routines are actually built up from the low-level file I/O services. As a result, you can choose which one best suits the task at hand.

The ANSI Standard and File I/O

The ANSI standard does not include the low-level file I/O functions as part of the standard library. The committee felt that because many of the low-level I/O routines are an integral part of the operating system (for example, the UNIX operating system), including them in the standard library would cause duplication of resources. The writers of the ANSI standard also felt that the minor performance difference between low- and high-level I/O didn't justify including the low-level functions in the standard library.

This omission poses certain problems, however. There is a lot of C code in the real world that makes use of low-level library functions. Just maintaining this existing body of code assumes the presence of the low-level functions.

Fortunately, most compiler vendors also recognize the need for continuing the low-level file I/O functions. This is especially true for operating systems that do not have the functions inherent in the operating system. QC provides the low-level functions you need. Still, if you plan to develop a large application, and future portability is important, consider using high-level file I/O functions for most of your development efforts.

The FILE Structure for High-Level File I/O

Any program for which you expect to use any of the high-level file functions must include the stdio.h header file. The reason is that high-level file functions rely on a structure declared in that header file. If you browse through the stdio.h header file, you will see the following #define in the header file

```
#define  FILE  struct _iobuf
```

Later on in the stdio.h header file, you see a structure defined using the FILE symbolic constant. If you perform the text substitution just as the preprocessor does, you find that the result is a FILE structure similar to that shown in Code Fragment 10-1.

Code Fragment 10-1. The _iob[] Structure

```
extern struct _iobuf {
        char *_ptr;      /* Next character in buffer   */
        int    cnt;      /* Characters left in buffer  */
        char * base;     /* Start of the file buffer   */
        char    flag;    /* The mode being used        */
        char    file;    /* File descriptor            */
        }  iob[];
```

A function that uses high-level file I/O has a FILE structure similar to that shown in Code Fragment 10-1, which maintains the file information for you. In effect, the FILE structure becomes the communications link between your program and the file facilities of MS-DOS. The statement

```
FILE *fpin;
```

defines a variable named fpin that points to a structure of type FILE. Although you rarely have to keep track of the details yourself, I describe each member of the FILE structure.

The variable _ptr is a pointer that points to the next character in the file buffer. (The actual memory location of the buffer is determined by MS-DOS. The number of buffers available to you is determined by the BUFFERS command, probably set in your CONFIG.SYS file that is read when you turn your computer on. When writing C programs, you probably want BUFFERS set to at least 10, perhaps higher.) The content of the buffer depends on whether you are reading from or writing to the buffer. For example, if you are reading a disk file, MS-DOS fills the buffer automatically for you (for example, with 512 bytes of data at a time). The variable _ptr, however, always points to the next character that your program needs. Therefore, even though MS-DOS prefers to grab 512 characters at a time from the disk, _ptr lets you work with the data one character at a time.

This *buffered file I/O* is an efficient way to handle things. If your program needs to read 512 bytes from disk and you read the disk one character at a time, your program "hits the disk" 512 times. Using the buffered approach, the disk is only hit once, resulting in much less disk I/O. Because data can be read from memory faster than from disk, this buffering scheme is fairly fast.

The _cnt member of the structure keeps track of the number of characters in the buffer. This allows your program and MS-DOS to know how much of the buffer space is filled with data. For example, if you write data to disk and _cnt reaches 512, MS-DOS knows that it is time to write the contents of the buffer to disk (that is, "flush the buffer" to disk).

The member named _base always points to the start of the file buffer. Why not just use _ptr? If you increment _ptr as you process the data in the buffer, _ptr no longer points to the starting memory address of the buffer. The next time you need to fill the buffer from disk, how do you know where to start writing the data? As you might guess, _base and _ptr have the same rvalue when the buffer is first filled. As the data are processed, the rvalue of _ptr changes, but _base always tells you where the buffer starts in memory. Therefore, MS-DOS uses _base any time the buffer is filled from disk or the data is written to disk.

The variable _flag keeps track of the type of file operation being done on the file. The most basic file operations include reading, writing, and appending to a disk file. (I discuss the details later in this chapter.) _flag tells you which of these basic operations is being done on the file.

The last variable, _file, is the file descriptor. The file desciptor is an "identification number" provided by MS-DOS when the file is first opened. Simplifying things a bunch, if there are 100 files on the disk and you try to open one of those files, MS-DOS assigns the file a number if it is opened successfully. From that point on, MS-DOS and your program could not care less about the actual name of the file. All communications with the file take place via the file descriptor.

Fortunately, MS-DOS and QC work together, so you don't have to worry much about what goes on in the FILE structure. You are free to concentrate on other aspects of file I/O.

Streams and Standard Devices

If you hang around a group of C programmers long enough, you're bound to hear the word *stream* used in the conversation. Input and output in C are often visualized as a stream of data that can be directed to one or more physical devices. These devices are not limited to disk files. They can be the screen, printers, plotters, measurement instruments — almost any device that attaches to the computer. Indeed, one of the design goals of C was that streams could work with virtually any I/O device in a single manner. C has met that goal.

Table 10-1 presents a list of "standard" I/O devices that use streams defined for the QC compiler.

Table 10-1. Predefined I/O Streams

#define stdin (&_iob[0])

#define stdout (&_iob[1])

#define stderr (&_iob[2])

#define stdaux (&_iob[3])

#define stdprn (&_iob[4])

If you look at the #defines in Table 10-1, notice that each one is defined in terms of an _iob structure like that shown in Code Fragment 10-1. In other words, QC has defined five elements of the _iob[] array of FILE structures. stdin is the standard input device and is normally associated with the keyboard. stdout is the standard output device and is typically the display screen. stderr is the standard error device where errors are reported. This, too, is usually the screen, although directing stderr to a disk file is useful at times. stdaux is an auxiliary I/O device and could be associated with a variety of I/O devices (plotters, modems, fax machines — who knows?). Finally, stdprn is the standard print device and is almost always associated with the printer.

Notice that each of these standard I/O devices is capable of working with streams of data. Further along in this chapter, you can see how to use these variable names in your programs. The advantage of using these standard devices is twofold. First, most C compilers provide these standard device names regardless of the host operating system. Although the names may not be identical in all cases, the differences are minor. For example, one MS-DOS compiler refers to stdprn as stdlst — the standard list device. Regardless of such minor name differences, you can count on having these standard names available for use in your programs.

Second and more important, you can use the same code to communicate with almost any I/O stream. Whether the output is written to a disk, the screen, or a printer, the means of communication is consistent. This makes writing device-independent code much easier than in some other languages.

Using Streams in Programs — A Word of Caution

It is probably obvious to you from Table 10-1 that QC automatically allocates five standard I/O devices for processing streams in any C program. This could be a problem for some of you. If you have the FILES command in your CONFIG.SYS file set to fewer than five (for example, FILES=4), QC cannot allocate a FILE structure for the standard devices let alone any disk files you may wish to open. If you set the FILES command to 10, you cannot open more than five disk files at a time in a program. The reason is that the first five buffers have already been allocated to the standard I/O devices.

Most C programmers consider 10 to be the minimum number of file buffers that should be set in CONFIG.SYS. Therefore, you often see the following two lines in the CONFIG.SYS file for a system used by a C programmer:

```
BUFFERS=10
FILES=10
```

In fact, seeing 20 or more files and buffers allocated in CONFIG.SYS is common.

In any event, check your CONFIG.SYS file to see that the files and buffers commands are set to at least 10. If you don't have a CONFIG.SYS file in your root directory, create a text file named CONFIG.SYS and using the QC editor, type the BUFFERS and FILES statements into the file. After saving the file, make sure it is in the root directory of the disk that is used to boot your computer when you first turn it on. Next, reboot the system (press Ctrl-Alt-Del) to reset the files and buffers commands.

Proceeding now with the rest of the chapter, I begin with high-level file I/O.

Opening a Disk File

Before you can do anything with a disk file, you must open it using the `fopen()` standard library function. The prototype for the `fopen()` function is

```
FILE *fopen(const char *filename, const char *mode);
```

The `filename` variable is the name of the file that you wish to open. You can use a simple file name (for example, `test.txt`) or you can have a fully qualified path name (for example, `d:\source\test.txt`). The `filename` can be either a character string constant or a variable.

The second argument (`mode`) tells the program how the file is to be opened. The three basic types of file access are 1) reading, 2) writing, or 3) appending. Table 10-2 shows the various combinations that can be used for the file `mode`.

Table 10-2. Modes for Opening a File

Mode	Explanation
r	Open for reading
w	Open for writing; truncate to 0 length if file already exists
a	Open for writing at the end of the file or create if file does not exist
r+	Open existing file for read-write
w+	Open for updating (read or write) for an existing file or create a new file
a+	Open for updating at end of file or create new file

The QC compiler also recognizes the extensions `t` for text files and `b` for binary files. Therefore, you could have `rb` for reading a binary file or `wt` for writing text files. Finally, you could have `r+t` for updating a text file.

Once you've decided how to access the file, check whether the file was opened successfully. After all, the file might not be there or a hardware failure might have occurred. The conventional style for opening a file named `test.txt` is shown in Listing 10-1.

Listing 10-1. Checking for a Successful File Open

```
FILE *fpin;

if ( (fpin = fopen("test.txt", "r")) == NULL) {
    printf("\n*** Cannot open test.txt ***\n");
    exit(EXIT_FAILURE);
}
```

The prototype for `fopen()` appears in the `stdio.h` header file, and I assume that you always include this header file in your programs. Because the prototype is in `stdio.h`, QC knows that `fopen()` returns a pointer to a structure of type FILE. (Code Fragment 10-1 shows what is in the structure.)

Two things can happen when you call `fopen()`. First, if everything goes well, a pointer of type FILE points to all the overhead information contained in the FILE structure. Second, if things don't go well and you cannot open the file, the value returned by `fopen()` is a null pointer. In C, a null pointer is guaranteed not to point to anything useful. QC `#defines` the null pointer with the symbolic constant NULL.

In Listing 10-1, the pointer returned by `fopen()` either points to a FILE structure (that is, a non-NULL pointer) or it is a NULL pointer. The pointer returned from `fopen()` is assigned into `fpin`, which we have defined as a FILE pointer. The `if` statement checks to see whether the pointer held in `fpin` is a NULL pointer. If it is a NULL pointer, an error message prints, and you call the `exit()` function.

The *exit()* Function

Think of the `exit()` function as one that is designed to abort a program gracefully. In essence, `exit()` does any housekeeping tasks (for example, closing open files) that need to be done before the program ends.

The argument to `exit()` is either EXIT_FAILURE or EXIT_SUCCESS. These symbolic constants are `#defined` in the `stdlib.h` header file. Obviously, you should `#include` the `stdlib.h` header file any time you use the `exit()` function.

If the call to `fopen()` fails (that is, returns a NULL pointer) in Listing 10-1, `exit()` is called, the housekeeping is performed, and the program terminates.

If all goes well and `exit()` is not called, the file is opened and `fpin` contains a pointer to the FILE structure associated with the file name `test.txt`.

Reading a Disk File

After the disk file is opened, you are free to use the file in whatever manner you wish (provided it is consistent with the `mode` used to open the file). Listing 10-2 presents a short program that opens a text file and displays it on the screen.

Listing 10-2. Reading a Disk File

```
/*
      Program to read a text file
*/

#include <stdio.h>
#include <stdlib.h>


int main(void)
{
   char filename[50];
   int c;
   FILE *fpin;

   printf("Enter a file name: ");
   gets(filename);
   if ( (fpin = fopen(filename, "r")) == NULL) {
      printf("Cannot open input file: %s\n", filename);
      exit(EXIT_FAILURE);
   }

   while ( (c = fgetc(fpin)) != EOF) {
      putchar;
   }
   fclose(fpin);

}
```

There is not much to this program, and most of it should look familiar to you. First, you enter the file name to be displayed that is stored in filename[]. Next, attempt to open the file for reading. Notice that the default file type is a text file. That is, if a t or b is missing in the mode string, the file is assumed to be a text file. Type the name of an ASCII text file when you run this program.

If you open the file, fpin contains a pointer to the necessary FILE structure. The standard library function fgetc() is used to read a single character from a disk file. The FILE pointer, fpin, is the only argument to the function and serves as a communications link between your program and MS-DOS. The return value from fgetc() is the character read from the file.

Notice that the variable c is defined as an integer variable even though you are reading a single character. Although you should be able to use a char definition for c, convention calls for an int. Also, c must sense a negative value because that is the value returned when the end-of-file mark is read. To abstract from such magic numbers, most compilers #define the end-of-file mark as EOF, as shown in Listing 10-2. (Back in the "old days," not all compilers supported the unsigned char data type, so it was imperative to use an int to sense the negative value often associated with EOF.)

As long as fgetc() returns something other than EOF, the while continues to read the file. The putchar() function displays the character on the screen. Eventually, fgetc() reads EOF and the while loop terminates.

Closing a Disk File

The last thing in the program is closing the disk file. This is done using the standard library function fclose(). The argument to fclose() tells which file to close because multiple files may be open in more complex programs.

When fclose() is called, some clean-up tasks are done. For example, if you write data to the disk, flushing the buffer in the FILE structure may be necessary to make sure all the data in the buffer have been written to disk. After calling fclose(), you cannot gain access to the file again without using the fopen() function.

Closing a file as soon as you finish using it is a good idea for several reasons. First, the FILE pointer you were using is free for possible use with another file. Second and more important, the potential for losing data is diminished. If Murphy should strike before you close the file, there could be data sitting in the buffer that was not written to disk. (High-level file I/O writes the data only when the buffer becomes full.) Therefore, you could lose data if something happened to the system before your program closes the file.

If you write a complex disk-intensive program, consider calling fflush() to flush the FILE buffer(s) even though they are not full. This flushing reduces the likelihood of losing data between normal writing of the buffer to disk.

Writing a Binary Disk File

The example shown in Listing 10-2 was opened in the r mode for reading an ASCII text file. In this section, you will write a sequence of integers to a disk file and then read them back. Because you are writing integer data, you use the binary mode for reading and writing. The program that writes the integer data is presented in Listing 10-3.

Listing 10-3. Writing a Binary File

```
/*
      Program to write 100 integers to a file
*/

#include <stdio.h>
#include <stdlib.h>


int main(void)
{
   char filename[50];
   int i;
   FILE *fpout;

   printf("Enter a file name: ");
   gets(filename);
```

Listing 10-3 continues

Listing 10-3 continued

```
if ( (fpout = fopen(filename, "wb")) == NULL) {
    printf("Cannot open input file: %s\n", filename);
    exit(EXIT_FAILURE);
}

for (i = 0; i < 100; i++) {
    fwrite(&i, sizeof(int), 1, fpout);
}
fclose(fpout);
}
```

The program is straightforward. When you run the program, type the name of the file that is to receive the data (for example, `ints.dat`). Keep in mind that the file is truncated to zero length if it already exists. (This is a polite way of saying that you'll clobber the contents of any existing file that you use for the file name.)

The call to `fopen()` should create a new file and return a non-NULL pointer. Notice that I changed the mode of the file to `wb` because I want you to write binary data to the file.

The call to `fwrite()` can also be used to write data to a disk file. There are four arguments to `fwrite()`. The first argument is a pointer to whatever is to be written. In the example, you pass the `lvalue` of `i`. In the `fwrite()` function, the pointer receives the `lvalue` of `i`, goes to that address and fetches the `rvalue` of what is stored there. This means that you are writing the contents of `i` to the data file.

The second argument is the size (in bytes) of the data item you wish to write to disk. In the example, you want to write two bytes of data. Using the `sizeof` operator assures you that the proper number of bytes are written regardless of how QC views an integer.

The third argument is the number of these data items that you wish to write on this call to `fwrite()`. Because you write one integer at a time in a `for` loop, use the integer constant 1.

The final argument is the FILE pointer to the data file that is to receive the data. In the example, this FILE is named pointer `fpout`. (Notice the clever variable names — `fpout` for file pointer output and `fpin` in Listing 10-2 for file pointer input.)

(The way that I have used `fwrite()` is a bit sloppy because I am not checking to see whether the data was written to the disk. I am assuming that there have been no disk failures, open drive doors, etc. Rather than cloud the real issue here, I postpone a more complete discussion of such details until the next section.)

After 100 iterations of the `for` loop, the disk write is complete and the program calls `fclose()` to close the file. The disk file now contains 100 integer numbers . . . doesn't it?

Reading a Binary Data File

Now read back the contents of the data file you created with Listing 10-3. The program to do that is shown in Listing 10-4.

Listing 10-4. Reading a Binary Data File

```
/*
    Read a binary file
*/

#include <stdio.h>
#include <stdlib.h>


int main(void)
{
    char filename[50];
    int i, num_read;
    FILE *fpin;

    printf("Enter a file name: ");
    gets(filename);
    if ( (fpin = fopen(filename, "rb")) == NULL) {
        printf("Cannot open input file: %s\n", filename);
        exit(EXIT_FAILURE);
    }


    while (num_read = fread(&i, sizeof(int), 1, fpin) ) {
        if (num_read) {
            printf("%3d", i);
        if (i && (i % 20 == 0) )
```

Listing 10-4 continues

257

Listing 10-4 continues

```
printf("\n");
    } else {
        printf("Read error. Last value of i = %d", i);
    break;
    }
  }
  fclose(fpin);
}
```

A Quick Way to Create Similar Program Files

The program is almost identical to Listing 10-3. In fact, the easiest way to write the program is to use the Merge option of the QC File menu. To do this, invoke QC using the name you wish to call the program (for example, p10-4.c). The MS-DOS command is

```
QC P10-4.C
```

and QC asks whether to create the program. Answer Yes and QC creates a new source file for you. Now press the Alt-F-M keys to merge in the program you used for Listing 10-3. QC prompts you to type the old file name. After you enter the file name, QC loads the source code from Listing 10-3 into the new file for Listing 10-4. It is a simple task to edit the file to match that shown in Listing 10-4.

The *fread()* Function

Most of the code in Listing 10-4 should look very familiar to you by now. Notice that mode for fopen() was changed to rb to read the binary file data. The real work is done by fread().

The arguments to fread() are identical to fwrite(), except that the data flows from the disk into the first argument. Although many C programmers don't bother, the value returned from the call to fread() has been stored in num_read. The value returned from the call should match the third argument in fread(). Because you are reading one integer at a time, the return value should be 1. Any other value indicates an error. Note: The return value is not necessarily the number of bytes read from the disk. Rather, it is the number of *data items* read from the disk.

The same type of logic can be used with fwrite(). That is, fwrite() returns the number of data items written to the disk. To play it safe, modify Listing 10-3 to check the return value from fwrite() in much the same way as in Listing 10-4. This is left as an exercise for you.

Notice that there is no check for reading EOF as in Listing 10-1. The reason is that num_read is 0 when fread() has read all the data in the file. Because the value is 0 at end-of-file, the while loop expression becomes logical False and the loop ends. The call to fclose() closes the disk file and the program ends.

What is the purpose of the if test on i after the call to fread()? Try to figure it out before you run the program.

Using Random Access to Read a Disk File

So far you have been reading and writing data to the disk file using sequential access methods. *Sequential access* means that you start at the beginning of the file and read it from start to end with no "skipping" around within the file. Sequential access methods are similar to how you "read" a cassette tape — in a linear fashion with no skips.

In many applications, however, you want to be able to skip over the data that is not of interest to you and go immediately to some given place in the file. The process of indexing into some given spot within a data file requires using *random access* methods for reading (or writing) a disk file.

Listing 10-5 presents a program that can read a given integer from the data file that you created with Listing 10-3.

Listing 10-5. Using Random Access to Read a Disk File

```
/*
    Random access data read
*/

#include <stdio.h>
#include <stdlib.h>
int main(void)
{
```

Listing 10-5 continues

Listing 10-5 continued

```
char filename[50];
int i, record;
FILE *fpin;

printf("Enter the record to retrieve: ");
record = atoi(gets(filename));
printf("Enter a file name: ");
gets(filename);

if ( (fpin = fopen(filename, "rb")) == NULL) {
   printf("Cannot open input file: %s\n", filename);
   exit(EXIT_FAILURE);
}

fseek(fpin, (long) (record * sizeof(int) ), SEEK_SET);
fread(&i, sizeof(int), 1, fpin);
printf("\nThe value for the record is %d", i);
fclose(fpin);
}
```

The program first asks you to enter the record to be read from the disk. In this case, the record is the same as the numeric value written to the disk. The character array `filename` does double-duty in that you first use it to get the record number before getting the actual file name. There is no reason not to use the `filename[]` buffer because you don't need the ASCII representation of the record number later. After all, the record number (`record`) stored as an `int` is what we use later on; not its ASCII representation.

Assuming that the file is opened successfully, a call to the `fseek()` standard library function is made. There are three arguments to `fseek()`. The first is the FILE pointer for the file being used.

The second argument is an offset used to index into the file. The interpretation of this offset is the number of bytes you wish to "skip over" before you start reading the data. In the example, if you wish to read the forty-fifth record (that is, the integer number 45), you must skip over 45 integers (that is, 0 through 44 is 45 integers). Therefore, if `record` is 45, you must skip over 45 times `sizeof(int)` bytes of data. With certain restrictions (explained later), this offset can be a negative value.

Note that this second argument is a `long`. You must cast the expression

```
record * sizeof(int)
```

to a `long` for things to work properly. (A `long` is used so that the file can be larger than 64K in size.) You will forget to perform this cast at some time in your programming future! If `fseek()` seems to put you in strange places, the data type of the second argument is the first thing you should check.

The third argument is a constant for the location from which you wish to apply the offset found in the second argument. The three location possibilities are shown in Table 10-3.

Table 10-3. Locations for `fseek()`

Location	Explanation
SEEK_SET	Set location at the beginning of the file
SEEK_CUR	Set location at the current position in the file
SEEK_END	Set location at the end of the file

The symbolic constants shown in Table 10-3 are `#defined` in the `stdio.h` header file. The SEEK_SET and SEEK_END set the file and the beginning and end of the file, respectively. These two constants are easy to understand. SEEK_CUR needs a little more explanation.

SEEK_CUR uses the current position in the file from which the offset is applied. For example, suppose that each record in the file is 2 bytes long and you just read the twenty-fourth record in the file. The call

```
fseek(fpin, -2L, SEEK_CUR);
```

would read the same record again. The reason is that the offset is minus 2 bytes from the current record. Because you just read the twenty-fourth record, -2L bytes from the current position places you at the start of the twenty-fourth record again. SEEK_CUR saves disk access time if you are updating records that are close to each other in the file.

A little thought should convince you that reading the disk with a positive offset is not a good idea when SEEK_END is the location. (You are trying to read past the end of file.) Likewise, a negative offset with SEEK_SET doesn't make sense. (You are trying to read before the start of the file.) SEEK_CUR can have positive or negative offsets.

In Listing 10-5, the call to `fseek()` sets the disk head to the position you wish to read. Next, the call to `fread()` reads the record into variable `i`. The value is then displayed on the screen, the file is closed, and the program ends.

As an experiment, try writing a program similar to Listing 10-5 that writes a new value to one of the records. Then use the programs in Listings 10-4 and 10-5 to check your work.

Using *fgets()* and *fprintf()*

Many high-level file functions are available in the standard library. Two additional functions that are quite useful in a variety of file situations are `fgets()` and `fprintf()`. The prototype for `fgets()` is

```
char *fgets(char *buff, int n, FILE *fpin);
```

The `fgets()` function reads one line at a time from the text file pointed to by `fpin` and stores it in `buff`. The line being read from the disk file is terminated by either a newline (`\n`) character or a maximum of n characters. Therefore, make sure that `buff` is defined with sufficient storage to hold the longest line you expect to encounter in the file. For example, if you know the longest line is 80 characters, `buff` should be defined

```
char buff[81];
```

(Don't forget the null termination character for strings.) It follows that n would have a maximum value of 80.

Notice that `fgets()` is slightly different than `gets()`. When `gets()` is used and you press the Enter key (that is, a newline is read from the keyboard), `gets()` replaces the newline with the null termination character; the newline is not part of the input string with `gets()`. With `fgets()`, the null termination character is appended after the newline character is read from the file. Therefore, the newline character remains in the string with `fgets()`.

Keep in mind that three factors can terminate a file read by `fgets()`:

1. A newline character.

2. n characters are read.

3. EOF is encountered while reading the file.

If all goes well, `fgets()` returns a pointer to `buff`. If no characters are read due to a disk failure or on reading EOF, the return value is a NULL pointer. Therefore, typical code using `fgets()` looks like

```
while (fgets(buff, MAXSTR, fpin) != NULL) {
    /* Whatever... */
    }
```

The `fprintf()` function works much the same as `printf()`, except the output is written to a disk file rather than to the display screen. All the conversion characters associated with `printf()` are available to you. For example, if you want to copy from an input text file to an output file with line numbers, the following code fragment can be used:

```
count = 1;
while (fgets(buff, MAXSTR, fpin) != NULL) {
    fprintf(fpout, "%5d  %s", count++, buff);
}
```

The resulting output file has line numbers at the beginning of each line in the output file. If you write a program using this code fragment, don't forget to open each file in its proper mode and to call `fclose()` for each FILE pointer. A piece of cake.

Check Your Library Documentation

The high-level functions presented thus far in this chapter only scratch the surface of the high-level file I/O functions available to you. You should check Microsoft's *C for Yourself* documentation (especially the C Library Guide section on Input and Output Routines) for a list of available library functions. Indeed, you know enough C now to scout the library with a full appreciation of the gold mine that exists in the functions discussed there. A little reading time now can save you a lot of time re-inventing the wheel unnecessarily.

Low-Level File I/O

The term low-level file I/O conjures up different images for different people. Some think low-level I/O is inferior to high-level I/O. The fact that ANSI didn't bless low-level I/O by inclusion in the standard library reinforces this image. To others, low-level I/O means that these routines are closer to the operating system and hence, offer some performance gain in terms of I/O speed or code size. Actually, both positions have some merit.

Low-level routines are closer to the operating system than the high-level functions already discussed in this chapter. It is true that most of the high-level functions draw upon the low-level functions to accomplish their tasks. In some operating systems (for example, UNIX), many of the low-level I/O functions are part of the operating system. However, because the low-level routines are not built into MS-DOS, the low-level routines are "built up" from the available system resources (for example, BDOS). Because low-level routines are not associated with FILE pointers and all of the overhead associated with them, low-level file operations are often referred to as "unbuffered" or "raw" I/O.

Finally, a marginal performance increase is associated with the low-level routines. However, unless your program hits the disk constantly, you do not notice much of a difference.

The *open()* Function

As always, you cannot do anything with a disk file until it is opened. The open() function is used to open a disk file using low-level file I/O. It has the following prototype:

```
int open(char *filename, int flags, int mode);
```

The filename has the same interpretation as it does with fopen(). The flags variable has a number of possible combinations, as shown in Table 10-4.

Table 10-4. Symbolic Constants Defined for flags *in* open()

Constant	Definition
O_RDONLY	Open the file for reading only
O_WRONLY	Open the file for writing only
O_RDWR	Open the file for reading or writing
O_APPEND	Write to the end of the file
O_TRUNC	Truncate file to zero length if it exists
O_CREAT	Create a file
O_EXCL	lopen() fails if this flag is set with O_CREAT (for example, O_EXCL | O_CREAT)

The symbolic constants presented in Table 10-4 are defined in the standard library and found in the `fcntl.h` header file. QC also adds O_TEXT and O_BINARY to the list for use with text and binary files.

The flags can be used with the bitwise operators to produce various combinations. For example, the statement

```
fdin = open(filename, O_WRONLY | O_CREAT | O_EXCL, 0);
```

opens `filename` 1) in the write-only mode, 2) creates the file in the normal mode (`mode` = 0), but 3) creates the file only if it does not already exist. If you use the bitwise OR operator (|) and various combinations of the flags, you can work with just about any type of file you might need.

The `mode` variable determines the type of access that is allowed with the file. The values shown in Table 10-5 are specific to MS-DOS.

Table 10-5. Possible `mode` Values

Value	Explanation
0x00	No mode set (that is, the normal mode)
0x01	A read-only file
0x02	A hidden file
0x04	A system file
0x20	Set archive bit

If you are not familiar with MS-DOS, setting `mode` to 0 for any files that you open would be best.

Reading a Disk File Using Low-Level Functions

If the file is opened successfully, a file descriptor number is returned from the call to `open()`. This number is returned by MS-DOS and corresponds to the `_file` member of a FILE structure. (See Table 10-1.) If the file cannot be opened, [-]1 is returned to indicate that an error occurred.

Assuming that the file is opened, you can proceed to read it. Listing 10-6 presents a program that reads a text file using the low-level file I/O `read()` function.

Listing 10-6. Reading a File with Low-Level I/O

```
/*
    Low-level file read
*/

#include <stdio.h>
#include <stdlib.h>
#include <fcntl.h>

#define PMODE   0       /* Set mode to a normal disk file */

#ifndef ERROR
    #define ERROR -1
#endif

int main(void)
{
    char c, filename[50];
    int fdin;

    printf("Enter a file name: ");
    gets(filename);
    if ( (fdin = open(filename, O_RDONLY, PMODE)) == ERROR) {
        printf("Cannot open input file: %s\n", filename);
        exit(EXIT_FAILURE);
    }

    while (read(fdin, &c, 1u)) {
        putchar;
    }
    close(fdin);
}
```

The call to open() attempts to open the file for reading only. If the file is opened, fdin holds the file descriptor associated with the opened file. This becomes your communication link between the program and MS-DOS for the file. The read() function uses the file descriptor to read the file one character at a time. Notice that the second argument to read() is a pointer, so you must pass the lvalue of c to read(). The 1u is an unsigned int and says that you want to read the file one character at a time. The call to putchar() displays the character held in c on the screen.

How does the `while` loop terminate? Because `read()` returns the number of bytes read during the call to `read()`, 0 is returned when end-of-file is sensed. Again, the 0 is interpreted as a logical False condition and the `while` ends.

The call to the `close()` function closes the file and the program ends. Notice how similar the low-level program in Listing 10-6 is to the high-level programs. In fact, sticking an `f` in front of most of the low-level function calls yields the names of the high-level counterparts.

Writing a File with Low-Level Functions

The program in Listing 10-7 shows how you can write data using the low-level `write()` function.

Listing 10-7. Writing a Low-Level File

```
/*
        Writing with low-level file I/O
*/



#include <stdio.h>
#include <stdlib.h>
#include <fcntl.h>


#ifndef ERROR
    #define ERROR -1
#endif

int main(void)
{
    char c, filename[50];
    int fdout, flag, i;
    double x;

    printf("Enter a file name: ");
    gets(filename);
    if ((fdout = open(filename, O_WRONLY | O_CREAT, 0) == ERROR) {
```

Listing 10-7 continues

Listing 10-7 continued

```
    printf("Cannot open input file: %s\n", filename);
        exit(EXIT_FAILURE);
    }

    for (i = 0; i < 100; i++) {
        x = (double) i;
        flag = write(fdout, &x, sizeof(double) );
        if (flag != sizeof(double)) {
            printf(" *** Disk write failure. Abort ***\n");
        exit(EXIT_FAILURE);
        }
    }
    close(fdout);
}
```

The program first creates the file (O_CREAT) and then opens it for writing (O_WRONLY). If opened successfully, fdout contains a valid file descriptor.

Assuming that all goes well, the program enters a for loop that writes 100 doubles to the file. Because write() expects the second argument to be a pointer, you must pass the lvalue of x to the function. The value written is i, which is cast to a double and assigned into x. The third argument tells how many bytes to write to the file.

The return value from write() is the number of bytes actually written to the file. Obviously, if the number of bytes written is not equal to the sizeof(double), an error occurred. If an error did occur, you fall into the error message and the program aborts via the call to exit().

After 100 values are written to the file, the for loop ends, the file is closed by the call to close(), and the program terminates.

Listing 10-8 presents a program to read the file that was written by the program in Listing 10-7.

Listing 10-8. Reading a Low-Level Binary File

```
/*
     Reading a binary file (llio)
*/

#include <stdio.h>
#include <stdlib.h>
#include <fcntl.h>


#ifndef ERROR
   #define ERROR -1
#endif

int main(void)
{
   char c, filename[50];
   int fdin, flag, i;
   double x;

   printf("Enter a file name: ");
   gets(filename);
   if ( (fdin = open(filename, O_RDONLY, 0)) == ERROR) {
      printf("Cannot open input file: %s\n", filename);
      exit(EXIT_FAILURE);
   }

   while (read(fdin, &x, sizeof(double)) ) {
      printf("%8.2f", x);
   }
   close(fdin);
}
```

The program is almost identical to earlier versions, so I limit the discussion to the read() function. The arguments are the same as write(). The second argument (&x) can be thought of as a double-sized buffer that read() uses to store the sizeof(double) bytes of data. Therefore, read() grabs eight bytes from the disk and places them into the lvalue of x. The call to printf() displays each double as you read the file.

Because the read() function returns the number of bytes actually read from the disk, you can use the return value to control the while loop. After all the data are read, the return value is 0 (that is, logical False) and the while loop ends. The file is closed by the call to close() and the program terminates.

Mixing High- and Low-Level I/O

There is nothing in the rules of C that prevent you from mixing high and low-level I/O routines. Consider the example shown in Listing 10-9.

Listing 10-9. Using High-Level File Handle with Low-Level Functions

```
#include <stdio.h>


int main(void)
{
   char buff[100];

   puts("Enter up to 80 characters: ");
   gets(buff);

   write(fileno(stdout), buff, strlen(buff));
}
```

You are asked to enter up to 80 characters of text and the write() function writes the string to stdout. Recall from the discussion of standard input and output devices (Table 10-2) that stdout is a standard output device that writes its data to the screen. However, because stdout is a FILE pointer but write() expects a file descriptor, you use the fileno() function to retrieve the file descriptor member of stdout's FILE structure. In fact, you can modify the write() statement in Listing 10-9 to read

```
write(_iob[1]._file, buff, strlen(buff));
```

and the program performs exactly as before. The reason is that the stdio.h header file defines stdout to be _iob[1]. This also reinforces the idea that high-level I/O functions are built from the low-level routines.

You can, of course, use the high-level routines to accomplish the task. The equivalent statement for `write()` is

```
fwrite(buff, sizeof(char), strlen(buff), stdout);
```

which would write the string to the screen. If you want to write the output to the printer, the statement becomes

```
fwrite(buff, sizeof(char), strlen(buff), stdprn);
```

By making the last argument a FILE pointer variable (for example, `fpout`), you can redirect the output to the screen, printer, or a disk file without changing the source code. All you need to do is ask the user where the output should be sent. You can use

```
printf("Output to Screen, Printer, or Disk (S, P, D): ");
c = getch();
switch (toupper (c) ) {
   case 'S':
      fpout = stdout;
      break;
   case 'P':
      fpout = stdprn;
      break;
   case 'D':
      fpout = fopen(filename, "w");
      break;
   default:
      fpout = stdout;
      break;
}
```

This allows you to direct the output to any one of the three output devices. In "real life," check `fpout` when a disk file is used to make sure the call to `fopen()` did not return a NULL pointer. Still, C provides a much simpler means for sending output to different devices than other languages. (Don't you just hate PRINT and LPRINT?)

One more point. If you are writing to `stdprn`, `stdout`, or any of the other standard output devices, it is not a good idea to use these standard output devices as the argument to `fclose()`. In some cases, the call to `fclose()` locks up the system.

Choosing Between High- and Low-Level File I/O

How do you know which kind of file I/O to use? Good question, and I'm not sure I know the answer. With some compilers there is a significant difference when using write() to stdout rather than printf(). The program in Listing 10-9 with QC compiles to a program size of about 15K. The same program with Ecosoft's Eco-C88 C compiler is about 4K. If printf() is used rather than puts(), QC generates a 17K file, whereas Eco-C88 generates a 10K file. Therefore, low-level I/O using QC doesn't seem to make much difference in code size. As you might expect, the execution time with QC doesn't change much either. (The Eco-C88 compiler is a bit faster when write() is used rather than printf().)

Given that it doesn't make much difference in code size or execution speed when using QC, the choice seems to favor high-level I/O. The reason is that the high-level functions are defined in the ANSI standard. Therefore, you can count on those functions being available for virtually any machine that has a C compiler.

Finally, each programming task has its set of unique problems. The nature of those problems may dictate using one type of file I/O over the other. Clearly you should be familiar with both types and then select the one that best provides a solution to the task at hand.

Command Line Arguments

You have probably run programs that required you to type more than just the program name. For example, when you were testing the function that determined the number of columns on the screen in Chapter 9, you entered

```
mode co40
```

at the MS-DOS command line. The program is named mode and the co40 told mode the number of columns to be used on the screen. In other words, co40 is a command line argument to the program named mode.

A command line argument in C is one or more arguments to the function main(). Command line arguments allow you to supply information to the program when the program is started from MS-DOS. Up to this point, you have prototyped main() with a void argument list. If you wish to supply command line arguments to the program, change the `main()` prototype to

```
int main(int argc, char *argv[])
```

The first argument is the *argument counter*, which holds the total number of command line arguments supplied to the program. For example, when you use the MS-DOS COPY command, typical syntax is

```
copy test.c b:
```

This command has three command line arguments: 1) the program name (`copy`), 2) the input file (`test.c`), and 3) where the file is to be copied (`b:`). In this case, `argc` would equal 3. Note that each argument must be separated from the others by a blank space.

The second argument to `main()` is the *argument vector*. Using the Right-Left Rule for parsing a data declaration, you find that `argv[]` is "An array of pointers to `char`." Because `argc` is equal to three, there are three pointers to `char` in `argv[]`. If you use indirection from the three pointers, you find that they point to the command line arguments. Therefore,

```
argv[0] = "copy"
argv[1] = "test.c"
argv[2] = "b:"
```

With that in mind, write a program that duplicates the MS-DOS COPY command. The program is presented in Listing 10-10.

Listing 10-10. A High-Level Copy Program Using Command Line Arguments

```
/*
    Copy program with command line arguments
*/

#include <stdio.h>
#include <stdlib.h>


FILE *fpin, *fpout;
void check_and_open(int argc, char *argv[]);

int copy_file(void);

int main(int argc, char *argv[])
{
```

Listing 10-10 continues

Listing 10-10 continued

```
   int okay;

   check_and_open(argc, argv);     /* Right args? Open 'em. */
   okay = copy_file();             /* Copy 'em.            */
   if (okay == -1)
      exit(EXIT_FAILURE);

   fclose(fpin);                   /* Close 'em.           */
   fclose(fpout);
}


/*****

                        check_and_open()

   This function checks to see that the proper number of command line
arguments were supplied to the program. If so, the files are then opened.

   Argument list:    int argc      number of command line args
                     char *argv[]   the argument vector

   Return value:  void

*****/

void check_and_open(int argc, char *argv[])
{
   if (argc != 3) {
      printf("Usage: program infile outfile\n");
      exit(EXIT_FAILURE);
   }

   if ((fpin = fopen(argv[1], "r")) == NULL) {
      printf("Could not open %s\n", argv[1]);
      exit(EXIT_FAILURE);
   }

   if ((fpout = fopen(argv[2], "w")) == NULL) {
      printf("Could not open %s\n", argv[2]);
      exit(EXIT_FAILURE);
   }
}


   /*****
```

```
                       copy_file()

           This function copies the files.

      Argument list:     void

      Return value:      int          -1 on error, 0 otherwise

*****/

int copy_file(void)
{
    char c;
    int num;

    while (fread(&c, sizeof(char), 1u, fpin)) {
       num = fwrite(&c, sizeof(char), 1u, fpout);
       if (num != sizeof(char)) {
          printf("*** Error in disk write ***\n   Abort.\n");
          return -1;
       }
    }
    return 0;
}
```

The program begins by including the necessary header files and defining the FILE pointer to be used. You also declare that `check_and_open()` returns a `void`. Notice that you have defined `main()` to have the arguments required to process command line arguments.

The `check_and_open()` function first checks to see that three command line arguments were supplied to the program. If that is not the case, a message telling you what is expected to run the program helps you to try again. The program is then aborted.

If the proper number of arguments were supplied, the program opens the input and output files. If either `fopen()` fails, an appropriate error message is given.

Assuming the two files are opened, the `copy_file()` function copies the file. If an error occurs during the copy, an error message is displayed and the program terminates. Otherwise, the two files are closed, and the program terminates normally.

When I ran the program, I used the QC Debugger to set a watchpoint (Alt-D-W) to display the address of argv[0] (&argv[0]). When the program was single-stepped, the address of argv[0] was at offset 0x0e46. Therefore, the argv[] array appeared like that shown in Figure 10-1.

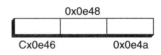

Figure 10-1. Memory Image of *agrv[]*

The pointers held in the pointer array shown in Figure 10-1 point to the three command line arguments.

Not all programs require command line arguments. In those cases in which your program does not need command line arguments, main() should be defined with a void argument list.

I have suggested several times that you haul out your *C for Yourself* documentation and review all the library routines available to you. However, don't forget that you can get information about each library function from within the QC editor. Place the cursor on the name of the function after you type it and press the F1 key. A summary of the function appears near the top of the screen.

When you first start programming in C, it takes some time to remember the function names, and even more time to learn the arguments and their order in the argument list. The online help function can be a real time-saver. However, you still must know the name of the function. For now, browse through the list of functions for an idea of the resources to be found there. You can use the F1 key later on to flesh in the details.

11

Tying It All Together

The goals of this chapter are

To use many of C's language features

To create a useful programming utility

In this chapter, you build a complete program that uses most of the C language constructs covered in this book. You see how a C language program is built and how the various elements of C fit together to form a working program. When you finish the chapter, you should have a better idea of how C is used to construct a program, and you have a useful programming tool called a *function finder.*

As your experience with C grows, you will develop larger and more complex programs. As the source code for such programs grows, you also will begin to appreciate the benefits of dividing the program into several smaller source code modules. One of the benefits of multiple source code modules is that you can use the NMAKE feature of QC (discussed in Chapter 12, "Debugging Programs") to compile only those modules that have changed since the QuickC program was last compiled. For example, suppose that you divided your program into six or seven smaller modules, and only one module is giving you problems. If NMAKE is used, each time you recompile the program to test it, QC (with NMAKE's help) recompiles only the module that is giving you trouble. The result is faster compile times, shorter turnaround time, and faster program development.

Although the benefits of small source code modules outweigh the drawbacks, there is one drawback that can be especially frustrating. When a program is divided into multiple source code modules, it is more difficult to remember which module contains a specific function definition. As a result, you waste time searching through the modules to locate the file containing the function you want to test next. A function finder can alleviate this drawback.

What Is a Function Finder?

If you have developed good C coding techniques, each function defines a specific task that is performed in the program. When you are debugging a program, you spend most of your time testing functions in an attempt to isolate and correct the bug. You save a lot of time if you have a list that tells which file contains each of the function definitions used in the program.

Of course as you write the program, you can simply write on a piece of paper the function names and the module in which they are defined. However, unless you are much more skilled than most of us, new modules are added and old modules are shifted around. As a result, the list is quickly outdated and useless. For the list to be of any significant benefit, you must rewrite it. Rather than write the list by hand, you can have the function finder create the list.

The program described here writes a list of function definitions for all C source files found in the current working directory. The listing presents the name of the source file containing the definition, as well as the line number where the start of the function definition appears in the source file. Additionally, the function names are presented in alphabetical order, so it is a simple task to find the information you are looking for. The list can be displayed on the screen or written to the printer. With these features, it is easy to find which modules contain the function definition that you want to test during a debugging session.

The program performance is sufficiently fast that you can run the program as often as necessary without waiting long for a new list to be generated. On one medium-sized project, I had almost 500K of source code spread across 18 files. The function finder read all 18 files, located, stored, sorted, and began to display the necessary information in just under 30 seconds. (The test was run on an 8Mhz AT compatible. On faster machines, it may not even be worth keeping a printed list; just rerun the program!)

Function Finder Restrictions

The function finder (ff from now on) operates by reading the C source files in the current working directory, searching those source files for function definitions, and saving the definitions that it finds. To do this, ff assumes a certain coding style is used.

As you might guess, ff's coding style is the same style used throughout this book. Specifically, I assume that each function definition begins on a new line with no tabs or blank spaces. I also assume that the first element of a function definition is a function type specifier, followed by a blank space and the function name, followed by a parenthesis. Figure 11-1 illustrates these coding style requirements.

```
Left margin



void my_function(void)
{
    /* Function body */
}
```

Figure 11-1. Coding Style Requirements

Notice that there is no white space (that is, tabs, blank spaces, etc.) between the left margin and the type specifier `void`. A blank space appears next, followed by the function name and the opening parenthesis for the argument list.

If you think about these style restrictions, you may discover that they are consistent with function declarations and prototypes. That is, the program output shows all function declarations and prototypes as part of the display. Although the program could be changed so that function declarations are not displayed, it may not be worth the effort. In fact, some may view this output as a benefit because it shows the source files that contain function prototypes and definitions.

If you use a coding style that is different from the style shown in Figure 11-1, don't give up. Read this chapter to learn how the program works; then modify it to suit your needs.

Now let's see how the program works.

Include Files, Symbolic Constants, and Global Definitions

Listing 11-1 shows all of the include files, symbolic constants, and global data definitions used in the program. Most of this should be familiar to you by now, but several items need some elaboration.

Listing 11-1. Includes, Constants, Globals

```
/*****
    PROGRAM: Function finder (funcf.c).

       This program searches C source files and displays a sorted list
    of all function definitions in each file, along with the function
          type specifier, line number, and name of the file in which
    the                      definition appears.

    USAGE: funcf filename tablesize [prn]
             example: funcf *.c 200

                          Outputs all function definitions in *.c
                          files to the screen. The maximum number of
                          function definitions is limited to 200.

    *****/

#include <stdio.h>          /* All of the include files         */
#include <malloc.h>
#include <stdlib.h>
#include <string.h>
#include <dos.h>

#define NAMESIZ 13          /* Maximum size of file name        */
#define MAXSTR  50          /* Maximum length of function name  */
#define MAXLINE 21          /* Maximum lines on screen          */

                            /* Prototype list                   */
int do_directory(char **argv);

void clrscr(void),
    correct_args(int argc),
    set_output_device(int num_args),
    open_files(int number, int size),
```

```
        show_results(void),
        sort_list(void);

                            /* List of function type specifiers */

char *table[] = {           /* See CAUTION in read_file()       */
    "FILE",   "char",       "double",    "int",    "long",
    "static", "struct",     "unsigned",  "void"
    };

                            /* Global data items                */

char *tptr;                 /* Pointer to file names            */

int room_left;              /* How many entries are left        */

FILE *fpin,                 /* Input-output FILE pointers        */
     *fpout;

struct record {
    char name[MAXSTR];      /* Name of function                 */
    char type[NAMESIZ];     /* Type specifier for function      */
    char file[NAMESIZ];     /* Name of C source file            */
    unsigned int line;      /* Line number of function def      */

    } list, *tbl1, *tbl2;
```

The program begins with a brief explanation of what it does and how it should be invoked from the command line. Although this may seem like overkill, you can forget such simple things in the course of time.

#includes and #defines

The program actually begins with a series of #include preprocessor directives. Every program should include the stdio.h header file. I explain why the other files are included when I discuss the relevant functions that use them.

The #defines set various screen and string sizes. MAXSTR causes long function definitions to be truncated to a maximum of 50 characters so that no function definition exceeds one line on the output display, yet leaves enough room on the line for the other required information.

Function Declarations and Prototypes

After the #defines is a list of the function declaration and prototypes for those functions defined in the file. As you have probably noticed, QC complains (as it should) whenever a function returns a noninteger data type and no function declaration is present (that is, a "redefinition" error). You should create a function declaration and prototype for every function in the file, even if the function returns an integer data type. This insures that the function arguments can be type checked by the compiler.

If you are creating a large program, you might want to move the function declarations and prototypes into a program header file. This makes it easy to have the function declarations and prototypes present in each of the separate modules. Also, if a header file is used, editing one entry in the header file is much easier (and less prone to errors) than editing multiple source code modules.

Global Data Items

The first data definition is table[], which is an array of pointers to char. This variable could have been defined as

```
char table[9][9];
```

and then initialized with the string constants shown in Listing 11-1. However, if you do this, you end up using more memory than is necessary. Figure 11-2 shows why this is true.

F	i	l	e	\0				
c	h	a	r	\0				
d	o	u	b	l	e	\0		
i	n	t	\0					
l	o	n	g	\0				
s	t	a	t	i	c	\0		
s	t	r	u	c	t	\0		
u	n	s	i	g	n	e	d	\0
v	o	i	d	\0				

Figure 11-2. Memory Image of char table[9][9]

As you can see, the bytes that appear after the null termination character (shown as \0 in Figure 11-2) are wasted, because the double-dimensioned array must allocate all elements to be the size of the longest string in the list. With the definition used in Listing 11-1 and assuming the small memory model with two-byte pointers, the memory image would be as shown in Figure 11-3. (It is assumed that the compiler places the array of pointers starting at memory address 30,000.)

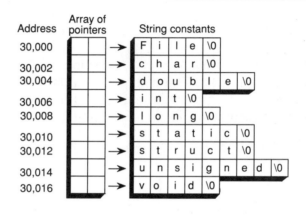

Figure 11-3. Memory Image of `char *table[]`

Even counting the additional bytes used for the pointers, you still save memory by using the array of pointers to the string constants. The compiler initializes the string, using the least amount of memory possible.

Another thing to notice about `table[]` is that the entries are in alphabetical order. (`FILE` appears before `char` because capital letters appear before lowercase letters in the ASCII character set.) If you use `typedef`s of your own making, simply add them to the initialized list for `table[]`. Make sure, however, that they are entered in (ASCII) alphabetical order.

Several other working variables are defined after `table[]`, most of which become obvious as the program is presented.

The last global definition is a structure of type `record` which has four members. These members hold the name of the function, the type specifier for the function, the name of the source file where the definition appears, and the line number where the definition was found in the source file. Note that the first member actually stores more than just the function name. Because this member can hold MAXSTR (that is, 50) characters, it usually holds most of the function prototype in addition to the function name. Although it is a simple matter to limit the member to just the function name, seeing the argument list is often very helpful when debugging programs.

With the preliminaries out of the way, you now enter the main() program function.

The *main()* Function

Listing 11-2 shows the main() function, which is little more than a series of function calls. The comments explain the general purpose of each function call. Note that command-line arguments are used when the program is first loaded. I present each function call as it appears in main().

Listing 11-2. The main() Function

```
int main(int argc, char **argv)
{
    int i, lcompar();

    clrscr();                        /* Clear screen function            */
    correct_args(argc);              /* Correct command line?            */
    i = do_directory(argv);          /* Get list of files in directory   */
    set_output_device(argc);         /* Output to screen or printer?     */
    room_left = atoi(argv[2]);           /* Allocation needed            */
    open_files(i, room_left);        /* Open and read i source files     */
    sort_list();                     /* Sort function names
    show_results();                  /* Show sorted results              */
    free(tptr);                      /* Free the allocations
    free(tbl1);
}
```

Clear Screen Function

The first function called in main() is clrscr(). The clrscr() function simply clears the display screen; however, the purpose of this function here is to show you how to use C to call an interrupt. Before examining the clrscr() function, you should inspect the dos.h header file.

If you examine the dos.h header file, you find one section that looks similar to that shown in Listing 11-3.

Listing 11-3. Part of the dos.h Header File

```
                        /* Word registers */
                        struct WORDREGS {
                                unsigned int ax;
                                unsigned int bx;
                                unsigned int cx;
                                unsigned int dx;
                                unsigned int si;
                                unsigned int di;
                                unsigned int cflag;
                        };


                        /* byte registers */

                        struct BYTEREGS {
                                unsigned char al, ah;
                                unsigned char bl, bh;
                                unsigned char cl, ch;
                                unsigned char dl, dh;
                        };

        /* general purpose registers union -
         * overlays the corresponding word and byte
           registers.
        */

                        union REGS {
                                struct WORDREGS x;
                                struct BYTEREGS h;

                        };
```

First, two structures are declared: one representing the word registers of the Central Processing Unit (CPU), the other representing the byte registers of the CPU. Next, a union with the union tag REGS is declared using the word and byte structures as members of the union. In other words, a

REGS union is allocated sufficient space to hold either a word (WORDREGS) or byte (BYTEREGS) structure. QC then uses this information to fill in the necessary register information prior to an interrupt call.

Now examine the clrscr() function, as shown in Listing 11-4.

Listing 11-4. The clrscr() *Function*

```
/*****
                                    clrscr()

      Function to clear the display screen

   Argument list:      void

   Return value:       void

*****/


void clrscr(void)
{
   union REGS ireg;

   ireg.h.ah = 6;                    /* Scroll screen up      */
   ireg.h.al = 0;                    /* Do all lines          */
   ireg.h.ch = 0;                    /* Row position          */
   ireg.h.cl = 0;                    /* Col position          */
   ireg.h.dh = 25;                   /* Assume normal size    */
   ireg.h.dl = 80;
   ireg.h.bh = 0;                    /* Attribute byte        */

   int86(0x10, &ireg, &ireg);
}
```

In Listing 11-4, I define ireg to be a union of type REGS and then proceed to fill in the byte values necessary to call the interrupt. Interrupt 0x10 is the video interrupt, and the QC library function int86() is used to call the interrupt. Function 6 of the video interrupt is used to scroll the screen. By setting ireg.h.al to 0, the entire screen is cleared. The union members ireg.h.ch and ireg.h.cl define the upper left corner of the window, whereas ireg.h.dh and ireg.h.dl define the number of lines and columns to be scrolled. Member ireg.h.bh defines the attribute to be used when the screen is scrolled: black in this case. If a nonzero value is used, you can set the background to a variety of different colors.

You now can call int86() to process the interrupt. The first argument tells QC which interrupt is being called. The second argument contains the setup values used to process the interrupt. This must be a pointer to the union and explains why the address-of operator (&) is used.

The last argument is used to return values from the interrupt call. However, because you can ignore the return values from interrupt 0x10, function 6, ireg performs double-duty. The first instance of ireg in the int86() call passes the values to the interrupt. The interrupt uses these values to process the interrupt. Function 6 of interrupt 0x10 does not return any values, so rather than define a second REGS union to hold the return values, ireg is used for the third argument. If you must retain both the setup and return values from a call using int86(), you should define two variables of type REGS.

Most interrupt calls work in a manner similar to that shown in Listing 11-4. The variables are initialized to the correct values and the interrupt is called. The scroll function (number 6) of interrupt 0x10 is not necessarily the fastest way to clear the screen (see function 0 of interrupt 0x10); but Listing 11-4 shows you how to set up an interrupt call, and it clears the screen fairly quickly.

Checking Command-Line Arguments, *correct_args()*

The next function called is correct_args(). The code for this function appears in Listing 11-5.

Listing 11-5. correct_args() *Function*

```
/*****

                                correct_args()

        This function ensures that at least three command-line
    arguments are used with the program. More may be used, but
    three are required.
        (Also see set_output_device() ).

        Argument list    int argc    the number of command-line arguments
```

Listing 11-5 continues

Listing 11-5 continued

```
   Return value:      void

*****/

void correct_args(int argc)
{
   if (argc < 3) {
    printf("Usage: FF filemask tablesize [printer]");
      exit(EXIT_FAILURE);
   }

}
```

As you can tell from the comment at the top of Listing 11-1, the program requires three command-line arguments. The first argument is always the name of the program. The second command-line argument is the file mask to be used to search the source files. The file mask can use wild cards, and in most situations, the file mask is *.c. This causes ff to search all the source files in the current working directory.

The third argument is the maximum number of function definitions to be processed by the program. The number supplied for this command-line argument is used to allocate memory for storing the results of the search. Once again, there are more elegant ways to do memory allocations, but this approach is simple and works quite well. Usually, I use the value 200 for the maximum number of entries; it does not hurt to overestimate the number needed.

The fourth command-line argument is optional. If a fourth argument is supplied, it indicates that a user wants the list sent to the printer. If the fourth argument is not supplied, output is sent to the screen.

It should be clear from Listing 11-5 that you need at least three command-line arguments for the program to function properly. If less than three command-line arguments are supplied, an error message is given and the program ends. (EXIT_FAILURE is #defined in the stdlib.h header file.) Note that the error message attempts to tell a user the proper way to invoke the program using command-line arguments. This is fairly common and has its origins in UNIX; many users are familiar with this style of error message.

Find the Files, *do_directory( )*

Assuming that there were at least three command-line arguments, control returns to `main()` and the `do_directory()` function is called. The source code for `do_directory()` appears in Listing 11-6.

Listing 11-6. `do_directory( )` Function

```
/*****
                            do_directory()

    This function searches the current working directory using the string
    pointed to by argv[1] as the search mask (for example, "*.c"). The third
    argument (argv[2]) is used to set the allocation that holds the file names.

    Argument list:    char **argv      command-line argument vector

    Return value:     int              number of files found

    CAUTION:
    The findfirst() and findnext() functions are not portable.
    Other compilers may use other functions. Likely candidates for substitution
    are opendir() and readdir(). QuickC uses _dos_findfirst() and
    _dos_findnext().

 *****/

int do_directory(char **argv)
{
    char *bptr, buff[NAMESIZ];
    int empty;
    unsigned i, size;
    struct find_t find;            /* Defined in dos.h */

    empty = _dos_findfirst(argv [1], _A_NORMAL, &find);/* Open the file directory   */
    size = atoi(argv[2]);
                                    /* Allocate for file names       */
    bptr = tptr = (char *) calloc(size, sizeof(buff));

    if (tptr == NULL) {
        printf("Out of filename memory");
        exit(0);
    }
```

Listing 11-6 continues

Listing 11-6 continued

```
for (i = 0; i < size; i++) {        /* Copy matching filenames   */
    if (!empty) {                    /* More matching files?      */
        strncpy(tptr + (NAMESIZ * i), find.name, sizeof(find.name));
        empty = _dos_findnext(&find);
    } else {
        break;                       /* If not, quit              */
    }
}
return i;
}
```

First, several working variables are defined in the function. Note the find_t structure definition. The structure declaration appears in the dos.h header file, part of which is shown in Listing 11-7.

Listing 11-7. Part of the dos.h *Header File*

```
/* _dos_findfirst structure */


struct find_t {
    char reserved[21];
    char attrib;
    unsigned wr_time;
    unsigned wr_date;
    long size;
    char name[13];
    };


/* File attribute constants */

#define _A_NORMAL    0x00    /* Normal file - No read/write restrictions */
#define _A_RDONLY    0x01    /* Read only file */
#define _A_HIDDEN    0x02    /* Hidden file */
#define _A_SYSTEM    0x04    /* System file */
#define _A_VOLID     0x08    /* Volume ID file */
#define _A_SUBDIR    0x10    /* Subdirectory */
#define _A_ARCH      0x20    /* Archive file */
```

The first function call in do_directory() is a call to _dos_findfirst(). The _dos_findfirst() call searches the directory for files that match the first and second arguments in the function call. In this example, the second command-line argument (argv[1] which is often *.c) is the file mask used in the directory search. The second argument uses a symbolic constant (_A_NORMAL) to find all "normal" files in the directory. (See the second half of Listing 11-7.) In most cases, C source files are "normal" files. These two arguments are the search criteria used in searching the file directory.

If _dos_findfirst() finds a file that matches the restrictions imposed by the first two arguments, the find structure is filled in with specific information about the file match. If the search was successful, the value 0 is returned. If no match is found, a nonzero value is returned by _dos_findfirst().

Assuming that at least one file meets the search criteria, you convert argv[2] to an integer and assign it into size. As you might recall, argv[2] tells the program the maximum number of definitions you wish to store. Next, size is used in a call to calloc() to reserve enough storage to hold size file names. If there is enough free memory to accommodate the call, calloc() returns a pointer to the free block of memory. The pointer is assigned into bptr (that is, a base pointer) and tptr (that is, a temporary, or working, pointer). Check to see that the pointers are non-null, indicating that the memory request was successful.

Next you enter a "double-duty" for loop. The for loop first copies the file names that match the search criteria into the memory block pointed to by tptr. Second, a call to _dos_findnext() is used to find any additional files that meet the search criteria established by the call to _dos_findfirst(). In other words, _dos_findfirst() sets up the proper directory search and finds the first match (if any) in the directory. Then _dos_findnext() continues the search, filling in the find structure on each subsequent call. As long as _dos_findnext() continues to return a value of 0, new files are being found that match the search criteria.

The statement

```
if (!empty)
```

causes additional calls to _dos_findnext() as long as a 0 (that is, a successful search) value is returned. When no additional files meet the search criteria, _dos_findnext() returns a nonzero value and the break statement is executed. When this happens, the program has copied all the file names that meet the search criteria into the block of memory pointed to by tptr.

The value returned from do_directory() is the number of files that matched the search criteria. Notice that the number of iterations through the loop tell you this number. That is, i is the return value.

Where To Send the Output, *set_output_device()*

Remember that if there is a fourth argument supplied on the command line, output is directed to the printer. The purpose of the set_output_device() function is to set the FILE pointer to the proper output device. Listing 11-8 shows the source code for the function.

Listing 11-8. Setting the Output Device

```
/*****
                            set_output_device()

        This function determines whether output is sent to the screen
or the standard list device, which is assumed to be stdlst. If argc
is 4, output is directed to the printer. (The corresponding argv[]
does not matter.) Any other number of command-line arguments sends
output to the screen.

    Argument list:     int argc       the number of command-line arguments

    Return value:    void

    CAUTION:
        This function assumes stdprn is the FILE pointer for the
standard list device. Other compilers may use different names (for
example, stdlst). Check stdio.h to see what is defined.

*****/

void set_output_device(int argc)
{
    if (argc == 4)
        fpout = stdprn;
    else
        fpout = stdout;
}
```

Variable fpout is a pointer of type FILE. If the command line has four arguments, fpout is initialized to the printer. Otherwise, the output is sent to the standard output device (the display screen). Obviously, four command-line arguments should be used when you want a hard copy and three arguments when you just want to find a specific function quickly.

After the output device is set, control returns to main(). Notice that room_left is set to equal the integer value of the third command-line argument. As you might recall from an earlier section, the third command-line argument is the number of entries used in the search.

Variable room_left and the number of files that match the search criteria (that is, the return value from do_directory()) are used as function arguments in the next function call in main().

Open and Read Source Code Files, *open_files()*

The next function call in main() opens the various source files that match the directory search performed earlier. The code for open_files() is shown in Listing 11-9.

Listing 11-9. Open and Read Source Files

```
/*****
                              open_files()

     This function opens for reading the files pointed to by tptr. The list of
files was created by the do_directory() function. The list of source files
pointed to by tptr are those that match the second command-line argument for the
current working directory.

     Argument list:     int number     the number of file names in the
                                        list.

                        int size       number of entries in name table

     Return value:      void

*****/

void open_files(int number, int size)
{
    int j;
```

Listing 11-9 continues

Listing 11-9 continued

```
   void read_file(char *fname);

                     /* Allocate for function info */
   tbl2 = tbl1 = (struct record *) calloc(size, sizeof(list));
   if (tbl1 == NULL) {
      printf("Out of table memory");
      exit(0);
   }
                             /* Open the files in list for reading */
   for (j = 0; j < number; j++) {
      if ( (fpin = fopen(tptr + (NAMESIZ * j), "r") ) == NULL) {
         printf("\n            Cannot open %s", tptr + (NAMESIZ * j));
         exit(0);
      }
      read_file(tptr + (NAMESIZ * j));   /* Read it; add to function list */
      fclose(fpin);                  /* Free FILE pointer for reuse  */
      if (room_left <= 0)
         return;
   }
}
```

The function begins by requesting a block of memory large enough to hold the requested number of structures for the function definitions. In other words, `calloc()` is called for a block of memory that holds `size` entries of structure type `record`. (The structure definition for `list` appears at the bottom of Listing 11-1.)

If there is no more available memory, the `tbl1` pointer is null, an error message is displayed, and the program ends. If there is sufficient memory available, `tbl1` and `tbl2` are initialized to point to the block of memory.

Next, a `for` loop is used to read each of the files that were found to meet the search criteria in `do_directory()`. Recall that `tptr` points to a list of these files. A call to `fopen()` attempts to open the first file in the list of file names pointed to by `tptr`. If the file cannot be opened, an error message is given and the program ends. If the file is opened, `fpin` is the FILE pointer for the file.

If you study the `fopen()` statement:

```
if ( (fpin = fopen(tptr + (NAMESIZ * j), "r") ) == NULL) {
```

you see that each iteration of the `for` loop opens the next file in the list. The key is the expression

```
tptr + (NAMESIZ * j)
```

Given that NAMESIZ is #defined as 13, multiplying this constant by j and adding it to tptr is a simple method of indexing off tptr in the same manner as indexing in an array. Each pass through the for loop causes the next file in the list to be read.

After the file is opened successfully, the call to read_file() (discussed in the next section) reads the contents of the file, looking for function definitions. After the file is read by read_file(), the file is closed, freeing fpin to be used again on the next iteration of the for loop. After the file is closed, room_left is checked to make sure the table still contains unused entries.

The for loop continues to process files until all files have been read or until the table has no more free entries (that is, room_left is zero).

Reading the Source Files, *read_ file()*

The real work in the program is done by the read_file() function. The source code for read_file() is shown in Listing 11-10.

Listing 11-10. The read_file() *Function*

```
/*****
                              read_file()

     This function reads the source code from the file named fname
and searches for function definitions within that file. Matched type
specifiers and function definitions are copied into a global
structure allocation pointed to by tptr.

   Argument list:    char *fname    the source code file name being
                                    read

   Return value:    void


   CAUTION:
     This function makes certain assumptions about how function
definitions appear in a source file. See text.

*****/
```

Listing 11-10 continues

Listing 11-10 continued

```
#define MAXBUFF 250

void read_file(char *fname)
{
    char *bptr, buff[300], buff2[300], *c, *sptr, temp[50];
    int len, compar(char*s1, char**s2);
    unsigned lines, num_elem, wide;

    wide = sizeof(table[0]);
    nel = sizeof(table) / sizeof(table[0]);
    lines = 0;

    printf("\nReading %s", fname);
    while (fgets(buff, MAXBUFF, fpin) != NULL) {
        strcpy(buff2, buff);
        sptr = strchr(buff2, '('); /* Look for opening paren          */
        lines++;
        if (sptr == NULL)          /* No paren, keep marching          */
            continue;
        if (buff2[0] == ' ' || buff2[0] == '\t' || buff2[0] == '\n')
            continue;
        sptr = strtok(buff, " ");  /* Look for spaces                  */
                                   /* If 1st character not white space */
        if (sptr != NULL) {        /* Now search type specifier list   */
            bptr = bsearch(sptr, table, nel, wide, compar);
            if (bptr != NULL) {
                len = strlen(buff2);
                if (len > MAXSTR) {
                    len = MAXSTR - 1;  /* Chop the string if too long      */
                } else {
                    len--;             /* Get rid of newline if too short...*/
                }
                buff2[len] = '\0';   /* ...and make it a string          */
                strncpy(temp, buff2, len);
                                     /* Get a pointer to space between   */
                                     /* type specifier and name          */
                c = strchr(buff2, ' ');
                while (*(c + 1) == ' ') {  /* Strip space away           */
                    c++;
                }
                                     /* Copy the function name to table  */
                strcpy(tbl1->name, c);
```

```
                    /* Now do type specifier            */
        strncpy(tbll->type, buff2, c - buff2);

                    /* Now do source file name           */
        strncpy(tbll->file, fname, NAMESIZ);

                    /* Finally the line number of def    */
        tbll->line = lines;
        room_left--;
        if (room_left <= 0) {    /* Check for unused space left */
            clrscr();
            tbll->name[0] = '\0';
            printf("\n\n    Out of memory\n");
            return;
        }
        tbll++;             /* Ready for next one          */
    } else
        continue;

    }
  }
}
```

The function begins by initializing wide to the size of one entry in the table[] array. Actually, this could be done with a constant because table[] is simply an array of pointers. However, using the sizeof operator ensures that the code works properly, regardless of the size of the pointer used (for example, a two-byte pointer for small model or a four-byte pointer in large model). Likewise, the assignment for nel

```
nel = sizeof(table) / sizeof(table[0]);
```

is a portable way of determining the number of elements in an initialized array. If you add new type specifiers to table[] (perhaps new typedefs of your own), dividing the size of the array by one of its elements always provides the number of elements in an initialized array.

A while loop is used to read the open file by calls to fgets(). The function fgets() reads the file one line at a time, up to a maximum of MAXBUFF characters per line. The line read is stuffed into buff[]. If the call was successful, a pointer to the string is returned from the call. If end-of-file (EOF) or an error occurs, a NULL pointer is returned. Therefore, the while loop terminates on sensing EOF or an error, and the call to read_file() ends.

Assuming that a line was read successfully, the standard library function strcpy() is used to make a copy of the line and place it in buff2[]. (You need to work with a copy of the string, for reasons that I explain shortly.)

The function strchr() is used to search the string contained in buff2[] for an opening parenthesis. If the string does not contain an opening parenthesis, it cannot be the start of a function definition. If strchr() fails to find the opening parenthesis, the search of the string fails, and the return value from strchr() is a NULL pointer. The line variable is incremented to keep a count of where each function definition occurs in the file.

The statement:

```
if (sptr == NULL)
    continue;
```

says, "If you don't find an opening parenthesis in the string, you are done with this line; continue to read the next line of the source file."

If sptr is not NULL, you know the program found an opening parenthesis, but you cannot be sure that the opening parenthesis is the beginning of a function definition. After all, it could be part of if, for, while, or other keywords and parenthesized expressions. For the most part, the rest of the code in the while loop is used to eliminate the other possibilities associated with an opening parenthesis.

White Space Characters

The first check determines whether the first character of the line is a *white space*. A white space in C is a blank, tab, newline, return, formfeed, or vertical tab character. Because it is unusual for the return, formfeed, or vertical tab white space characters to appear in a C source code file, you need to check only for a blank, tab, or newline character.

If any white space characters are found in the first character position of the string, you know (from your assumptions about coding style) that the line cannot be the start of a function definition. If that is the case, you can continue the while loop to read the next line in the file.

Dissecting a String, *strtok( )*

If you do have a function definition in the current line, the first word of the line must be a type specifier. The list of valid type specifiers is held in the `table[]` array. If your programs use other type specifiers, such as `typedef`s, add them to the `table[]` array. Just make sure you place them in (ASCII) alphabetical order.

Now you must find out whether the first word in the line is a valid type specifier matching one of those found in the `table[]` array. To do this, you should check the first word in the line with the list held in `table[]`. You also must create a substring that consists of the first word of the line held in `buff[]`. The `strtok()` function is perfectly suited for the task.

`strtok()` searches the first argument (`buff[]`) for a character match with a character in the second argument. The second argument is a string of delimiter characters that you want to find. In this case, the second argument is a single blank space because you simply want to find the end of the first word in the line. If `strtok()` finds a match between the string and a character in the delimiter string, it overwrites the delimiter with a null termination character (`\0`). The result is a substring of the original string.

This is the reason you created a copy of the original line in `buff2`: `strtok()` "chops up" the original line into substrings. Because you must use the original string later on, you make a copy of it. (The formal definition of `strtok()` implies that the original string is destroyed. Actually, some implementations of `strtok()` appear to create a copy of the string before any action is taken, leaving the original string intact. QC, however, does alter the original string.)

The return value from `strtok()` is a pointer to the start of the new substring. In this example, `sptr` points to the first word in the line. If no word exists in the line, a `NULL` pointer is returned and the next iteration of the `while` loop is executed.

Searching an Ordered List, *bsearch( )*

If `sptr` is not `NULL`, a call to the standard library function `bsearch()` is made. The `bsearch()` function performs a binary search of a sorted list of items. In this case, the sorted list contains the type specifiers held in `table[]`. As can be seen from the statement

```
bptr = bsearch(&sptr, table, nel, wide, compar);
```

there are five arguments for bsearch(). The first argument (sptr) is a pointer to the item, or key, you wish to match in the list. In this program, it is a pointer to the first word of the line. The second argument is a pointer to the list to be searched: the list of type specifiers contained in table[]. The third argument is the number of elements in the list, and the fourth argument is the width of each item in the list, specified in bytes.

The Comparison Support Function, *bsearch( )*

The fifth argument to bsearch() is a pointer to a function that performs the actual test for a match between the first and second function arguments. The code for the function that performs the comparison is shown in Listing 11-11.

Listing 11-11. The Comparison Function for bsearch()

```
/*****
                              compar()

     This function is used to compare type specifiers in the global
  table[] array with those read from the input source file. It is
  called by the bsearch() function as a pointer to function. Double
  indirection is needed because table[] is an array of pointers to
  char.

  Argument list: char *s1    pointer to the type specifier
                             read in the source file.

                 char **s2   pointer to the type specifier
                             found in table being searched
                             (table[]).

  Return value: int          0 if a match, nonzero otherwise

*****/

int compar(char *s1, char **s2)
{
    return (strcmp(s1, *s2));
}
```

In C, any time you use a function name without its associated parentheses, the compiler uses the `lvalue` of the function. That is, instead of actually calling the function, the compiler generates the address of the start of the function in memory. This memory address is then passed to `bsearch()` for use as needed using indirection.

Why pass a pointer to a function? Think about it. By using a pointer to function, `bsearch()` does not have to know anything about the actual name of the function; all it needs is a memory address to branch to as it sees fit. This also means that you can use `bsearch()` with as many different comparison functions as you need. By not using another function name as the last argument, `bsearch()` is made more flexible because it can search a list of any data type. If you need to search a list of integers and then a list of strings, `bsearch()` can handle the job. All you need to do is write two different comparison functions: one for integers and one for strings.

In the comparison function, `compar()`, the arguments may seem a bit strange. That is, in

```
int compar(char *s1, char **s2)
```

the first argument should look familiar by now. However, `**s2` may be unfamiliar. This is simply the syntax utilized when two levels of indirection ("double indirection") are used. Some details should help you understand what double indirection implies.

First, remember that `s1` is a pointer to the first word in the source code line. It points to the word you want to find in the list. Second, remember that `s2` is the list of type specifiers held in `table[]`; `table[]`, however, is an array of pointers. Specifically, `table[]` is an array of pointers to the strings that contain the list of type specifiers. But what is a string? A string is an array of characters. Because you can view the name of a character array as a pointer, you can say that `table[]` is defined as "an array of pointers to pointers to `char`." If only one level of indirection were used with `table[]`, you would only succeed in finding the `lvalue` where the strings are stored, not the strings themselves. If you want, add a `printf()` in the compare function or use the debugger to print the relevant `lvalue`s.

The purpose of the `compar()` function is to return an integer that is equal to zero if the two strings are equal. If the two strings do not match, `compar()` returns a nonzero value — the sign of which determines how `bsearch()` proceeds with the binary search.

When `bsearch()` is done, it returns a pointer to a match in the list if the search found a match. A `NULL` pointer means the word being searched was not in the list contained in `table[]`.

A Non-NULL *bsearch()*

When `bsearch()` returns a non-NULL pointer, you know that a type specifier is the first word in the line. Although this could be a function prototype, you still treat this as a success. The call to `strlen()` is done to determine whether the function name and its arguments are too long to fit within the 50-character maximum (`MAXSTR`). If they are too long, the line is truncated and turned into a 50-character string. If the line is fewer than 50 characters, the newline is replaced with a null termination character. (The null termination character from the call to `fgets()` is placed after the newline character. By overwriting the newline character with the null termination character, the output is not double-spaced when it is displayed.) A call to `strncpy()` copies the new string into a temporary storage space.

The call to `strchr()` again searches for the blank space between the type specifier and the function name, returning a pointer to the blank space character that is assigned into `c`. A small `while` loop strips away multiple blank spaces if they exist. When this loop is finished, `c` points to the first character of the function name. The function name is now copied into the entry table with a call to `strcpy()`. `c` (the pointer to the function name) and `tptr` (the pointer to the table) are used as the arguments in the call.

The call

```
strncpy(tbl1->type, buff2, c - buff2);
```

copies the type specifier into the `type` member of the structure pointed to by `tbl1`. The statements

```
strncpy(tbl1->file, fname, NAMESIZ);
```

and

```
tbl1->line = lines;
```

copy the file name and the line number in the source file where the definition appeared in the structure.

Next, `room_left` is decremented and checked to make sure that there are still free entries in the table. If there is no more space, a message is displayed, and the function ends. If there are still unused entries, the table pointer is incremented (`tbl1`), and more lines are examined from the file.

Eventually, all lines in the file are read and `fgets()` returns a null pointer. At that point, the `while` loop and the `read_file()` function end.

Note that each call to `read_file()` reads the entire file before control returns to `open_files()` to process another file. In other words, program control goes from open_files() to read_file() each time it is necessary to read a C source code file. Eventually, all the files are read, the for loop in open_files() ends, and control returns to main().

Sorting the Output, *sort_list( )*

At this point in the program, all the information has been collected on the function definitions. Unfortunately, the information is stored in the order in which it was read, making it difficult to read the output. The purpose of the sort_list() function is to sort the information into alphabetical order for easy review. The sort_list() function is shown in Listing 11-12.

Listing 11-12. The sort_list() *Function*

```
/*****
                            sort_list()

     This function sorts the list of function names into
     alphabetical order using the qsort() function (UNIX System V
     compatible). The function assumes that the comparison function,
     lcompar(), exists.

     Argument list:    void

     Return value:     void

*****/

void sort_list(void)
{
    int lcompar(char*s1, char*s2);
    unsigned j;

    j = tbl1 - tbl2;       /* How big is the list?        */
    tbl1 = tbl2;           /* Point back to start of list */
    clrscr();
    printf("Sorting...");  /* Now sort it...              */
    qsort(tbl1, j, sizeof(list), lcompar);

}
```

When `sort_list()` is called, pointer `tbl1` points to the next empty space that can be used to store a new entry. Because you are finished making entries in the list, `tbl1` points just past the last entry in the list. `tbl2` points to the start of the list. Therefore, `tbl1` minus `tbl2` yields the total size of the list as it now exists in memory. The first statement in `sort_list()` assigns the table size into variable `j`.

Next, the `tbl1` pointer is reset so that it also points to the start of the list. The screen is cleared and a message is displayed to inform a user that the list is being sorted. (Any time there might be a lengthy pause in the program, tell users that things are progressing as planned. Otherwise, they might think something is amiss and attempt to break out of the program.)

The last statement in `sort_list()` calls the standard library function `qsort()` which sorts the data. There are four arguments to the function. In the statement

```
qsort(tbl1, j, sizeof(list), lcompar);
```

`tbl1` is always a pointer to the first element in the list to be sorted. The second argument (`j`) is the overall size of the list, in bytes. (Remember that the size of the list was determined using the first statement in the `sort_list()` function.) The third argument is the size of one element in the list. The argument `sizeof(list)` returns the size of one structure of type `record` as defined just before `main()`. The fourth argument is a pointer to the function that performs the comparison to determine the sort order.

These four arguments tell `qsort()` all it needs to know to sort virtually any type of information. Working through the argument list, the arguments tell `qsort()` where the list starts in memory, how many bytes are in the list, how big each element is in the list, and how to arrange the list. All you need to write is the compare function (`lcompar()`).

The Comparison Function, *lcompar()*

The code for `lcompar()` is shown in Listing 11-13.

Listing 11-13. Comparison Function, `lcompar()`

```
/*****

                              lcompar()

     This function is called by the qsort() function as a pointer
  to function. It is used to sort the structure array pointed to by
```

tptr. The sort is on function name. The actual value of each
argument used in a comparison is set by the internal workings of
the qsort() function.

Argument list: char **s1   first function name used in the
                                    sort comparison

                  char **s2   second function name used in the
                                    sort comparison

Return value: int   0 if a match, nonzero otherwise

*****/


```
int lcompar(char *s1, char *s2)
{
    return (strcmp(s1, s2));
}
```

The lcompar() function shows how simple it is to use the standard
library qsort () function. The first member of the record structure is the
name of the function definition and is the key by which you sort, because
the function name is a string, you can use the standard library function
strcmp() to do the comparison. The comparison function used by qsort()
must return one of three possible values:

- negative means that the item pointed to by s1 is less than s2
- 0 means that the item pointed to by s1 is equal to s2
- positive means that the item pointed to by s1 is greater than s2

The return values from strcmp() are consistent with the comparison
requirements of qsort(), so the function simply calls strcmp() with the two
arguments and returns to qsort() the return value from strcmp().
What would happen if you changed the statement in lcompar() to

return (strcmp(s2, s1));

(Notice that the order of the arguments is reversed in the call.) Think about
it. If you are not sure of the outcome of the change, edit the line as shown
previously, recompile the program, and observe the output. You should
be able to explain the changes you now see on the screen.

Displaying the Output, *show_result( )*

The purpose of the `show_result()` function is to display the output on the selected output device (either the screen or the printer). The code for `show_result()` is presented in Listing 11-14.

Listing 11-14. The `show_results()` *Function*

```
/*****
                                show_results()

        Function to display the sorted list of function definitions.
    The function is fairly dumb (no fancy headers or printer paging),
    but it does pause when MAXLINEs of output are sent to the screen.

    Argument list:    void

    Return value:     void

*****/

void show_results(void)
{
    int count;

    count = 0;
    clrscr();
    while (tbl2->name[0] != '\0') {
        fprintf(fpout, "\n%-50s    %-8s    %4d   %s",
        tbl2->name, tbl2->type, tbl2->line, tbl2->file);
        tbl2++;
        count++;                /* Pause when needed    */
        if (count > MAXLINE && fpout == stdout) {
            printf("\n\n Press any key to continue");
            getch();
            clrscr();
            count = 0;
        }                       /* Space between letter groups    */
        if (tbl2->name[1] != (tbl2 - 1)->name[1]) {
            fprintf(fpout, "\n");
            count++;
        }
    }
}
```

The program begins by setting `count` to 0 and clearing the screen. A `while` loop is used to march through the (now sorted) list that is pointed to by `tbl2`. The statement

```
while (tbl2->name[0] != '\0') {
```

shows how the `while` loop is controlled. As long as the first member of the `record` structure pointed to by `tbl2` is not a null termination character, there are more entries in the list. When the `name[]` member is empty (that is, the first character is a null termination character), the `while` loop ends, and control returns to `main()`.

In the `while` loop, the standard library function `fprintf()` is used to display the output. `fprintf()` works the same as `printf()`, except the output is sent to the output device pointed to by the `FILE` pointer `fpout`. If a user selects the screen for output, `fpout` is equal to the standard output device, `stdout`. For the QC compiler (and virtually any other C compiler), the standard output device is the screen.

If the printer was selected, output is sent to the standard list device, `stdprn`. For some C compilers, the standard list device is `stdlst`. If you change to another compiler, look in the `stdio.h` header file to find the name for the standard list device.

The next two statements increment the line counter (`count`) and the pointer to the list of entries (`tptr2`). The `if` statement checks to see whether `MAXLINE` lines of output have been sent to the standard output device. If so, the screen is paused via a call to `getch()` until a key is pressed. At that point, the line counter is reset to 0 and the process continues until all entries have been displayed. If a user selects the printer as the output device, there is no need to pause the program, and the output is written to the printer uninterrupted.

The last `if` statement is used to add an extra newline character each time an entry begins with a different letter. This groups together all function names that begin with the same letter but adds a blank line whenever the function name starts with a letter different from the one previously displayed. This makes it a little easier for a user to view the output.

Freeing Up Dynamically Allocated Memory, *free()*

After all output has been sent to the desired output device, program control returns to the `main()` function. The last two function calls in `main()`

are calls to the standard library function named `free()`. Any time you request a block of memory from the operating system at runtime, you should call the `free()` function to release that storage when you are finished with it.

Requesting storage while the program is running is called *dynamic memory allocation* and frequently uses one of the standard library functions (for example, `calloc()`, `malloc()`, `realloc()` or similar functions). A dynamic memory allocation should be "freed" before the program ends. Although most modern compilers release dynamic memory allocations on sensing program termination, some older compilers still in use do not.

Finally, when you do call `free()`, make sure you use the name of the pointer that was used in the memory allocation call. Freeing a pointer that does not point to dynamically-allocated storage can cause some nasty bugs and possibly some undesirable side effects.

Improvements in ff

I have mentioned some of the changes that I have been meaning to add to the ff program, but over the years, it has served me well without them. However, you may want to try to implement some of the changes yourself.

First, it would be more elegant if a user did not have to supply the maximum number of entries as part of the command line. For example, the standard library function `realloc()` is designed to reallocate storage for a new size. Each time a new function definition is read, calls to `realloc()` could be performed to allocate just enough new storage to hold the new entry. This would free users from having to guess how many entries might be needed.

Second, it might be useful to allow the output to be directed to a disk file. The program would add code to prompt for the file name and direct the output to the disk file on completion. This would allow for quicker copies of the output if the printed copy was not handy. Also, this option might be added at the end of the program, so a user can decide after seeing the output whether to make a more permanent copy of the output (printer or disk file).

Third, the program could be more resourceful in sorting out the distinctions between true function definitions and function declarations. This has never been a problem for me and has on occasion made me aware of passing incorrect variables to a function, even though the data types were correct.

Fourth, the program could be written to recognize more than one coding style. Again, most people write C code in the style presented in this book, but other styles do exist. The program is not so complex that it could not be modified to handle other styles.

Fifth, create a table of function prototypes from the function definitions or even write the prototypes automatically to a header file, because the only difference between a function definition and a prototype is the semicolon at the end.

Finally, there may be algorithm changes that could improve performance, although it should be fast enough for most projects. Even though there is a great deal of truth to the adage: "If it ain't broke, don't fix it," there is always room for improvement. If you make an improvement, I hope you will share it with me.

12

Debugging Programs

I n this chapter, you learn

The different types of program errors

The difference between syntactic and semantic errors

Common programming errors

How to use the QC Debugger

For a writer, program errors and debugging in general are frustrating topics. It would be great to be able to warn you about the types of errors you will (surely) make before you make them. Unfortunately, that isn't the most practical approach. Instead, this topic must be deferred until you have enough C experience to understand why the errors occur in the first place.

No doubt you already have experienced a number of the errors discussed in this chapter. The good news, then, is that you already have some debugging experience. In this chapter some of the more common mistakes, plus a few of the subtle ones, are discussed. As you progress through the chapter, I suggest some defensive coding techniques that might help you avoid some of the bugs that all programmers make at one time or another.

Programming Expertise, Comfort, and You

Now that you have invested this much effort to learn C, I admit that C is not the easiest language to learn. Furthermore, the ease with which you learn C is influenced significantly by your programming experience. Programmers with Pascal or assembly language experience, for example, tend to have much less difficulty than those whose programming experience is with less structured languages (for example, BASIC).

Your programming background also influences your "comfort" level with C. A good indication of your progress is by noting what language you choose when you have a quick-and-dirty programming task. For example, if you come from a BASIC or Pascal background and you want to write a short program that you estimate will take only ten or fifteen minutes to write, which language do you choose? When you choose C over the alternatives, it is because you are comfortable with the language.

An important element of your comfort level is your confidence in correcting a program when something goes wrong. When you start choosing C for all your programming efforts, you probably will be confident in your ability to debug a C program. Some debugging techniques can be taught; others are learned from experience. (Although out of print, *Debugging C* by Robert Ward is a masterpiece that belongs on your bookshelf. It can be ordered from *The C User's Journal*.) Debugging requires a methodical approach to the problem and a clear understanding of its nature.

In the rest of this chapter, I build a base for the general types of program bugs and point out some common errors that beginning programmers make, so you can advance to more sophisticated bugs. The chapter ends with a discussion of the QC Debugger.

Level 1 Errors

To keep things simple, I assume that there are only three levels of coding errors. A Level 1 error is a *syntactic* error. A syntactic error occurs because the source code statement does not conform to the C language rules. You can reasonably expect all syntactic errors to be caught by QC and virtually any other commercial C compiler.

Because Level 1 errors are detected by the compiler, they are usually easy to figure out and correct. All beginning C programmers experience Level 1 errors, and there is no reason for you to expect to be different. Chances are pretty good that you have had your fair share of syntactic errors already. It is fairly safe to assume that many of these were typing mistakes.

Redefinition Errors

Some of the error messages issued by QC, however, are a bit obtuse. Perhaps you have seen the "redefinition error" message while writing a program. The reason for this message is clear when you have two variables in scope with the same name. However, QC also uses this message when you forget to declare a function that has a return value other than `int`. This error usually occurs when you neglect to `#include` the proper header file for the function or when you forget to declare a function that you defined in the program. The fix is simple: either include the proper header file or place a function declaration at the top of the program.

The redefinition error message would be more meaningful if it said either "Function return value mismatch" or "No function declaration" when the return type is not `int`. Eventually, you get used to the message; after you figure it out, you can easily set things straight.

On-line Function Help

If you do get a redefinition error message on a QC library function, chances are pretty good that you did not include the proper header file. If you are not sure which header file is required for a function, move the cursor to the start of the function name and press the F1 key. This gives you on-line information about the function. If you need more help or want to see the function used in an example, press the F6 key to move to the Help window and use the Tab key to select the type of help you need.

Most Level 1 errors are easily recognized because QC does a good job of highlighting the offending line in the program. Usually, syntactic errors are of the "flat-forehead" variety—after you see it you slap your hand to your forehead and admonish yourself for making the mistake. However, if you are like most programmers, you pass through Level 1 fairly quickly—and move on to bigger and better errors!

Level 2 Errors

After programmers master Level 1 errors, they move on to Level 2 errors. I define Level 2 errors as *semantic* errors. Whereas the syntax of a language defines the rules of the language, the semantics of the language define how those rules are properly applied. For example, the sentence, "The cat barked," obeys the syntactic rules of the English language (that is, the sentence has a noun and a verb). However, because cats do not bark, the sentence is semantically incorrect. Either the noun (cat) or the verb (barked) is not used in the proper context and an error results.

Semantic errors are more difficult to detect. QC must concern itself not only with the rules of the program statement (syntax), but also of the context (semantics) within which the statement is used. This is especially difficult in C because certain operators have multiple meanings depending on the context within which the operator is used. The classic example in C is the asterisk. The asterisk can indicate multiplication, pointer definition, or indirection, depending on how the operator is used.

The end result is that compilers can shed only so much light on a semantic error. QC does a good job in most cases of pointing you in the right direction. (The UNIX utility named Lint does an excellent job of pointing out such errors, and commercial versions do exist for the PC market.)

Consider the sample program presented in Listing 12-1.

Listing 12-1. Program Example with Semantic Errors

```
main()
{
    double x;

    x = sqrt(5);
    printf("The square root of 5 is %f", x);
}
```

If you type this program and compile it, no error messages are given. However, two common Level 2 errors are present in the program.

What the Preprocessor Does: /P Switch

The first step in compiling a program is the preprocessor pass. You have seen in previous chapters how the compiler responds to preprocessor directives like #include and #define. The important thing to remember is that the preprocessor can change how the compiler views your C source code.

If you want to see what the C source file looks like after the preprocessor pass, use the /P switch. For example, to see the preprocessor output file for a program named `test.c`, use the QC command-line compiler and type

```
QCL /P TEST.C
```

at the MS-DOS command line. This command line causes an output file name `test.i` to be written that contains the C source code plus the changes (if any) caused by the preprocessor. Note that this command does not compile the program; it only writes out the C source file along with any possible preprocessor changes.

What happens when the program presented in Listing 12-1 is run through the `/P` switch? If you examine the preprocessor output file for Listing 12-1, you find that there is no change at all to the source code. Next, you see why the program has errors even after the preprocessor has had a crack at it.

When the preprocessor makes its pass over the code, QC finds the argument to `sqrt()` as the numeric constant 5. Because the default data type for numeric constants is an integer, QC treats the value 5 as an integer. The `sqrt()` function, however, "expects" 5 to be a floating point constant. This expectation can create a mess of things.

Pushing and Popping the Stack

When the code is generated for the call to the `sqrt()` function, QC sees the constant 5 and not knowing any differently, places the integer constant 5 on the *stack*. The stack can be thought of as a small section of memory used to pass arguments to a function as well as where the return value from a function call is placed. This memory works like a stack of trays in a cafeteria. A value is "pushed" onto the stack and the stack grows downward (toward lower memory addresses). When a value is taken ("popped") from the stack, the value also is taken from the top. Therefore "pushing" an integer on the stack places 2 bytes on the stack. If you immediately pop a 2-byte value from the stack, you retrieve the same value that was just pushed onto the stack.

How *sqrt( )* Works

Figure 12-1(a) shows how the stack might look after the call to `sqrt()` using the integer constant 5. Trouble first occurs when you reach the `sqrt()` code itself. The `sqrt()` function knows that to work properly, an argument must be on the stack to be used in the function. sqrt() also assumes that the argument on the stack is a double-precision, floating-point number. Therefore, sqrt() dutifully pops off 8 bytes from the stack. This is shown in Figure 12-1(b). The result, however, is 2 bytes of integer-sized data (that is, the constant 5) plus 6 bytes of junk.

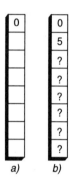

a)   b)

Figure 12-1. Stack Operations for a Function Argument

Assuming that the eight bytes represent a valid double value, sqrt() proceeds to take the square root of the (junk) value. After the square root is calculated, sqrt() places the eight-byte (double) answer back on the stack. (The sqrt() function returns a double.) Program control then returns to main().

The Second Part of the *sqrt()* Problem

Back in main(), the return value is assigned into x. However, QC assumes that sqrt() returns an int and proceeds to pop two bytes off the stack. However, because QC knows that the return value is being assigned into the double named x, QC casts the integer return value to a double and assigns it into x. The answer is virtually certain to be a nonsense value. The call to printf() then displays the (nonsense) square root on the screen.

Note that QC never offers a clue to these problems during the compilation process. When I ran the program, I obeyed the syntactic rules of C, but violated several semantic rules. QC did, however, issue a runtime error message saying DOMAIN error in the sqrt() function. (You may or may not get the same error message. It depends on how the stack looks when `sqrt()` pops off the six bytes of junk from the stack.) The most likely cause of a domain error in the `sqrt()` is an improper function argument, such as a negative value.

You can test this theory very simply. If you are passing an improper value to `sqrt()` and that is what is causing the DOMAIN error, telling QC that the numeric constant is a floating point value of 5 should cause the DOMAIN error to disappear. What you need is a way to tell QC that the 5 is a `double` data type. To do this, you must change the argument for `sqrt()` to

```
x = sqrt(5.0);
```

Because of the decimal point in the constant, QC can now form the `double` in the proper manner. The result is that eight bytes are pushed onto the stack as a `double` rather than an `int`. Now the stack is set up properly, and `sqrt()` is at least receiving the proper value. When I recompiled the program and ran it, the DOMAIN error did, in fact, disappear. The answer is still wrong, but at least the DOMAIN error is fixed.

The remaining problem is that QC does not know that `sqrt()` returns a `double` rather than an `int`. The correct answer from `sqrt()` is sitting on the stack as an eight-byte value, but QC is only popping off two bytes from the stack. Obviously, the displayed answer is still going to be junk.

To solve this, you need to tell QC that `sqrt()` returns a `double` rather than an `int`. This is the purpose of a function declaration. Therefore, if you change the statement

```
double x;
```

to

```
double x, sqrt();
```

and recompile the program, you should get the proper answer, because QC now knows that it must pop an eight-byte value from the stack to form the proper answer. Compile and run the modified program and the answer will be correct.

Prototyping to the Rescue

Perhaps you noticed that you can avoid these problems by making a full function declaration and prototype for `sqrt()` available to QC when the program is compiled. The line

```
double sqrt(double);
```

added near the top of the program includes the declaration and prototype. These tell QC that the function argument is a `double`. This means that QC views the `5` as `5.0` and places eight bytes on the stack. This takes care of the DOMAIN error. Because the function type specifier is `double`, QC knows that the return value from `sqrt()` is a `double` and that eight bytes must be popped off the stack. This takes care of getting the proper return value from the stack.

Header Files

In short, function declarations with prototyping can help eliminate many semantic errors that cannot be caught otherwise. For example, a simple

```
#include <math.h>
```

at the top of Listing 12-1 would solve all your problems.

Fortunately, function prototypes for the QC library functions already exist in the various header files provided with the compiler. If you do not know the proper header file associated with the function, move the cursor to the function name in the source code and press the F1 key. The on-line Help function tells you the name of the required header file.

Any time you write a function that uses a noninteger argument or returns a value other than `int`, write a function prototype for that function and place it near the top of the program. (Often, the prototypes are placed immediately after the `#include` directives.) If you find yourself writing more than five or six prototypes, you might want to move them into their own header file and `#include` the header file into the program. This is especially useful when the program involves multiple source modules that are compiled separately.

An Important Digression

Before progressing to Level 3 type errors, an important point must be reemphasized. I have been very careful when using the terms *declaration* and *definition*. Many C programmers use these two terms as though they mean the same thing, but they don't. An example might clarify the differences.

Suppose that you see the following statement in a program:

```
char c, *gets();
```

You know that the statement allows you to use c as a character variable in your program and that the function gets() has pointer to char as the return data type.

What QC does with each of these two pieces of information in the statement, however, is very different. When the compiler sees the char c, it goes about the task of creating a spot in memory for the variable c. That is, the compiler allocates storage for c.

When QC reads the *gets() part of the statement, it simply makes a note to itself that gets() returns a pointer to char rather than an int (the default data type). Unlike variable c, no storage is allocated for gets(). Therefore, there is a very real difference between a data definition (c) and a data declaration (*gets()):

definition	causes QC to allocate memory for the data item being defined.
declaration	gives QC information about a data item, but does not allocate memory for that data item.

Consider a second example:

```
extern int i;
int j;
```

In this fragment, the statement extern int i is a data declaration that tells QC: "Variable i is defined in some other file; just make a note of it and let me use i as an int in this section of code." Therefore, the extern int i statement is a declaration. This type of declaration is little more than a message to the linker to provide the proper memory address (lvalue) for i at a later time. The second line, on the other hand, defines variable j and causes storage to be allocated for j.

The real difference between data declarations and data definitions should be clear. You need to understand the difference, because it can help you in your debugging efforts.

Now proceed to Level 3 errors.

Level 3 Errors

Level 3 errors are all the other types of errors that can creep into a program and that are not obviously Level 1 or Level 2. Level 3 errors are not the technical type of semantic errors that you associate with Level 2 errors discussed earlier. Rather, Level 3 is a catch-all for errors that do not fit into the other error classifications. An experienced C programmer probably has not made some of the following Level 3 types of errors for years. On the other hand, I make some Level 3 errors on a daily basis. What follows is a list of common Level 3 errors that beginning C programmers often make.

Trailing Semicolons

One of the first things you learned as a budding C programmer is that C statements end with a semicolon. Forgetting a semicolon at the end of a statement is a common Level 1 error. Sometimes, however, a programmer learns the lesson too well and places the semicolon where it doesn't belong. A common example is

```
if (a == b);
    ++i;
```

The intent of the programmer is to increment variable i if a and b are equal. You can see the effects of the trailing semicolon more clearly if the error is "beautified":

```
if (a == b)
    ;
++i;
```

The "lonely" semicolon is actually a null statement in C and is perfectly legal syntax. The problem is that you always increment i regardless of the values of a and b.

A similar example is:

```
for (i = 0; i < MAXVAL; i++);
    if ( (i % 2) == 0)
        s[i] = i;
```

In this code fragment, the programmer probably wanted to set every other element in the s[] array. Another look shows what the code is actually doing:

```
for (i = 0; i < MAXVAL; i++)
    ;
if ( (i % 2) == 0)
    s[i] = i;
```

Again, the code that was to be controlled by the `for` loop is not being executed within the loop.

Trailing semicolons occur most often with `for`, `if`, and `while` statements. The effect of the trailing semicolon is that a null program statement is executed. The trailing semicolon is one of the first things to look for whenever it appears that your program is bypassing a section of code.

Missing Braces

A similar error is to omit braces when a C control statement is being used. For example

```
while (i < END)
    s[i] = value(i);
    ++i;
```

which probably means to fill in the `s[]` array with some value calculated by the `value()` function as long as `i` is less than the symbolic constant `END`. What actually happens is

```
while (i < END)
    s[i] = value(i);


++i;
```

If `i` is less than `END` to begin with, the program enters an infinite loop because `i` is never incremented past its starting value. The program calls `value()` with the same `i` value forever. What was intended was

```
while (i < END) {
    s[i] = value(i);
    ++i;
}
```

The braces group the necessary increment on `i` so that it is now controlled by the `while` statement.

Although braces are not necessary when a `while`, `if`, `for`, or `do-while` controls a single statement, you might find it advantageous to *always* use braces with these keywords even when they control a single program statement.

Assignment Versus Relational Test

If you have experience with other programming languages, it may take a while to become accustomed to using a double equal sign (==) when doing a relational test for equality in C. Even though programmers know better, sometimes things creep into the code, as in the following:

```
for (i = 0; i = MAXVAL; i++) {
   .
   /* Some C statements controlled by the for */
   .
}
```

In this example, if MAXVAL is nonzero the loop is executed forever because an assignment operator (=) was used in the second expression rather than the test for equality (==). Similar mistakes can occur in while, do-while, and if statements. The best evidence that this type of bug is present is when a program seems to have skipped a section of code.

A related error involves something like

```
c = d == 5;
```

In this case, the programmer might be trying to assign 5 into d and c. However, because the test for equality (==) has higher precedence than does the assignment operator (=), the logical test is performed first. If d does equal 5, the test is logically True and 1 is the result of the expression. Therefore, 1 is assigned into c, not 5. If d is not equal to 5, the test is logically False and 0 is the result of the expression. In this case, c ends up equal to 0.

Complicating the problem is that you can look at the error several times before you notice the double equal sign. Often it is the forest-for-the-trees syndrome. Many times taking a short break from the code or having a colleague look at it quickly uncovers the bug.

This type of bug is especially nasty because it sends you down a false trail looking for a variable that has the value 0 or 1. If a variable never has a value other than 0 or 1 and you think it should have other values, look for the relational-assignment error shown previously.

A similar problem can occur in loop structures. Consider the following code fragment:

```
letter = getchar();
while (c = letter != 'A') {
   switch (c) {
      case 'A':
```

```
        /* The rest of the code fragment */
    }
}
```

The relational test is performed first because relational operators have higher precedence than does assignment. In this case, if c is not equal to 'A', the statement is logical True and the result of the test is 1. A 1 (logical True) is assigned into c, not the letter 'A'. Because the case statement expects a letter rather than integer 1, the program falls through the cases and repeats the `while`. Because the `getchar()` is outside the loop, the system hangs. Clearly, a `default` statement would catch this error.

Given all the operators in C and that they are scattered among 15 levels of precedence, you can easily make this kind of error, even after considerable experience with C. Because QC cannot catch these (or other Level 3 errors), tracking down the error is more difficult.

Pointer Bugs

Without a doubt, pointers are the single most troublesome topic the beginning C programmer must tackle. The key to understanding pointers is a clear understanding of `lvalues` and `rvalues`. (Refer to Chapter 8 to see how `lvalues` and `rvalues` relate to pointers.) In this section, some of the most common mistakes made when using pointers are discussed.

Not Initializing a Pointer

The first common pointer mistake is forgetting that pointers do not automatically point to something useful. Consider the diagram of the statements shown in Figure 12-2.

The first statement defines and initializes the value of i. This is why both the lvalue and rvalue of i are known after the statement is executed. The second statement, however, simply defines an integer pointer named ptr. QC defines a storage location for the pointer (for example, 60,000), but the rvalue of the pointer is whatever random bit pattern exists in memory when the program is run. In other words, the pointer could point to any location and you would have no idea where it is pointing.

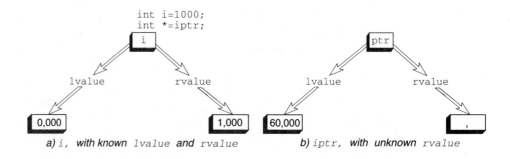

a) `i`, **with known** `lvalue` **and** `rvalue`   b) `iptr`, **with unknown** `rvalue`

Figure 12-2. Pointer Diagrams

If you try to use `ptr` in an assignment statement in its present state, such as

```
*ptr = 5;
```

who knows where the value 5 is stored? The 5 is assigned into whatever memory address is formed by the random bit patterns stored in `ptr`'s `rvalue` when the program begins executing. Suddenly, a 5 might appear in the middle of your program, the operating system (perhaps locking it up), or anywhere. Regardless, the program probably will not perform as expected.

You must initialize a pointer to point to some valid data item for things to work properly.

Improper Pointer Initialization

The second type of pointer error is improper pointer initialization. Use the same initializing code as before:

```
int i = 1000;
int *ptr;
```

Now suppose that you learned your lesson from pointer mistake number one, and that you want to initialize the pointer to point to something useful. You try

```
ptr = i;
```

As I said before, you always progress to bigger and better mistakes! The statement does initialize the pointer, but is it correct? To discover what you have actually done, look at how QC views this statement. As it stands now, QC is told to assign the value of i (1,000) into the rvalue of ptr. The diagram in Figure 12-3 displays what is now in memory.

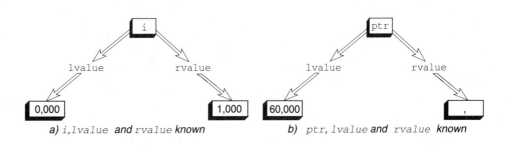

a) i, lvalue and rvalue known   b) ptr, lvalue and rvalue known

Figure 12-3. Improper Pointer Initialization

Most likely, this is not how you intended the code to work. If you now try something like

```
*ptr = 3;
```

the asterisk indicates that indirection is to be used when making the assignment. QC now proceeds to the memory location stored in ptr's rvalue (1,000) and places an integer constant 3 at that address. Quite possibly, you once again assigned a 3 into the middle of your program (or the operating system?) while it is executing!

To correct the problem, the pointer initialization must be

```
ptr = &i;
```

The ampersand (&) tells QC to assign the lvalue of i into the rvalue of ptr. This is the only way to initialize a pointer properly. The lesson is two-pronged:

1. Always initialize a pointer before you use it.
2. Make sure the pointer is initialized to a proper memory address.

Confusing Pointers and Array Names

If you hang around C programmers long enough, eventually you hear one (or more) of them say, "You can treat the name of an array the same as a pointer." This is one of those half-truths that can come back to haunt you.

It is true that when an array is referenced, QC uses the `lvalue` of the array for referencing. For example, if you define an array

```
char uname[30];
```

you can use `uname` in certain expressions, and QC uses `uname` as a shorthand for the memory address of element `uname[0]`. This means that the `lvalue` of `uname` is the same as the address of `uname[0]` (that is, `uname = &uname[0]`). Therefore, the statements

```
char uname[30], *ptr;
```

```
ptr = uname;
```

are perfectly legal C syntax because `uname` is a form of compiler shorthand for the `lvalue` of the starting element of the `uname[]` array (`&uname[0]`). Variable `ptr` now points to the start of the `uname[]` array.

Because you can use the name of an array to initialize a pointer, some programmers assume the sameness of pointers and arrays. If carried too far, you soon run into problems.

For example, if pointers and array names are the same, the statements

```
char *ptr, uname[30];
```

```
ptr = uname;
++ptr;
++uname;
```

should be processed without complaint. However, when QC gets to the last statement, it issues the error message

```
'++' needs lvalue
```

QC is saying that the increment operation on `uname` cannot be done because QC does not have a valid `lvalue` for `uname`. To understand the error message, think about what an `lvalue` is. It is the address of a variable's storage location in memory. Likewise, an `lvalue` is the only way QC can find a variable. If you try to increment an `lvalue`, QC cannot find the variable.

Tracking this kind of error is even more difficult because the QC error message is rather ambiguous to the beginner. Other compilers issue the error message `Cannot increment a constant lvalue`. This conveys the idea that the `lvalue` of a variable is a constant and should not be changed. This should cause you to look at the statement and realize that you have tried to increment the `lvalue` of `uname`.

Another variation of this mistake is:

```
uname = 'A';
```

If `uname` and `uname[0]` are identical, this statement should be legal, but it isn't. The nature of the mistake is the same. If you assume that the array is stored at memory address 50,000 and you know that an ASCII `'A'` is 65 decimal, the previous statement is attempting to change QC's shorthand label for the `lvalue` of `uname[0]` to memory address 65. Clearly, if QC allowed this, it would lose track of where the array is actually stored in memory.

The lesson here is that you cannot change the address where the compiler stores something. These addresses are "constant `lvalues`" that are etched in stone and cannot be incremented or decremented.

Careless Pointer Usage

Flushed with earlier pointer success, a programmer sets about using pointers with more regularity. Take a moment to study Listing 12-2 to see whether you can see the problem.

Listing 12-2. Overrunning the Pointer

```
int main()                      void func1(int s[])
{                               {

    int *ptr, n;
                                    int i = 0;
    ptr = &n;                       while (i < 10)
    func1(ptr);                         s[i++] = i;

}                               }
```

This can be a real nasty bug, because sometimes the code works and other times it might not. The programmer initializes `ptr` to point to `n` (that is, the `rvalue` of `ptr` is the `lvalue` of `n`). However, when `func1()` gets the `lvalue` held in `ptr`, the `int s[]` declaration in `func1()` says that it has the `lvalue` of an `array`. The function then stuffs the integers `0` through `9` into what it thinks is an array.

Only one problem: there is no array to stuff. Variable n in main() is a single integer, whereas func1() "thinks" it has an array of integers. What happens is that n gets the value 0 on the first pass through the while loop (that is, n = 0 = s[0]) because func1() has n's lvalue. However, on the second pass through the while, whatever is stored in memory after n now has an integer 1 stored there. Eight more integers continue to be stored after the second one, blowing away whatever was stored after variable n in memory.

What makes this bug especially difficult is that, if nothing is stored after n in memory, the program might appear to work. In fact, the following statements can be added to main():

```
for (n = 0; n < 10; n++, ++ptr)
    printf("%d ", *ptr);
```

and we may or may not see the expected output. This type of bug can lay dormant for years before anything goes wrong.

Define Versus Declare Again

Part of the reason that the last example usually blows up is because func1() declares that it has been passed an array (that is, func1() has the lvalue of an array of int's). Note what this means: func1() *assumes* that there is a definition of an integer array somewhere in the program that corresponds to the lvalue it just received.

It follows that a declaration refers to some previously defined quantity. Programmers often misuse functions because the function's arguments declare that specific data items should be used by the function, but the program has passed arguments that have different data definitions.

A Sample Debug Problem

Now see how you handle a simple debugging problem in light of the things that have been discussed in this chapter thus far. Examine the program shown in Listing 12-3.

Listing 12-3. A Debugging Problem

```
#include <stdio.h>
int main(void)
{
   char buff[20];
   int num, sq;

   printf("Enter a number: ");    /* Get the number to square * /
   num = atoi(gets(buff));
   sq = square(num);              /* Try to square it */
   printf("\nThe square of %d is %d", num, sq);
}
int square(int n)
{
   n = n * n;                     /* Do the square */
   return n;

}
```

If you type this program and try to compile it, QC complains:

```
fatal error C1004: unexpected end-of-file
```

and the line with the first `printf()` function call is highlighted. What's the problem?

This should be an easy error to find, because QC has detected a syntax error and has even highlighted the line. Several years ago I had a similar bug in a very complex piece of code, and I probably spent an hour trying to identify the bug. (It was a different compiler, but the error message was almost identical.)

I finally gave up, went to lunch, came back, and found the error within 10 seconds. Sometimes a break is one of the most productive debugging techniques.

So what's the error? If you look closely at the end of the comment in the line with the first `printf()` call, you see that there is a blank space between the comment character pair. The * / should actually be */. Because * / does not designate a close-of-comment character sequence, QC keeps reading the source code, looking for the close-of-comment. Eventually, QC reads the entire file without detecting the close-of-comment characters. At this point, QC has no choice but to give up and issue an error message. The `unexpected end-of-file` message tells you that QC ran out of source code. Any time you see this message, you should check to see whether there is an "unclosed" comment.

Using the QC Debugger

Some bugs are sufficiently well hidden that simple inspection of the source code still leaves you scratching your head. The program compiles, and no compile, link, or runtime error messages are given. Everything seems to work, but the results of the program are not what you expected. It is time to call out the Big Gun: the QC Debugger.

Note that you can use the Debugger only when the program has been compiled successfully into an executable (`.exe`) program. In order for the Debugger to do its job, certain overhead files (for example, `*.sym`, `*.ilk`, and `*.mdt`) must be generated. These Debugger support files are generated automatically during compilation if the Debug flag is on. If the Debug flag is turned off (that is, released), compilation is somewhat faster and less disk space is used. The first step, then, is to make sure that the Debug flag is set.

Turning On the Debugger Support Files

From the main QC menu, select the Options menu item and then select the Make feature from the options submenu (Alt-O-M). The screen will look similar to the one shown in Figure 12-4.

If the Debug flag is not set, the cursor will be sitting in the Release field. This indicates that the Debug flag is not on and the Debugger support files are not being written. Press the left arrow key to set the Debug flag on and press Enter to return to the source window. If the Debug flag is on, simply press the Escape key. Now you are certain that the necessary Debugger files will be written when the program is compiled.

The program used here has a deceptively simple bug in it, but it nonetheless illustrates how the Debugger is used. The sample program appears in Listing 12-4.

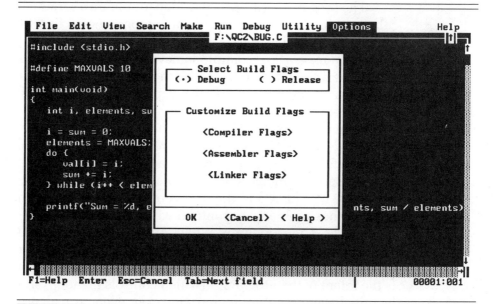

Figure 12-4. Setting the Debug Flag

Listing 12-4. A Debugging Program Example

```
#include <stdio.h>

#define MAXVALS 10

int main(void)
{
   int i, elements, sum, val[MAXVALS];

   i = sum = 0;
   elements = MAXVALS;
   do {
      val[i] = i;
      sum += i;
   } while (i++ < elements);
   printf("Sum = %d, elements = %d, mean = %d",
          sum,         elements,         sum / elements);
}
```

The program uses a `do-while` loop to sum up a series of numbers and calculate the `mean`. When you run this program, you find that the sum is 20, the number of elements is 10, and the mean is 2. That is one of the things that makes this example somewhat interesting: The answer agrees with what is shown on the screen. If the numbers were more complex, this could be a serious bug because the display output suggests that the results are correct.

Actually, the sum of the digits from 1 to 10 is 55 and the mean is 27.5. This suggests the first error. It is probably better to use floating point numbers for `sum`, and display `mean` as a `double`. If the data is other than the sum of a series of integers, you also want `val[]` to be `doubles`. These things should be considered in the design of the algorithm, but now there are more serious problems to contend with.

The next questions are "What is the intent of the sum? Is it to sum the digits 0 through ten or 1 through 10?" Again, this is an algorithm decision, but the intent here was to present the sum of the digits 1 through 10. If that is the intent of the program, `i` (which controls the loop) should probably be initialized to 1 rather than 0. However, even with algorithm changes, the program does not produce the correct answers for `sum` and `mean`. Obviously, there is still something wrong with the program.

Using the Locals Window of the Debugger

Assume that the bug remains hidden after close inspection of the source code. A good starting point for almost any debug problem is to activate the *Locals Window* of the Debugger. The Locals Window is controlled by the Debugger and displays all the local variables that are in scope as the program executes.

To activate the Locals Window, select the View option from the main QC menu and then select the Windows options from the submenu (Alt-V-W). Your screen should look similar to Figure 12-5.

Press the L key to highlight the Locals options and then press the Enter key. A small window appears near the top of the display screen. Before the program is run, the Locals Window is empty. However, as different local variables come into scope (for example, you enter a function), the variables with local scope appear in the Locals Window near the top of the screen.

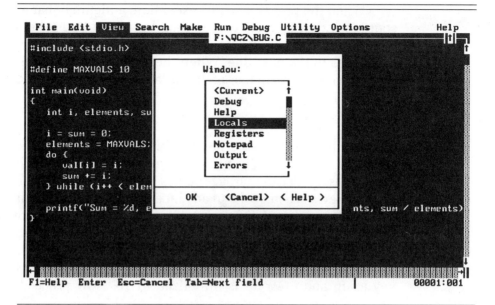

```
 File  Edit  View  Search  Make  Run  Debug  Utility  Options        Help
                            F:\QC2\BUG.C
#include <stdio.h>

#define MAXVALS 10              Window:

int main(void)
{                                <Current>
    int i, elements, su          Debug
                                 Help
    i = sum = 0;                 Locals
    elements = MAXVALS;          Registers
    do {                         Notepad
        val[i] = i;              Output
        sum += i;                Errors
    } while (i++ < elem

                             OK     <Cancel>  < Help >
    printf("Sum = %d, e                                  nts, sum / elements)
}

 F1=Help  Enter  Esc=Cancel  Tab=Next field                    00001:001
```

Figure 12-5. The View-Window Menu Options

If you have not compiled the program shown in Listing 12-4, you should do so now. When QC finishes, the necessary debug files are available so that you can use the Debugger to shed some light on the problem.

Single-Step: The F10 Key

When debugging a program, it is helpful to be able to slow the program down so that you can examine it more closely as it executes. This is the purpose of the *single-step* function of the Debugger. To begin single-stepping the program, press the F10 key. QC loads the program and begins executing it one line at a time.

Note that the single-step process is limited to a one-line step. Although some C programmers code with multiple statements on a line, this is not a good practice when you want to use a debugger. If a line contains multiple program statements (or other expressions), you cannot evaluate each statement in isolation. In some instances, multiple statements per line can reduce the effectiveness of the debugger.

When the program begins execution, a highlight bar appears in the source window so that you can monitor which line is being evaluated. Note that the highlighted line does not evaluated until *after* the highlight bar moves to the next line. When the highlight bar first moves into the main() function, the names of the variables appear in the Locals Window, but each has

```
<unknown identifier>
```

written after the variable name. This suggests that QC knows which variables are in scope, but has not yet evaluated the data definitions in main(). Also notice the garbage values for each of the variables. Now press the F10 key a second time to advance to the next statement.

After the data definition statements are evaluated, notice how the val[] array is shown in the Locals Window. All ten elements of the array are shown (even though they are junk at this point in the program). Press the F10 again and the initialized values for i and sum are set. Press the F10 key again and elements is initialized to 10. Now proceed to enter the do-while loop.

Notice that the highlight bar does not stop on the line with the do keyword. Instead, the highlight bar advances to the assignment of i into the val[] array. This is because there is nothing to evaluate with respect to the do keyword. In fact, each iteration of the loop ignores the line with the do keyword. (This also suggests that there is no code generated for the do keyword. The keyword is simply used as a marker for the start of the loop.) Also notice that the first element of the val[] array has the proper value written into it.

Another press of the F10 key causes i to be added to sum. One more press advances the highlight bar to the while part of the do-while loop and the evaluation of the test between i and elements. If you watch the Locals Window, you see that i is incremented as part of the relational test against elements.

Press the F10 key again, and the highlight bar jumps back up to the assignment of i into val[]. Figure 12-6 shows how the Locals Window looks after several iterations through the loop.

Moving to the Locals Window

If you have more than three local variables in scope at one time, some of the variables will not be visible in the Locals Window. Press the F6 key to move the cursor to the Locals Window. Now use the arrow keys to scroll

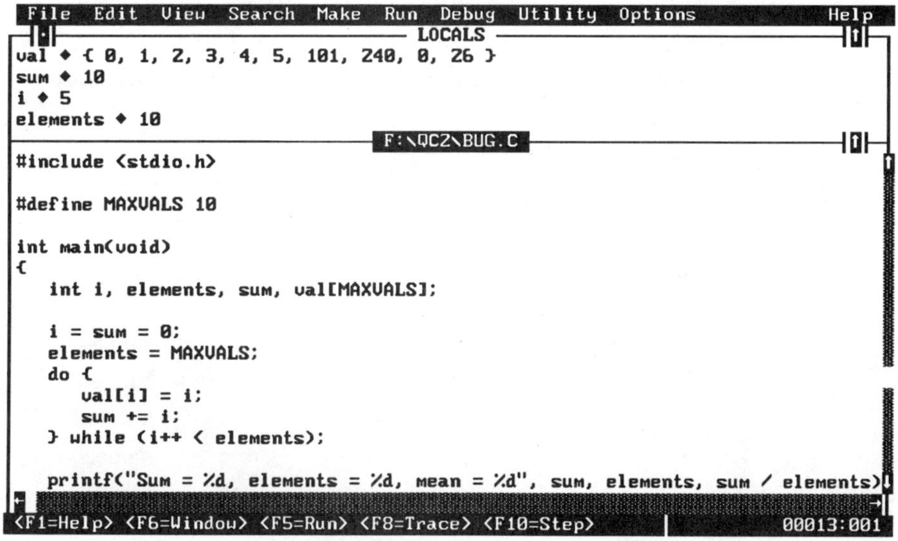

```
 File  Edit  View  Search  Make  Run  Debug  Utility  Options         Help
┤╫├─────────────────────── LOCALS ───────────────────────────────┤╫├
val ◆ { 0, 1, 2, 3, 4, 5, 101, 240, 0, 26 }
sum ◆ 10
i ◆ 5
elements ◆ 10
                         ┤ F:\QC2\BUG.C ├─────────────────────────┤□├
#include <stdio.h>

#define MAXVALS 10

int main(void)
{
    int i, elements, sum, val[MAXVALS];

    i = sum = 0;
    elements = MAXVALS;
    do {
        val[i] = i;
        sum += i;
    } while (i++ < elements);

    printf("Sum = %d, elements = %d, mean = %d", sum, elements, sum / elements)
 <F1=Help> <F6=Window> <F5=Run> <F8=Trace> <F10=Step>          00013:001
```

Figure 12-6. The QC Screen After Several Loop Iterations

the window up and down until the variable you are interested in is visible. A second F6 press moves the cursor back to the edit window.

By the way, you can change how the variables in the Locals Window are displayed. For example, I was using the Debugger on a program that was working with several `char` variables. In some cases, the value of these variables were nonprinting characters, which made it difficult to determine their values. I pressed the F6 key to move to the Locals Window and scrolled the window for the variable I was interested in. I then changed the variable from a simple `char`, such as

```
c
```

to

```
c,x
```

which causes variable `c` to be displayed as a hexadecimal value. Table 12-1 lists the conversion characters that can be used.

*Table 12-1. Conversion Characters for Alternate Display
in Debug Windows*

Character	Effect	Example
d or i	signed decimal	c,d or c,i
u	unsigned decimal	j,u
o	octal value	j,o
x	hexadecimal value	j,x
f	floating point (f.p.)	sum,f
e	scientific notation f.p.	sum,e
g	shortest of e or f	sum,g
c	signed char	letter,c
s	string	name,s
z	structure names	record,z

By default, the variables shown in the Locals Window are displayed using the conversion character normally associated with the variable's data type. That is, an integer variable automatically uses the d conversion in Table 12-1 without having to write it into the window. (Note that these conversion characters can be used in all of the View and Debugger windows, not just the Locals Window.)

Although not mentioned in the documentation, you also can use a cast to force the output to another data type. For example, the integer cast of a character variable named c:

```
(int) c
```

has the same effect on the display output as

```
c,d
```

You must obey the proper syntax rules for casts, but casts can come in handy on occasion.

Using the Watch Window

As you single-step the program, pay close attention to the values of the variables shown in the Locals window. It appears that sum is being reset towards the end of the do-while loop. Concentrate on the values of the variables as they march through the loop. Although you could continue to do this with the Locals Window, use the Watch Value window just to see how it works.

First, if you are currently in the Edit window, select the Debug option from the main QC menu and then select the Watch Value option from the submenu (Atl-D-W). After you enter these keystrokes, you see the input field for the Watch Value option as shown in Figure 12-7.

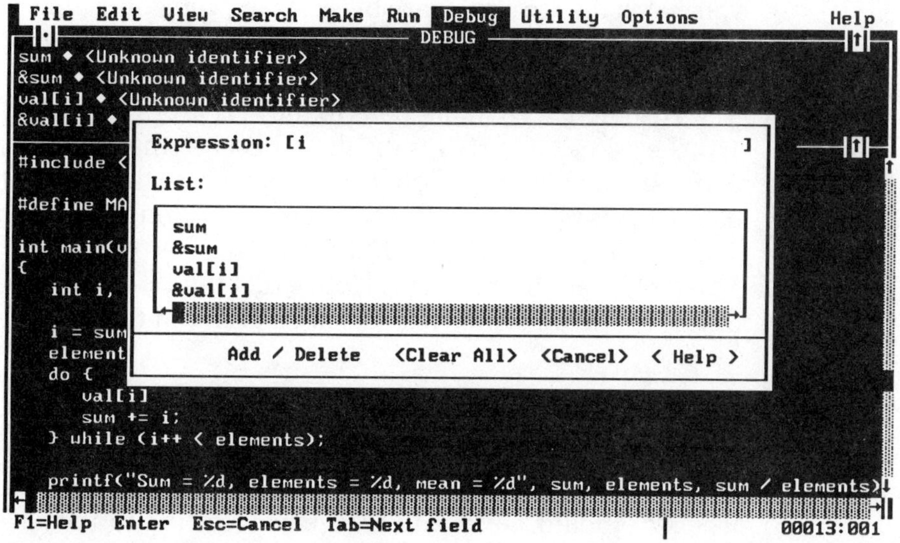

```
 File   Edit   View   Search   Make   Run   Debug   Utility   Options          Help
─╫·╫─────────────────────────── DEBUG ────────────────────────────────────╫t╫─
sum ♦ <Unknown identifier>
&sum ♦ <Unknown identifier>
val[i] ♦ <Unknown identifier>
&val[i] ♦
               ┌──────────────────────────────────────────────┐
#include <     │  Expression: [i                              ]│        ─╫□╫─
               │                                               │           ↑
#define MA     │  List:                                        │
               │  ┌──────────────────────────────────────────┐ │
int main(v     │  │ sum                                       │ │
{              │  │ &sum                                      │ │
    int i,     │  │ val[i]                                    │ │
               │  │ &val[i]                                   │ │
    i = sum    │  └▓▓▓▓▓▓▓▓▓▓▓▓▓▓▓▓▓▓▓▓▓▓▓▓▓▓▓▓▓▓▓▓▓▓▓▓▓▓▓▓▓▓┘ │
    element    │      Add / Delete   <Clear All>   <Cancel>   < Help > │
    do {       └──────────────────────────────────────────────┘
        val[i]
        sum += i;
    } while (i++ < elements);

    printf("Sum = %d, elements = %d, mean = %d", sum, elements, sum / elements)↓
▓▓▓▓▓▓▓▓▓▓▓▓▓▓▓▓▓▓▓▓▓▓▓▓▓▓▓▓▓▓▓▓▓▓▓▓▓▓▓▓▓▓▓▓▓▓▓▓▓▓▓▓▓▓▓▓▓▓▓▓▓▓▓▓▓▓▓▓▓▓▓▓▓▓╫
 F1=Help   Enter   Esc=Cancel   Tab=Next field          |        00013:001
```

Figure 12-7. Using the Watch Value Window

The input field is filled with the first word that was under the cursor in the Edit window. Because this often is not the variable name that you want to view in the Watch Value window, start typing the name of the variable to watch. After each entry is typed, press the Enter key, and the variable appears in the Watch Value window near the top of the display screen.

In this particular example, there seems to be a relationship between the sum and val variables and i. If you look closely at Figure 12-7, you notice that the following variables have been entered into the Watch Value window:

```
sum
&sum
val[i]
&val[i]
i
```

337

Why display the lvalues of the variables? Any time a variable seems to be changing mysteriously on its own, you should watch both its rvalue and its lvalue. After all, something has got to be changing it other than what is obvious in the source code. Also notice that the Debugger allows you to use the value of i as an index into the val[] array. This is a very useful feature not always found in inexpensive debuggers.

Now that the Watch Value window is loaded with the variables mentioned above, start single-stepping the program using the F10 key. If you watch the sum and i variables closely, you notice that sum is reset to 10 when i equals 10. (This occurs on the iteration of the loop just after sum equals 45.)

Also notice what happens to the lvalue of val[] when sum is reset to 10. The lvalue of val[0] is 0x0de6. (Because the program was compiled using the small memory model, you can ignore the segment address.) Just before sum is reset to 10, the lvalue of val[i] (on my machine) is 0x0de6. This can be seen in Figure 12-8.

Notice anything weird? Notice that the lvalue of sum and the lvalue of val[i] are the same. This means that the statement

```
val[i] = i;
```

is assigning the value of i into the same memory location occupied by sum! In other words, too many values are being written into val[], and the value in sum is being clobbered. Even though val[] was defined to hold 10 integers, i should never equal 10 when writing to the val[] array. Only elements val[0] through val[9] are valid indices for val[].

Why does sum have a higher memory address (lvalue) than val[0]? The reason is that QC allocates memory for variables with local scope starting at high memory and working toward low memory (that is, a stack mechanism). Therefore, even though sum appears in the data definition statement before val[], it actually occupies a higher memory address. The last valid memory location for the val[] array is 0x0de4 (that is, &val[9] = 0x0de4). Therefore, writing to val[10] at 0x0de6 is attempting to address the same memory location that QC allocated to sum. This can be seen in Figure 12-9.

You should be able to see that the reason you get the incorrect sum and mean is because you are writing past the end of the val[] array. One of the reasons that C is so powerful is that there are relatively few rules. In this case, because C does not do boundary checking on arrays, you simply overwrite the next data item in memory.

The fix is simple enough: change the do-while loop to a for loop that checks to see that i never exceeds 10 (i < MAXVALS). Ask yourself this question:

"If I change the postincrement on i to a preincrement, does this solve the problem?" Give it a try.

Figure 12-8. The Watch Value Window Just Before sum *is Reset*

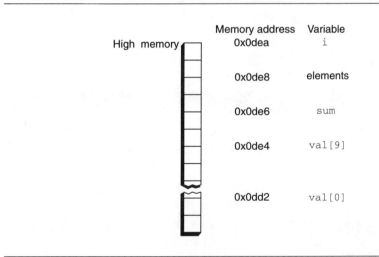

Figure 12-9. How QC Allocates Memory for the Local Variables in Listing 12-4

Other Debug Features

The QC Debugger has many other useful features that were not used in the debugging example already discussed. They are discussed briefly in this section. However, this section is more meaningful if you use QC, load a program source file, and try each of the options yourself. (The function finder program presented in Chapter 11 is sufficiently large to make the tests more interesting.) It is one thing to read about the features; it is quite another to see them in action.

Figure 12-10 shows the submenu that appears when the Debug option from the main menu (Alt-D) is activated.

Each of the options as they appear in Figure 12-10 is discussed in the following sections.

```
 File   Edit   View   Search   Make   Run   Debug   Utility   Options          Help
├■┤─────────────────────────── DEBUG: main ───────────────────────────────├■┤
sum ◆ 45
&sum ◆ 0x585b:0x0de6
val[i] ◆ 9
&val[i] ◆ 0x585b:0x0de4
i ◆ 9
                              ┤ F:\QC2\BUG.C ├                              ┤■├
#include <stdio.h>

#define MAXVALS 10

int main(void)
{
   int i, elements, sum, val[MAXVALS];

   i = sum = 0;
   elements = MAXVALS;
   do {
      val[i] = i;
      sum += i;
   } while (i++ < elements);

<F1=Help> <F6=Window> <F5=Run> <F8=Trace> <F10=Step>            │     00014:001
```

Figure 12-10. The Debug Submenu Options

Calls Command

The Calls command shows which functions have been called during program execution. For example, if you have single-stepped to a certain line in the program and want to know the series of functions that were executed to reach that point, you would use this command (Alt-D-C).

One nice feature of the Calls command is that you also can see the values of any arguments that were passed to the function. Too often, you get buried in the logic of a program and later find that you need to know the specific argument values that caused you to be where you are. Having the function argument values available can be very useful.

Breakpoint Command

A *breakpoint* is a line in a C source file where you want the program to halt execution. In most programs you write, it becomes very tiresome pressing the F10 key a hundred times to get to the section of code where you need to begin your debugging in earnest. Instead, you can set a breakpoint on the line where you would like to pause the program while you inspect different variables, expressions, or whatever.

To set a breakpoint, move the cursor to the line where you want to pause the program. Press the F9 key. The line under the cursor changes color (to red if you have a color monitor). Now press the F5 key to execute the program. The program executes at normal speed to the point where the breakpoint was set and then pauses the program. You can now use other debugger options and windows to examine the variables under consideration. To resume program execution, press the F5 key again.

To remove a breakpoint, move the cursor to the line with the breakpoint and press the F9 key a second time. The breakpoint is removed. (You can tell the breakpoint has been removed visually because the line returns to the normal text color.)

You also can remove a breakpoint by using the Breakpoint option of the Debug menu (Alt-D-B). A list of all the active breakpoints in the program appears in the List field of the dialog box. Each entry shows the name of the source file and the line number where a breakpoint has been set. To remove a breakpoint, press the Tab key to move to the List field in the dialog box. Then use the cursor keys to highlight the breakpoint that you want to remove. When the breakpoint is highlighted, press the Enter key and the breakpoint is removed.

Watchpoint and Quickwatch Commands

A *watchpoint* is not much different from a breakpoint, except that the program pauses only when some test condition is logically True. For example, in the sample debugging program, things seemed to progress normally until i reached the value of 9. Although you could set a breakpoint somewhere in the do-while loop, you still must press the F5 key eight times before arriving at the section of the loop you want. A better way is to use a watchpoint.

You can think of a watchpoint as a conditional breakpoint. To use the sample program, select the Watchpoint option of the Debug submenu (Alt-D-p) and type the expression

```
i > 8
```

and press the Enter key. Then press F5. The program runs at normal speed until i is greater than 8. At that moment, the program pauses and QC displays a dialog box telling you that the watchpoint has been reached. You now can use the other features of the Debugger to inspect the variables of interest. If you press F5 again, the program continues to execute, but stops at the watchpoint as long as i is greater than 8.

To remove a watchpoint, select the Watchpoint option (Alt-D-p), press the Tab key to move to the List field, and press the arrow keys to highlight the watchpoint to be removed. Press the Enter key and the highlighted watchpoint is removed.

A Quickwatch command allows you to modify the variables and expressions that are in the Watch window as the program runs. When you start a debug session, you have a preconceived notion of the variables and expressions that you want in the Watch window. However, as you see things unfold, you might want to investigate additional variables or expressions. If you press the Shift-F9 key combination, you can test these new expressions as the program executes.

Watch Value and Modify Value Commands

The Watch Value debug option was used earlier in the debugging example. The Watch Value command is similar to the watchpoint discussed earlier, except a Watch Value does *not* pause the program. To enter a Watch Value, select the Watch Value option from the Debug submenu (Alt-D-W) and enter the variable name or expression to be watched. (See

Figure 12-7.) The Watch variables and expressions in the Debug window are updated constantly as the program executes. (Figure 12-8 shows an example.)

The Modify Value command enables you to modify the contents of the Watch Value expressions while the program executes. This is useful when you notice some variable or expression that you want to modify as the program executes.

Note that when a logical expression is viewed, the logical result of the expression is displayed in the Debug window. For example, if you enter the expression

```
i == 9
```

and then single-step the program, you see

```
i == 9 : 0
```

until i does equal 9. That is, the expression is logical False. When i does equal 9, the result is displayed as

```
i == 9 : 1
```

saying that i does equal 9.

Debug History

It is not uncommon for a bug to show up only when a certain sequence of program statements is executed or certain input values are supplied by the user. Unless these special conditions are met, the bug does not show itself. The problem here is that you might not remember the special sequences that caused the bug to appear. In situations like this, the History option can be very useful. The History option records the commands given to the Debugger as well as any input supplied by a user as the program executes. Each of the debug commands stored in the history file is called a *history point*. The History option lets you record the Debugger history points at some later time.

To activate the Debug History option, select the History option from the Debug submenu (Alt-D-H). After the History option is activated, QC records the debug and user input information in two files that use the secondary file names of his and inp. Therefore, if you are running a program named test.c that requires user input, the history file is test.his and the user input data file is test.inp.

When the History option is active, a small dot appears in front of the History option on the Debug submenu. Also, if you are saving or replaying the history file, the letter D appears near the lower right corner of the screen. If user input is being saved or used, the letter I appears next to the D on the screen.

Special Debug History Keys — Shift-F8 and Shift-F10

When you record a debug history, you can use the Shift-F8 key to display the previous history point. This key sequence causes the display to back up to the previous history point. Obviously, you cannot do a Shift-F8 until after at least one history point is recorded. The Undo command on the Debug submenu is functionally the same as Shift-F8.

Whereas the Shift-F8 key combination moves the display backward one history point, you can use Shift-F10 to advance the display to the next history point. For example, if you are at some point in a history recording session and realize that you need to back up two history points, press the Shift-F8 key combination twice. Note that when you want to resume the debug session, two Shift-F10 presses advance you to the current point in the debug history being recorded. In other words, the Shift-F8 and Shift-F10 keys allow you to move backward and forward during a history recording session without saving these movements in the history file.

Replay a Debug History

You can replay a previously-recorded debug history by selecting the Replay option of the Debug submenu (Alt-D-R). Note that the History option also must be active to replay a debug history. If your recording session had no pauses in it (for example, a breakpoint or similar command), the history session is played back very quickly—perhaps too quickly to see what is happening. You can slow the replay down by selecting the Run/Debug option of the Options submenu. Advance the cursor to the Animate field and use the cursor keys to play the radio button in the Slow field. This enables you to follow the history more easily.

Truncate User Input

The last option of the Debug submenu allows you to alter the user input that is stored in the user input file (for example, test.inp). You can change all or part of the user input. To clear all the user input, select Shift-F5 or select the Truncate User Input option. You also can erase the user input file (for example, `test.inp`).

If you want to clear part of the user input file, use the Shift-F8 or Shift-F10 keys to move to the point where you want to clear the user input. Select the Replay option from the Debug submenu (Alt-D-R) to rerun the debug session to the history point where the new input is to begin. Then select the Truncate User Input option from the Debug submenu (Alt-D-T). All subsequent history points that involve user input are now cleared, but previous inputs are saved.

The Debugger history options are quite powerful and can help track down some of the hardest types of bugs to find (for example, the "sequence-input" sensitive types of bugs). In most debug sessions, you probably will not use the History option. If that is the case, make sure the debug History option is off. This saves you a little time and disk space because the history files do not have to be written. Also, you should clean off the *.his and *.inp files from time to time when you are finished with them.

Conclusion

The material presented in this chapter merely scratched the surface of the art and science of debugging a program. In some ways, debugging a program is an art form, and some individuals are incredibly skilled at it. The skill required to elevate debugging to an art form requires years of experience. Each debugging problem you solve adds to your knowledge base and makes you more skillful in the future.

However, debugging is also a science in that successful debugging benefits from a methodical approach to the problem. Robert Ward's book *Debugging C* shows how a methodical approach to a debugging problem makes the task much simpler than it would be otherwise.

The debugging tools provided with the QC compiler should help you quickly advance your debugging skills, especially relative to those programmers that do not have access to a debugger. Like any other tool, it takes time to become proficient with it, but once you do, debugging becomes a much more manageable task.

13

Unturned Stones and Tools

In this chapter, you will learn about

Additional preprocessor directives

Parametized macros

The Make utility

The QC librarian

Using assembler code with C

It is unfair to view the contents of this chapter as leftovers, because each topic has value in its own right. These topics were postponed until now for one of several reasons. First, some of the elements of C discussed in this chapter are not used frequently. Rather than clutter your first impression of the C landscape, these topics were deferred until you had a better grasp of the language. Another reason for delaying some concepts is that they do not fit in well with the primary thrust of any other chapter. Now that you are familiar with virtually all elements of the language, you can skip around a bit.

More Preprocessor Directives

Several preprocessor directives (for example, `#define` and `#include`) are discussed in earlier chapters. Some of the ones presented here build on directives already discussed.

#if

In Chapter 7, the #ifdef preprocessor directive was used to toggle the keyword extern into a program when working with multiple source files. #ifdef toggles between data declarations and definitions in the various source files. (The support files require the keyword extern, but the primary module with main() does not.) The #if directive is similar to the if keyword in operation, but can be used with global scope. That is, you cannot use the if keyword unless it appears within the body of a function. At times, however, you must have the control structure of an if outside a function body. Consider the following example.

```
#if SUPPORT == 2
    #include "support2.h"
#endif
```

This code fragment enables the support2.h header file to be read into the program only if the symbolic constant SUPPORT equals 2. The #if performs the test and takes appropriate action. In the example, if SUPPORT equals 2, the appropriate header file is #included.

The #if directive must (eventually) be followed by #endif. The purpose of the #endif is to tell the preprocessor which lines are controlled by the #if. The #endif is used with all of the #if-type constructs (for example, #ifdef, #ifndef, etc.).

The #if can control multiple source lines. For example:

```
#if DRIVES == 2
    #define DRIVEA   "a:"
    #define DRIVEB   "b:"
#endif
```

In this example, if DRIVES equals 2, the two symbolic constants for DRIVEA and DRIVEB are defined.

The ANSI standard has added a new flavor to the #if directive by allowing the following preprocessor directive:

```
#if !defined (TRUE)
    #define TRUE 1
#endif
```

Notice that this directive has the same effect as the #ifndef directive. You also can use the #if defined without the logical NOT operator. If the NOT operator is absent, the #if defined directive behaves the same as #ifdef. Therefore, you can also write the previous example as

```
#ifndef TRUE
    #define TRUE 1
#endif
```

Either form of the directive causes the same action to occur in the program. Because the meaning of the ANSI version is a little more obvious, the #ifdef and #ifndef will likely fade away and be replaced by the #if defined and #if !defined.

#elif

Suppose that your program is fairly complex and you want the preprocessor to control multiple #include files. For example, assume that each source file requires a special header file. Rather than write multiple .#include statements in the header file, the #elif directive can simplify the code.

If there are four source modules and each module has its own header file (perhaps for prototypes and variables that are unique to that module), you might use something like:

```
#if SUPPORT == 1
    #include "support1.h"
#elif SUPPORT == 2
    #include "support2.h"
#elif SUPPORT == 3
    #include "support3.h"
#elif SUPPORT == 4
    #include "support4.h"
#endif
```

The #elif is the preprocessor equivalent of the if-else construct. How do you use the example? Assume that the *previous* #elif sequence is in a header file named prog.h. At the top of source module 1, you write

```
#define SUPPORT
#include "PROG.H"
/* The rest of the source code for module 1 */
```

In source module 2, you write:

```
#define SUPPORT 2
#include "PROG.H"
/* The rest of the source code for module 2 */
```

and so on for all the source files. This causes the required support header files to be read by the preprocessor into the source file. Although you can use an #if to include the appropriate file, the #elif simplifies things a little.

#undef

The #undef directive enables you to undefine something that was previously #defined. A common use is when you are writing code for the debugging process, and you want to inspect the values in an array during a debug session. You might write:

```
#ifdef DEBUG
    for (i = 0; i < MAXVAL; i++) {
        printf("%d ", array[i]);
    }
#endif
```

You might have a number of these debug statements sprinkled throughout your program. Rather than remove the debug code, you can leave all of it in the program but only allow certain ones to be active. For example,

```
#define DEBUG
#ifdef DEBUG
    for (i = 0; i < MAXVAL; i++) {
        printf("%d ", array[i]);
    }
#endif
#undef DEBUG
```

causes this for loop to execute. The #undef at the end of the code fragment, however, "undefines" DEBUG so that any remaining debug code is not compiled into the program. The #undef has the effect of removing a definition from QC's symbol table, thus making that definition invisible to the remainder of the program.

Another use of the #undef is to undefine one instance of a symbolic constant so that a new version of the constant can replace it. For example, QC defines the symbolic constant NULL as

```
define NULL ((void *) 0)
```

However, if you write programs for Microsoft's Windows operating system, it expects NULL to be defined

```
define NULL 0
```

You can solve this problem with the following preprocessor directives:

```
#if defined WINDOWS
    #undef NULL
    #define NULL 0
#endif
```

This enables you to control which definition of NULL is used in a program, depending on whether WINDOWS is defined.

Parametized Macros

With a parametized macro, you can define a sequence of replacement text with arguments. Suppose that you want to write a function to calculate the reciprocal of a number. Consider the code presented in Listing 11.1.

Listing 13.1. reciprocal() *Macro*

```
#include <stdio.h>

#define reciprocal(x) ( (double) (1.0 / (x)))


int main(void)
{
    printf("The reciprocal of 5 is %g\n", reciprocal(5));
    printf("The reciprocal of .5 is %g\n", reciprocal(.5));
}
```

Notice that a macro called reciprocal() is #defined with an argument x. Immediately after the name of the macro (reciprocal()), the contents of the macro is defined. In this example, the value of x is divided into 1.0, and the result is cast as a double. When the preprocessor sees the first printf() in the program, it looks in its macro symbol table to see whether reciprocal() is already defined. Because it is defined, the preprocessor *substitutes* the text of the reciprocal() macro for the macro name in the printf() statement. After the preprocessor finishes the statement, it is as though the source code was typed as:

```
printf("The reciprocal of 5 is %g\n", ( (double) (1.0 / (x))));
```

The answer displayed when the line is executed is .2.

Why Are All the Parentheses in Macros?

The reason for the parentheses in macro definitions is to prevent side effects that can really cause problems. For example, suppose that reciprocal() is defined as

```
#define reciprocal(x)   (double) 1.0 / x
```

Now you perform the assignment:

```
y = reciprocal(y);
```

If y equals 3, after the preprocessor pass you have

```
y = reciprocal((double) 1.0 / 3);
```

which works out fine. Glowing with success, you place it in a header file and tell your colleagues a reciprocal() macro is available now. A colleague uses it in

```
y = reciprocal(y + 1);
```

Still assuming that y equals 3, the statement now reads

```
y = reciprocal((double) 1.0 / 3 + 1);
```

Rather than the correct answer of .25, you get the answer of 1.33. The parentheses assure us that the two operands in the argument are added first, and then its reciprocal is calculated.

Why Are Macros Different from Functions?

The most important distinction between macros and functions is that a macro is a *textual substitution* that takes place in the source code. In the example above, if your program invokes the reciprocal() macro 100 times in a program, the code to perform the reciprocal is repeated 100 times.

When you call a function, its code appears only once in the program. Therefore, macros tend to increase code size if the macro is invoked more than once.

On the other hand, because a macro substitution takes place, function overhead is associated with a macro. In other words, you don't have to make a copy of the argument, push it on the stack, place the result back on the stack, and then pop it off the stack when you are done. All that overhead costs time. As a result, macros are a bit faster than functions because they avoid the overhead of a function call. As always, a programmer is faced with the choice between speed and code size when choosing between macros and functions.

There is, however, another issue to consider in the choice between macros and functions. Macros are data inspecific but functions are not. If you write a function, you must state in the function definition the type of data that is being passed to the function. Therefore, you must write one reciprocal function for each data type that must calculate a reciprocal.

Macros don't "care" what the argument data type is—one macro serves all! Therefore, macros are especially attractive when you must perform the same operation on several different types of data. Macros can actually save you code space by avoiding duplicate functions.

The original ANSI draft proposal stated that there should be an underlying function for every macro whenever possible. (The `assert()` macro cannot be written as a function.) Therefore, you should be able to #undef virtually any macro and let the linker pull in the code from the function libraries. For example, in Chapter 10 ("Working with Disk Files"), the function called `fileno()` was used to convert the FILE pointer associated with `stdout` to a file descriptor for use with the `write()` function. In reality, `fileno()` is a parametized macro in the `stdio.h` header file; not a function from the standard library. Therefore,

```
#include <stdio.h>

#undef fileno

/* some code */

    fd = fileno(stdout);
```

should cause the linker to pull the code from a library (`.lib`) file because the macro for `fileno()` that appears in `stdio.h` has been #undef'ed. Unfortunately, QC does not have `fileno()` defined in the standard libraries; it is implemented only as a macro. You could, of course, write your own replacement for `fileno()` using the method illustrated in Chapter 10.

It is worthwhile for you to view the `stdio.h` header file at this time and browse through the macros that are defined in that file. (Use the Alt-V-I sequence to view a header file. QC accepts path names for the include files.) If you are feeling confident, try writing replacement functions for the macros. Write a program to test the macros, and then `#undef` them and see whether your functions provide the same results.

The *#line* Directive

The `#line` directive usually is used in conjunction with some form of debugging. The format for the `#line` directive is

```
#line line_number "filename"
```

where `line_number` is the starting line number used to reference the file, and `filename` is the name of the source file. Listing 13-2 shows how `#line` is used.

Listing 13-2. Using the #line Directive

```
/*
     Testing #line
*/

#include <stdio.h>

#line 100 "module.c"

int main(void)
{
   int i

   printf("i = %d", i);
}
```

When I tested this file, I named it `line.c`. Notice that I omitted the semicolon after the definition of `i`. The `#line` directive states that I want the line where this `#line` occurs to be referenced as line 100. Further, I want this file to be known as `module.c`. The error message issued by QC was

```
module.c(105):error C2061: syntax error: identifier 'printf'
```

The #line directive caused QC to find the error at line 105 in module.c even though the file is actually named line.c and clearly does not contain 105 lines of source code.

This scheme is useful in files where you are editing at lower line numbers. Suppose that you delete line 5 in a source file, but your list of error messages was generated before you deleted the line. All the line numbers for the error messages are now off by 1. The #line directive lets you "force" the line number to a specific value. By setting the line number with #line, all subsequent error messages are relative to this (constant) line number. Normally the file name is the same name as the source file. However, if output is being redirected (such as to a disk file rather than to the screen), you might want to use a different name. For example, line.c might have the errors directed to a file named line.ers.

Predefined Preprocessor Identifiers

ANSI has defined five preprocessor identifiers that can be used in your programs. Listing 13-3 illustrates each of these.

Listing 13-3. Predefined Preprocessor Identifiers

```
/*
    Test of preprocessor ids
*/

#include <stdio.h>

int main(void)
{
    printf("\ntime = %s", __TIME__);
    printf("\ndate = %s", __DATE__);
    printf("\nfile = %s", __FILE__);
    printf("\nline = %d", __LINE__);
    printf("\nstdc = %d", __STDC__);
}
```

All of the identifiers begin and end with a double underscore to avoid collision with other variables that you might use in your programs. The purpose of each identifier is fairly clear from its name. __TIME__ and __DATE__ provide the current time and date as kept by the system clock. __FILE__ holds the name of the current source file. Note that the first three identifiers are string variables. __LINE__ is the line in the source where the identifier is used and is an integer variable.

__STDC__ stands for "Standard C" and is an integer value that can assume one of two values. If the compiler used to compile the source code is an ANSI conforming compiler, __STDC__ returns a value of 1. If the compiler does not meet all the ANSI requirements, the value returned is 0. The QC compiler returns a value of 0 for __STDC__.

Perhaps the reason you do not often see these variables used is because programmers forget about them. Keep them in mind: they might offer an easy solution to some common programming tasks.

#pragma

The #pragma directive was created by ANSI to allow C compiler vendors to add useful features to their compilers that are not part of the ANSI standard. For example, some vendors use #pragma's to allow a programmer greater control over the code and data segments. Such control has little meaning for CPUs that do not use a segmented architecture like the 80x86 family.

There are four #pragmas supported by QC, as shown in Table 13-1.

Table 13-1. #pragmas Defined for QC

#pragma	Descriptions
#pragma check_stack(on)	Check to see whether enough storage is in the stack for args
#pragma check_pointer(on)	Check NULL pointers
#pragma message ("hello")	Show this message on-screen during compilation
#pragma pack(1)	Byte packing for structures (arg may be 1, 2, or 4)

In Table 13-1, you can substitute the word *off* where you see the word *on* as an argument to disable the features of the #pragma. It appears that some pragmas found in earlier releases of QC are not available in Release 2.5.

Building Your Own Libraries with LIB

As you develop more C programs, you also develop a core of functions that you can reuse in other programs. These reusable functions belong in your personal function library. For example, assume that you have five functions which your programs always seem to require. For simplicity, call them f1.c through f5.c. When you compile these functions, QC produces an intermediate file called an *object file* (.obj) that is used by the linker. If you use the Make facility of QC, the project list compiles f1.c through f5.c into f1.obj through f5.obj. The linker then combines these function modules into the final (.exe) program.

A librarian is a program that gathers all these intermediate object (.obj) files into one convenient place. This "one convenient place" is called a function library. A function library used with the QC linker has a secondary file name of .lib (for example, myfuncs.lib). You can use the QC librarian to create a library and modify (that is, add, delete, and replace) functions in the library file.

The advantage of creating a library is that you do not have to name explicitly each function using the MAKE facility. You simply tell QC to search the new library for any missing (unresolved) functions.

Creating a Library

Now let's create a library from the five functions mentioned earlier. Compile the five functions so that you have five .obj files. The Library Manager (LM from now on) is stored in the file named lib.exe. The LM is run from the MS-DOS command line rather than from within the QC compiler. Log onto the directory that contains the compiled functions and type

```
lib mylib +f1 +f2 +f3 +f4 +f5
```

The LM creates a library named mylib.lib from the object files (f1.obj, f2.obj, etc.). This library now contains the five new functions. If LIB cannot find a file named mylib.lib, it creates a new file with that name. Because this is the first time you have tried to create a library, LIB creates a new library.

As you might guess, the plus sign (+) before a function module name indicates that the module is to be added to the library. The other command symbols for LIB are shown in Table 13-2.

Table 13-2. LIB Command Symbols

Command Symbol	Descriptions
+	Add a module to the library
–	Delete a module from the library
–+	Delete the module from the library and add the new version of the module
*	Copy a module from the library into an `.obj` file with the same name
––*	Copy a module from the library and then delete it

Granularity of the Library

Notice that I refer to the arguments on the LIB command line as *modules* rather than functions. This is because `f1.c` can contain more than a single function. If that is so, why not just pull `f1.c` through `f5.c` into one big file (such as, `f1-5.c`), compile it, and put it into the library? It certainly simplifies the LIB command.

Shortcutting now often makes you pay the price later. Figure 13-1 has a simplified view of what a library file contains. To make the example easier to understand, assume that each module would compile to a 3K OBJ file, or 15K total.

If the five functions are combined and placed in the library, you might have something similar to that shown in Figure 13-1. At the start of the file `mylib.lib` is a table that gives the linker the information it must have to find the code it requires from the library. Figure 13-1 shows that the module named `f1-5` starts 3,233 bytes from the beginning of the file and is 15,000 bytes long. The information table at the beginning of the file resembles the table of contents in a book. Figure 13-1 displays the chapter headings, and within the chapter heading named `f1-5` are the subchapter titles. In this case, these are the function names found in `f1.c` through `f5.c`.

Now suppose that your program uses only one function (for example, f3) from the `f1-5` module. The QC linker (LINK) has no choice but to yank the entire `f1-5` module from the library and shove it into your program. Even though your program only needed 3,000 bytes of code, LINK was forced to extract all 15,000 bytes and place it into your program. This is an example of not creating a "granular" library.

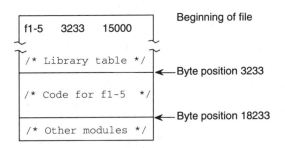

Figure 13-1. File Picture of a *.LIB Library File

The *granularity* of a library refers to the degree to which you break down each module into its smallest possible parts. Most programmers prefer to have one function for each module added to a library. This approach ensures that only the code you requested to be linked into the program ends up in the program. This is one reason why different compilers can yield such widely divergent .exe file sizes.

Granularity and File Size

Depending on which compiler is used, different program files can be significantly different sizes. Consider the following two programs:

```
int main(void)                    int main(void)
{                                 {
    puts("Hello");                }
}
```

The program shown on the left simply prints the word "Hello" on the screen, whereas the program shown on the right does absolutely nothing. The second example provides some indication of the "start-up" code used by the compiler. For the QC compiler, this "empty" program generates a 13,594-byte .exe file. Another compiler generates a 1778-byte file for this same program. However, in the version that calls the `puts()` function, the QC-compiled program file does not change in size, but the other compiler generates a 3004-byte program file.

This little experiment suggests that the start-up code for the QC compiler includes a number of the commonly used functions from the standard library, whereas the other compiler does not. Usually, the larger

359

start-up code does not pose a problem. However, if you are writing code for, say, a programmable toaster, you want the code size as small as possible to keep costs down.

The point here is that when you are creating your own libraries, keep the library as granular as possible, so the code size doesn't bloat unnecessarily.

Other LIB Commands

Several additional command line options are available with LIB (see Chapter 6 of your QC *Toolkit* manual for full details), but four of the commands are worth repeating here.

Consistency Check

Whenever you create a new library, perform a consistency check of the library. This test ensures that the library is in a format that can be used correctly with the QC linker. To run a consistency check, simply type:

```
LIB MYFUNCS;
```

where MYFUNCS is the newly-created library. If the library checks out properly, LIB simply ends the program. If inconsistencies are found, LIB issues an error message. A consistency check is most useful when you have a third-party library that might not have been created with LIB. (LIB performs a consistency check of the OBJ modules before adding them to the library. Therefore, it is unlikely that you will find inconsistencies in a library built with LIB.)

Extended Dictionary Option

If you invoke LIB with the /NOE option, LIB does not generate an extended dictionary for the library. An extended dictionary enables the linker to search a library somewhat faster; however, the extended dictionary uses more memory. If you see the error message

```
Insufficient Memory
```

or

```
No more virtual memory
```

use the /NOE option.

Page Size

When LIB creates a library, each module in the library must start on a new *page*. A page must be an integer value that is a power of 2 within the range of 16 and 32,768. The default page size for a library is 16. Larger page sizes enable LIB to hold more modules in the library. However, because each new module must start on a new page, large page sizes result in wasted space. Some early linkers had a default page size of 512 bytes. Therefore, if one OBJ file was only 50 bytes long, 462 bytes of the page were "empty" because there can be only one module per page.

Because few libraries benefit from large page sizes, you should use the default page size when building a new library. If you use a third-party library (especially one that was created under MS-DOS 2.0), you might save some disk space by extracting the modules and recreating the library with a smaller page size.

Cross-Reference Listing File

If you want to re-create a library, you must have a list of the public symbols and modules that make up the library file. For example, to create a cross-referencing listing of the contents of the `slibce.lib` file, you use the following command line:

```
LIB SLIBCE, LIBLIST.LST;
```

The result is an alphabetized listing of all the public symbols in the library followed by a list of the modules in the library. The module listing also provides information about the size of each module and its offset in the file. (The output listing file is over 120K!)

The Missing Library Option

By the way, the next time you are at a cocktail party talking with Bill Gates, ask him whether he would add wild cards to LIB. That is, the command

```
LIB MYLIB +.OBJ
```

would add all OBJ files in the current directory to the library. Even inexpensive librarians have this feature, and it saves a great deal of typing.

Using Your Library with LINK

Suppose you have compiled a program named `test` that draws functions from a library you created. The `link` command at the MS-DOS prompt is

```
LINK TEST MYLIB.LIB
```

The end result is a program named `test.exe` which extracts the necessary code from `mylib.lib`.

Inline Assembler Code in C Programs

QC's code generation is pretty good, and most application programs never require any assembler code. Still, there are times when a program develops "hot spots" that might benefit from the speed increase provided by assembler code. The old adage that "90 percent of a program's time is spent in 10 percent of the code" rings true in many situations. Obviously, identifying a program's hot spots is one of the first steps in deciding if it is worthwhile using assembler in a function.

What Is a Program Profile?

Profilers are programming tools used to determine how much time is spent in each part of a program. Even though QC does not provide a profiler, you get a pretty good idea of where most of a program's time is spent by placing calls to `clock()` before and after each function call you want to time. Listing 13-4 presents an example.

Listing 13-4. Crude Timing of Function Calls

```
/*
     One way to measure function execution times
*/

#include <time.h>
#include <stdio.h>
#include <limits.h>
```

```
void func1(void), func2(void), cprofile(time_t, time_t, char *);

int main(void)
{
   time_t start, end;
   long t1, t2, t3, t4;

   start = clock();                    /* Start measuring time */
   func1();
   end = clock();                      /* End measuring time   */
   cprofile(start, end, "func1()");    /* Show the results     */

   start = clock();
   func2();
   end = clock();
   cprofile(start, end, "func2()");

}

void func1(void)               /* Several dummy functions */
{
   unsigned int i;

   for (i = 0; i < UINT_MAX; i++)     /* #define's in limits.h */
      ;
}

void func2(void)
{
   unsigned long int i;

   for (i = 0; i < UINT_MAX; i++)
      ;

}

/*****

   A cheap profile function that gives the amount of time spent
   in a function. The two variables are return values from earlier
   calls to clock().
   Argument list:  time_t start        start time
                   time_t end          end    "
                   char *fn            timed function name
```

Listing 13–4 continues

Listing 13–4 continued

```
    Return value:    void

*****/

void cprofile(time_t start, time_t end, char *fn)
{
    printf("\nTime in %s: %4.2f",
                fn, (double) (end - start) / CLK_TCK );
}
```

This program calls the `clock()` function prior to entering a function and then calls `clock()` a second time after returning from the function. The `cprofile()` function (that is, cheap profiler) simply reports the time difference along with the function name. The symbolic constant CLK_TCK is defined in the `time.h` header file, whereas UINT_MAX is defined in `limits.h`.

Notice that `func2()` uses a `long` data type versus the `unsigned int` in `func1()`. Both functions perform the same number of iterations through the loop. As you might expect, twice as much time is spent in `func2()` because processing a `long` requires shuffling twice as much data as an `int`. You might try the same experiment using `float` and `double` data types to see whether the results are as expected. (Hint: Remember what was said about floating point operations being done in double-precision arithmetic, even if you use the `float` data type.)

This program can be embellished considerably if you choose. For example, you can call `clock()` at the start of the program (`prog_start`) and call it again at the end (`prog_end`); thus recording total elapsed time for the program. Having done this, you can allocate an array and store each function's time. At the end of the program you can report what fraction of total execution time was spent in each function.

Finally, it is useful to write a program "filter" that reads the C source file and automatically inserts the prefunction and postfunction calls to `clock()`, plus adds the necessary calls to `cprofile()`. Although this still is not as elegant as a commercial profiler, it provides useful timing information to help identify program hot spots.

Using Inline Assembler with QC

Assume that you have identified (by whatever means) a function that would significantly improve program performance if it were written in assembler. How can you mix assembler and C in the same program? Easy!

QC has added the keyword _asm to signify that what follows is an assembler instruction. Listing 13-5 presents an assembler function for cursor addressing.

Listing 13-5. Cursor Addressing Using Inline Assembler

```
/*
        Cursor addressing function using inline assembler
*/

#include <stdio.h>

void cursor(char row, char col);


int main(void)
{
    cursor(10, 40);
    printf("Done!");
}


void cursor(char row, char col)
{
    row -= 1;            /* Assume 1,1 for upper left */
    col -= 1;

    _asm {
        mov ah, 2               ;Function number for setting cursor
        mov bh, 0               ;Video page number (assume 0 only)
        mov dh, byte ptr row    ;Assume 1,1 is upper left
        mov dl, byte ptr col
        int 0x10                ;Video interrupt
        }
}
```

You can use the _asm in either of two ways: before each assembler instruction, or before an opening brace that marks the start of a block of assembler instructions. If the block method is used, note that the block must end with a closing brace. The latter style is used in Listing 13-5. The first style requires the code to be written:

```
_asm mov ah, 2          ;Function number for setting cursor
_asm mov bh, 0          ;Video page number (assume 0 only)
_asm mov dh, byte ptr row
_asm mov dl, byte ptr col
_asm int 0x10                   ;Video interrupt
```

In most cases, the block form is easier to use. Also note that comments are preceded by a semicolon in an _asm block. Unlike the C comment form, there is no closing comment character. The newline character marks the end of the comment.

In the cursor() function, 1 is subtracted from the row-column positions so that the upper left corner of the screen is position 1,1 rather than the 0,0 that MS-DOS expects. The rest of the code simply draws on the services of video interrupt 0x10, function 0x02 to position the cursor on the screen.

A More Complex Example of Inline Assembler

The example shown in Listing 13-6 was written by Davie Reed of Software Masters. The function uses inline assembler to determine the type and speed of the host CPU at runtime. Listing 13-6 shows a more complex, yet useful, example of how to use inline assembler than does Listing 13-5.

Listing 13-6. Determining CPU Type and Speed with Inline Assembler

```
/*
    Find CPU type and speed.
*/

#include <stdio.h>

void getcpuspeed(double *cpuspeed),
    getcputype(int *cputype, char *cpuname),
    chiptype(int far *),
    chipspeed(int far *);
char *cpuid[] = {
```

```
_   "8088", "8086", "NEC v20", "NEC v30",
    "80188", "80186", "80386", "80286"};

int main(void)              /* Small test shell for CPU tests */
{
    char name[20];
    int cpu;
    double x;

    getcpuspeed(&x);
    printf("CPU Speed = %g Mhz\n", x);
    getcputype(&cpu, name);
    printf("CPU Name = %s\nCPU Index Number = %d\n", name, cpu);
}
```

```
/*****

                            getcpuspeed()

        Function to determine the approximate speed at which the CPU
chip is operating. The CPU speed is stated in Mhz.

    Argument list:  double *cpuspeed      pointer to cpu speed variable

    Return value:   void

*****/
```

```
void getcpuspeed(double *cpuspeed)
{
    char cpuname[20];
    double rx, r0, r1;
    unsigned int cpuhash;
    int cpu;
    getcputype(&cpu, cpuname);
    chipspeed(&cpuhash);
    r1 = cpuhash;
    switch (cpu) {
        case 2:              /* If NEC V20 or NEC V30 then divide by  */
        case 3:              /* factors that were empirically derived */
            r1 /= 283;
            break;
```

Listing 13–6 continues

Listing 13–6 continued

```
    case 6:              /* 80386 */
        r1 /= 452.5;
        break;
    case 7:              /* 80286 */
        r1 /= 404;
        break;
    default:             /* and the rest */
        r1 /= 260;
        break;
    }
    *cpuspeed = r1;
}
/*****
                                getcputype()
    Function to determine the type of CPU.

    Argument list:     int *cputype       index for cpu type
                       char cpuname       buffer for cpu name

    Return value:      void
*****/
void getcputype(int *cputype, char cpuname[])
{
    chiptype(cputype);
    strcpy(cpuname, cpuid[*cputype]);
}
/*****
                                chiptype()
    Function that executes a series of assembler instructions in an
attempt to decipher the CPU type.

    Argument list:     int far *cputype      to hold cpu index

    Return value:      void

*****/

void chiptype(int far *cputype)
{
_asm \
        {
```

```
        ;
        ; check the processor type!
        ;

                push    ds
                push    si              ;save stuff
                push    di
                jmp     dorealcode      ;jump around routines to main asm stuff
10cba:
        ;
        ; check for possible presence of 386
        ; could return cx<>0 because of segment prefix if not a 386
        ;
                mov     cx,0ffffh
                sti
                push    ax
                mov     cs:nop1,0f3h            ;fake a repz lodsb es:
                mov     cs:nop2,026h            ;kludge for making db's
                mov     cs:nop3,0ach
                push    si
nop1:           nop                             ;db 0f3h
nop2:           nop                             ;db 026h
nop3:           nop                             ;db 0ach
                pop     si
                pop     ax
                ret
10cc6:
        ;
        ; check for 8086 or 80186
        ;
        ; tests the processor's pre-fetch queue
        ;
                push    cs
                pop     ds
                push    cs
                pop     es
                std
                mov     di,offset 10cdd
                mov     al,byte ptr cs:10cdc
                cli
                mov     cx,3
                repz    stosb
                cld
```

Listing 13–6 continues

Listing 13–6 continued

```
            nop
            nop
            nop
            inc     cx
10cdc:  sti
10cdd:  sti
            mov     byte ptr ds:[di+1],41h
            ret

dorealcode:
lcpu:
            mov     bx,6
            push    sp
            pop     ax
            cmp     ax,sp
            jnz     10134
;
; 286 or 386
;
            pushf
            xor     ax,ax
            mov     ax,0f000h
            push    ax
            popf
            pushf
            pop     ax
            and     ax,0f000h
            jnz     1012a
            popf
            jmp     1014a
;
; 386
;
1012a:  popf
            mov     bx,66h
            jmp     1015x
;
; 8088 or nec chip
;
10134:  mov     bx,4
            mov     cl,21h
            mov     al,0ffh
            shl     al,cl
            jnz     1014a
```

```
        mov     bx,2
        call    10cba
        jcxz    1014a
        mov     bx,0
;
;
;
1014a:  call    10cc6
        jcxz    1015x
        or      bx,1
1015x:  cmp     bx,6
        jnz     1286
        mov     bx,7
;       jnz     1cpu
1286:   and     bx,07h
        sti
;
; bx=0 8088
; bx=1 8086
; bx=2 nec v20
; bx=3 nec v30
; bx=4 80188
; bx=5 80186
; bx=6 80386
; bx=7 80286
;
        lds     si,cputype          ;get address of cputype
        mov     ds:[si],bx          ;store answer
        pop     di
        pop     si
        pop     ds
    }
}
```

/*****

chipspeed()

This function attempts to measure the chipspeed of the CPU by executing a known set of instructions. While not absolutely accurate, it is close enough that you can figure timing loops using the value calculated by this routine.

Listing 13–6 continues

Listing 13–6 continued

```
    Argument list:    int far *speed    pointer to the speed constant

    Return value:    void

*****/

void chipspeed(int far *speed)
{
_asm \
        {
        push    ds
        sti
        mov     ax,40h
        mov     ds,ax
        mov     bx,ds:[6ch]
cslp1:
        cmp     bx,ds:[6ch]
        jz      cslp1
        add     bx,1+18*2
;
; loop for speed counter
;
        mov     ax,0
        mov     dx,0
cslp2:
        nop
        nop
        nop
        nop
        nop
        nop
        nop
        nop
        nop
        nop
        nop
        nop
        nop
        nop
        nop
        nop
        nop
        nop
```

```
        nop
        nop
        inc     ax
        jnz     cs3
        inc     dx
cs3:
        cmp     bx,ds:[6ch]
        jae     cslp2
        mov     bx,50
        div     bx
        lds     si,speed            ;load address of far(speed)
        mov     ds:[si],ax
        pop     ds
    }
}
```

Some "work-arounds" are present in the code. Some of them exist because QC does not allow data to be defined within an _asm block. That is, DB, DW, DD, DQ, DT, and DF directives are not permitted. It also appears that some specialized assembler instructions are not supported by QC. (Note the work-around to fake a `repz lodsb es` instruction.)

It takes approximately two seconds to run the test program on an AT-type machine. When the test is complete, the return value from `chiptype()` is used to index into the string array of chip types. The value returned from `chipspeed()` is a `double` and measures the approximate speed of the CPU. If you want to write delay loops without using the system clock, this code is one alternative.

Why Inline Assembler?

Assuming you understand why you might want to use a function written in assembler, why do it as a C function using inline assembler code? Why not just write the code in assembler and link it into the program?

If you have done any assembly language programming on the PC, you know that there is a lot of start-up code necessary to set things properly (for example, equates, data and segment definitions, etc.). By using inline assembler, QC takes care of all the details necessary to interface the assembler code with this program. QC makes using assembler code in a C program about as easy as it can get.

If you do decide to experiment with inline assembler, you should read all of Part 16 in the *C for Yourself* manual for guidelines and restrictions that may apply to your work.

Conclusion

There are other tools provided with the QC compiler. Throughout this text, the Integrated Environment was used to write, compile, and debug programs. However, you also can use the command-line version of the compiler (QCL) to accomplish the same tasks. The *Toolkit* manual supplied with QC devotes a 40-plus-page chapter to using the command-line version of the QC compiler. Most of that chapter is devoted to explaining how to use the many compiler options. During the learning phase of your C experience, you might not need to use any of the available options. As your experience grows, however, you might want to review Chapter 4 of the *Toolkit* manual to see whether these options can be useful in your program development.

14

Working with the Display Screen

In this chapter, you learn about

The extended character set

How to write directly to the display screen

How to write a pseudo-windowing system

Although the topics in this chapter are few, understanding these concepts and using them in your programs can add a touch of professionalism and significantly speed up programs that perform a great deal of screen I/O.

The IBM Extended Character Set

For the IBM family of PCs, a character (char) is defined as eight bits. This means that there are 256 binary bit patterns possible with an eight-bit data item (2 to the 8th power). The ASCII character set reserves the first 128 values for its own use. The eighth bit is not used in the ASCII character set.

For the PC, IBM created the *extended character set*, which includes the values 129 through 255. The extended character set is composed of symbols and graphic primitives. Some of the symbols are from other character sets (like the symbol for the British pound), some are Greek letters, and others have a double function (for example, the Greek letter sigma, which also is a standard math symbol). The remaining characters are a collection of lines, blocks, and other graphic primitives that can be used to build larger graphic representations.

Listing 14-1 presents a program that displays the extended character set.

Listing 14-1. Program to Display the Extended Character Set

```
#include <stdio.h>
#define LASTASCII 128
int main(void)
{
    int i, j;

for (i = 0; i < LASTASCII; i++) {
    if (i && i % 15 == 0) {                    /* Print 15 per line */
        printf("\n");
        for (j = i - 15; j < i; j++) {
            printf("%4d", j + LASTASCII);      /* Print number */
        }
        printf("\n");
        }
    printf("%4c", (char) i + LASTASCII);   /* Print char */
}
printf("\n");
for ( ; j < i; j++) {
    printf("%4d", j + LASTASCII);
}
printf("\n\n\n");
}
```

This program is controlled by a `for` loop that runs from 0 to `LAST_ASCII` (128). The `if` statement checks to see whether 15 characters have printed on the line. If 15 characters have been printed, a newline prints and a second `for` loop is entered. The purpose of this loop is to print the numeric value of the extended character set displayed on the line above. After the 15 numeric values are displayed, the next iteration of the loop is executed. Notice how a field specifier (%4c") is used in the `printf()` calls so that the output is aligned properly.

A sample run of the program appears in Figure 14-1.

Figure 14-1. The IBM Extended Character Set

The first series of extended characters are foreign characters, followed by various text graphics characters, and finally by a number of math symbols.

By combining certain text graphics characters, more complex images can be drawn. For example, character 218 looks like it could be used to draw the upper left corner of a box. Likewise, character 217 looks like the lower-right corner of a box. Using the proper characters (217, 218, 191, 192, 179, and 196), you can form a complete box.

A Program To Draw a Box with Text Graphics

Listing 14-2 displays a program that enables you to test the various combinations of text graphics characters that are used to draw a box.

Listing 14-2. Text Graphics Program To Draw a Box

```
/*

        Draw a box with extended character set.
*/

#include <stdio.h>
#include <stdlib.h>
#include <dos.h>

#define BLACK    0        /* Define some colors */
#define RED      4
unsigned char far *base;        /* Pointer to base of screen memory */
```

Listing 14–2 continues

Listing 14–2 continued

```
unsigned char far *find_screen_memory(int mode);
void get_box_characters(int *ul, int *ur, int *ll, int *lr, int *v, int *h);
void do_box(int row, int col, int deep, int wide, int ul, int ur,
            int ll, int lr, int v, int h, int fore, int back);
void clhm(int mode);

int main(void)
{
   char buff[20\];
   int ul, ur, ll, lr, v, h;
   int row, col, deep, wide, mode;

   mode = check_video_mode();
   if (!mode) {
      printf("Incorrect mode. Try the command line: MODE C080");
      exit(EXIT_FAILURE);
   }
   clhm(mode);
    get_box_characters(&ul, &ur, &ll, &lr, &v, &h);        /* Get characters  */
    printf("Enter row position: ");                        /* Get coordinates */
   row = atoi(gets(buff));
   printf("Enter column position: ");
   col = atoi(gets(buff));
   printf("Enter width: ");                                /* Get size */
   wide = atoi(gets(buff));
   printf("Enter depth: ");
   deep = atoi(gets(buff));
   base = find_screen_memory(mode);
   clhm(mode);
   do_box(row, col, deep, wide, ul, ur, ll, lr, v, h, RED, BLACK);

}

/*****
                              do_box()
```

Function draws a box at the specified row-column coordinates with foreground and background color attributes. The box characters are passed to the function.

```
Argument list:    int row      the row position on screen
                  int col      "  column      "
                  int deep     the number of rows deep
                  int wide     "       columns wide
                  int ul       upper left character of box
                  int ur       "  right       "
                  int ll       lower left       "
                  int lr       "  right        "
                  int v        vertical         "
                  int h        horizontal       "
                  int fore     foreground color
                  int back     background    "

Return value:     void

*****/

void do_box(int row, int col, int deep, int wide, int ul, int ur,
            int ll, int lr, int v, int h, int fore, int back)
{
    int offset, maxwide, maxdeep;
    register i;
    unsigned attribute;
    unsigned int far *ptr;

    attribute = ((back << 4) + fore) << 8;
    offset = row * 80 + col * 2;
    ptr = (unsigned int far *) base;
    maxwide = offset + wide;
    maxdeep = offset + (deep * 80);

    *(ptr + offset) = attribute + ul;              /* Do corners */
    *(ptr + maxwide) = attribute + ur;
    *(ptr + maxdeep) = attribute + ll;
    *(ptr + maxdeep + wide) = attribute + lr;

    for (i = 1; i < wide; i++) {                   /* Do horizontals */
        *(ptr + offset + i) = attribute + h;
        *(ptr + maxdeep + i) = attribute + h;
    }
    for (i = 1; i < deep; i++) {                   /* Do verticals */
        *(ptr + offset + 80 * i) = attribute + v;
        *(ptr + 80 * i + maxwide) = attribute + v;
```

Listing 14–2 continues

379

Listing 14–2 continued

```
   }
}

/*****
                     get_box_characters()

   Function gets the characters used to draw a box on-screen.

   Argument list:    int *ul        pointer to upper left character
                     int *ur        pointer to    "   right      "
                     int *ll        pointer to lower left        "
                     int *lr        pointer to    "   right      "
                     int *v         pointer to vertical          "
                     int *h         pointer to horizontal        "

   Return value:    void

*****/

void get_box_characters(int *ul, int *ur, int *ll, int *lr, int *v, int *h)
{
   char buff[20];
   static char *m[] = {
      "upper left", "upper right", "lower left", "lower right",
      "vertical", "horizontal", 0};
   int i, temp;

   for (i = 0; m[i]; i++) {
      printf("Enter %s character: ", m[i]);
      temp = atoi(gets(buff));
      switch (i) {
         case 0:
            *ul = temp;
            break;
         case 1:
            *ur = temp;
            break;
         case 2:
            *ll = temp;
            break;
```

```
        case 3:
            *lr = temp;
            break;
        case 4:
            *v = temp;
            break;
        case 5:
            *h = temp;
            break;
        }
    }
}
```

```
/*****
                        find_screen_memory()
```

Function determines the base memory address for the screen and sets a global character pointer to that address.

Argument list: int mode   the current screen mode

Return value: unsigned char far *   pointer to base screen
                                         memory

```
*****/

unsigned char far *find_screen_memory(int mode)
{
    return ( (mode == 7) ? (unsigned char far *) 0xb0000000L :
                           (unsigned char far *) 0xb8000000L);
}
```

```
/*****
                        check_video_mode()
```

Function checks that the video is in text mode. The video mode should be 2 or 3 for 80x25 text mode.

Argument list: void

Return value: int   the text video mode, 0 otherwise

```
*****/
```

Listing 14–2 continues

Listing 14–2 continued

```
int check_video_mode(void)
{
   int get_video_mode(void);
   int mode;

   mode = get_video_mode();
   if (mode == 2 || mode == 3 || mode == 7)
      return mode;
   else
      return 0;
}
/*****
                            get_video_mode()

   Function calls video interrupt 0x10, function 0x0f to see the
   current video mode.

   Argument list:    void

   Return value:     int     the video mode

*****/

int get_video_mode(void)
{
   union REGS ireg;

   ireg.h.ah = 0x0f;    /* Get video mode function */
   int86(0x10, &ireg, &ireg);
   return (ireg.h.al);
}

/*****
                            clrscr_home()

   Function calls video interrupt 0x10, function 0x00, to clear
   the screen and move the cursor to home.

   Argument list:    void

   Return value:     void
```

```
*****/

void clhm(int mode)
{
    union REGS ireg;

    ireg.h.ah = 0x00;
    ireg.h.al = mode;
    int86(0x10, &ireg, &ireg);

        }
```

Turning Off Pointer Checking

Because this program tinkers with video memory, QC issues the error message Illegal far pointer use when you run the program. To disable pointer checking by QC, you must turn off pointer checking in the appropriate dialog box. To do this, select the Make option from the Options submenu. Then select the Compiler Flags option (Alt-O-M-C). If you do the selections properly, your screen should look like Figure 14-2.

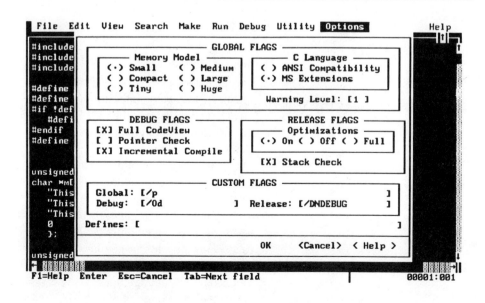

Figure 14-2. Turning Off Pointer Checks

Next, press the Tab key to move to the Pointer Check field of the Debug Flags. Unless you have changed this flag yourself, the Pointer Check box has an X in it. Press the space bar once to remove the X. This deactivates pointer checking. You can always reactivate pointer checking by repeating the process described in this section.

This program illustrates several new concepts and also displays variations of functions examined in earlier chapters. The program begins by including several header files that it requires. The remainder of the start-up code declares function prototypes, several symbolic constants, and one global variable. Note that base has been defined as a far character pointer. This must be done anytime you expect to reference a data item that lies outside the current data segment. The reason base is a far pointer is explained shortly.

check_video_mode()

If you expect to be doing text graphics, check the status of the video display to see whether it is in the text mode. The possible screen modes are presented in Table 14-1.

Table 14-1. Video Display Modes

Mode	Type
0	BW text, color card
1	40x25 color text
2	80x25 BW text
3	80x25 color text
4	320x200 four-color graphics
5	320x200 four-color graphics
6	640x200 two-color graphics
7	monochrome text
8	160x200 16-color graphics (PCjr)
9	320x200 16-color graphics (PCjr)
10	640x200 four-color graphics (PCjr)
13	320x200 16-color graphics (EGA)
14	640x200 16-color graphics (EGA)
15	640x350 monochrome graphics (EGA)
16	640x350 four- or 16-color graphics (EGA)
17	640x480 two-color graphics (VGA)
18	640x480 16-color graphics (VGA)
19	320x200 256-color graphics (VGA)

If you scan Table 14-1, you find that only modes 2, 3, and 7 support the standard 80 column by 25 row display screen. These modes should be included in your program.

In the `check_video_mode()` function, a call to `get_video_mode()` performs a video interrupt (0x10) to function 0x0f to return the current mode of the display screen. This is then returned to `check_video_mode()` and assigned into `mode`. The display mode value is returned only if the display screen is in text mode. Otherwise, a value of 0 is returned. (You also can set the video mode using an interrupt call.) On return from the function, the program checks to see whether `mode` is nonzero. If `mode` is zero, a message is displayed and the program ends. Otherwise, the program continues to execute.

clrscr_home()

The `clrscr_home()` function is a variation of the clear screen function `clrscr()` used in Chapter 11. The `clrscr_home()` function is different because it uses video interrupt 0x10, function 0x00, rather than function 0x06 or 0x07, which scroll the screen. Function 0x00 requires that the video mode be loaded into the AL register prior to the interrupt call. However, because of the call to `check_video_mode()`, the proper value is sitting in the `mode` variable. Note that fewer registers have to be loaded with function 0x00. As a result, this version is slightly faster.

get_box_characters()

The program calls `get_box_characters()` so that users can enter the extended character set numbers necessary to draw the box. Six characters are needed: four for the corners of the box, plus two for the horizontal and vertical sides. Rather than use six different prompt messages, I created an array of pointers to the prompts and placed the input in a `for` loop in conjunction with a `switch` statement.

Note that the message array `m[]` is defined with the `static` storage class. In the days before the ANSI C standard, you could not initialize arrays with the `auto` (default) storage class. The ANSI standard, however, enables you to initialize `auto` arrays, and QC supports the new standard. The old style is used here to help you understand why the keyword `static` is used in pre-ANSI code.

Variable i in the for loop is used to index into the m[] array and display the proper prompt message. A user then types the appropriate numeric value for the prompted extended character. The switch statement assigns the numeric value for the extended character into the appropriate variable by way of indirection.

After all values have been entered, control returns to main(). The program next asks users to enter the coordinates for the upper left corner of the box plus its width and depth. At this point in the program, all the information necessary to draw the box has been gathered.

find_screen_memory()

Now a design decision must be made. The box can be written to the display screen using the standard I/O facilities of MS-DOS (that is, the BIOS, or Basic Input/Output System), or the BIOS can be bypassed and the information written directly to the screen. The BIOS is notoriously slow when writing a character to the screen. A direct write of the character to video memory, on the other hand, is very fast. The catch here is that there are some MS-DOS systems still in use (for example, Tandy 2000 and Zenith 100) that do not have video memory where an IBM PC expects it to be. For this example, it is assumed that you have a true PC compatible and information can be written directly to video memory.

Some PC systems (monochrome and black and white) use mode 7 for the display screen and have video memory at segment address 0xb000. Systems using modes 2 and 3 have the video memory starting at segment 0xB800. If you reached this point in the program, you know that video memory must be at one of these segment addresses because of the call to check_video_mode().

In find_screen_memory(), the video mode is checked and the ternary operator is used to return the base address of video memory. The long data value

0xb0000000L

represents the video memory address at segment 0xb000, offset 0x0000 (0xb000:0000). Because you want to treat this number as a pointer outside the current data segment, the numeric constant is cast to an unsigned far character pointer. If the video mode is 7, memory address 0xb000:0000 is used. In all other cases, the base of video memory starts at address 0xb800:0000.

When you return from the call to `find_screen_memory()`, the address of video memory is assigned into `base`. All operations on video memory are referenced from this memory base.

Understanding Video Memory

In the text modes you want to use, the display screen consists of 25 lines, each capable of displaying 80 characters. This means that each screen is capable of displaying up to 2000 characters. What is not so obvious is that each of these characters has its own associated *attribute byte* with it. In other words, when you use the text screen mode, one byte holds the character being displayed on the screen while the next byte in memory holds the attribute byte for that character. The attribute byte determines what display characteristics are used to display the character. The value of the attribute byte determines the color of the character, whether it is displayed in high or normal intensity, and whether it is in "blink" mode.

Figure 14-3 shows how the word "Hello" on the display screen looks in video memory. Note in this figure that offset addresses appear above and below the art. Those above the art are attribute byte offset addresses and those below the art are character byte offset addresses.

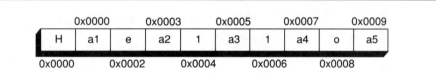

Figure 14-3. How the Word "Hello" Looks in Video Memory

Notice how each character's byte is on an even memory address, and its attribute byte (a1, a2, a3, etc.) is on an odd memory address. It should be clear from Figure 14-3 that one byte must be skipped after each character is written to video memory, in order to leave the attribute byte unchanged. Conversely, if you start at offset 0x0001 and skip every other byte, the characters would be unchanged, but the attribute bytes would be altered.

Alternatively, the character and the attribute byte together can be treated as an `unsigned int` if you want to write *both* the character and the attribute byte to video memory. That is how they are handled here.

do_box()

Back in `main()`, the program clears the screen and calls the `do_box()` function. There are many arguments to the `do_box()` function, but they should be fairly obvious from the comments in the function's description. Some of the function's code, however, needs elaboration.

The statement

```
attribute = ((back << 4) + fore) << 8;
```

is a bit unusual. To understand why the attribute byte is set in this manner, you need to understand how the attribute byte is used.

First, the top four bits (nibble) of the attribute byte define the background attribute of the character. The lowest nibble defines the foreground attributes of the character. The expression

```
back << 4
```

takes the background color passed to `do_box()` and shifts it four positions to the left. This moves the background color into the high nibble of the attribute byte. If `back` has a value of 4, its binary representation is

```
00000100 = 4
```

After shifting four positions, its binary representation is

```
01000000 = 64
```

The high nibble now has the background color. If the foreground color is 3, its binary representation is

```
00000011 = 3
```

Therefore, the expression

```
(back << 4) + fore)
```

results in

```
  01000000 = 64
+ 00000011 = 3
-------------------
  01000011 = 67
```

This is the value for the attribute byte. So what does the last part of the expression

```
attribute = ((back << 4) + fore) << 8
```

do? Keep in mind that `attribute` is defined as an `unsigned int` that requires two bytes of memory (16 bits). So far, `attribute` has the binary representation of

```
0000000001000011
```

If you are familiar with how integer values are stored in memory with the Intel 8088 and 80?86 families of CPU chips, you know that the low byte is always stored first. Therefore, shifting the bit pattern to the left ends up storing the value as

```
0100001100000000
```

and makes the value look like it does when stored in memory.

Calculating *offset*

The next statement in `do_box()` sets `offset` to the product of `row` times 80 plus `col` times two. In other words, if `row` equals 10 and `col` equals 5, `offset` equals 810. However, with two bytes per `unsigned int`, this equates to offset 1620, or address 0xb800:0654 in hexadecimal. This memory address is the place where the upper left corner of the box should be drawn in memory.

The statement

```
ptr = (unsigned int far *) base;
```

casts the memory address in `base` (which is a `far` pointer to `char`) to a `far` pointer to `unsigned int`. Now there is a pointer to the memory address for the upper left corner of the box in terms of an `unsigned int`. Variables `maxwide` and `maxdeep` are the offsets to the upper right and lower left corners of the box.

The next four statements

```
*(ptr + offset) = attribute + ul;
*(ptr + maxwide) = attribute + ur;
*(ptr + maxdeep) = attribute + ll;
*(ptr + maxdeep + wide) = attribute + lr;
```

simply write the four corners of the box to the proper addresses in video memory. To do this, the proper offset must be added to `ptr` and indirection used to set the value in memory. The parentheses are necessary because the indirection operator (*) has higher precedence than addition.

Note how `attribute` is added to the extended graphics character being drawn. `attribute` has the bit pattern

```
0100000110000000
```

If character 218 is being drawn for the upper left corner, its bit position is

```
11011010
```

Adding these two yields

```
0100001111011010
```

This means that the low byte has the graphics character and the high byte has the character's attribute byte. When the `unsigned int` is stored in memory, the low byte is stored first, followed by the high byte. In other words, the text graphics character is written to video memory first; then the attribute byte is written. This is exactly what you want.

After the corners of the box are written, a `for` loop is executed to write the top and bottom lines of the box. Note two things about variable `i`. First, the register storage class is used. If possible, QC stores `i` in a CPU register that makes the loop execute as fast as possible. Second, the offset to `ptr` begins with `i` equal to 1; not 0. This is so the corners of the box are not overwritten.

The second `for` loop functions the same as the first, only it writes the sides of the box. Obviously, the offset calculation for `ptr` is different for this loop because it is moving in a vertical direction. After this loop terminates, control returns to `main()` and the program ends.

If you feel like experimenting, put a loop around the call to `do_box()` in `main()` so that it is called several hundred times. Next, write a new `do_box()` function that uses `printf()` so that the data pass through the BIOS. Then time this version. You might find that the pointer version presented in Listing 14-2 is significantly faster. You also might try modifying the program to draw multiple boxes using different characters.

Pseudo Windows

As you run the QC compiler, you see dialog boxes come and go on the display screen. Typically, the dialog boxes overlay the contents of the edit window where the program source code appears. The same is true for the submenus that appear to scroll downward from the QC menu line. In this section, the basic concepts for writing such windows are presented. The task is not difficult and is a simple extension of the concepts presented earlier in this chapter.

How a Pseudo Window Works

These windows are called *pseudo windows* because they lack the bells and whistles that a real windowing system contains. There are no scroll bars or zoom features, and dragging is not possible (although an ambitious user could add these features). Instead, a pseudo window opens a box on the screen (perhaps in a contrasting color), displays a message, and waits for a user to press a key. When a key is pressed, the window closes and the display returns to its original state.

The algorithm to do all this contains the following steps:

1. Determine the window size necessary to display the message.
2. Identify the screen location where the message displays.
3. Save a copy of the current screen contents.
4. Display the message in a window.
5. Copy the original contents of the window back to the display screen after a user reads the message.

There are several ways that you can implement the third step in the algorithm. Most PC's have multiple display pages that can be used. In the text mode, up to eight pages are available, and it is relatively easy to switch between video pages. The video interrupt (0x10), function 0x0f, can get the current video page number, and function 0x05 can set the video page number. However, if this approach is used, the message window appears on a blank screen and does not look like a window.

Another method for creating a pseudo window is to copy the contents of the current video page to the alternate page and then overlay the message window. When the user finishes reading the message, the video page is reset to its previous video page number. Visually, changing video pages is sufficiently fast that the user probably would not know the difference. However, this approach was rejected for several reasons. First, it does not expose you to some useful concepts that are required with alternative methods. Second, time is wasted copying the contents of the first video page to the second page. Finally, this approach is not very elegant.

In the example here, the third step of the algorithm is accomplished by copying the contents of the screen where the window will appear to a chunk of memory. Step 4 of the algorithm displays the message in the window, and step 5 simply copies the original contents from memory back to the screen. A test program to write a pseudo window is presented in Listing 14-3.

Listing 14-3. A Test Program To Write a Pseudo Window

```
/*
     Program to write a pseudo window
*/

#include <stdio.h>
#include <stdlib.h>

#define BRIGHTWHITE   15
#define RED            4
#if !defined
   #define FALSE       0
#endif
#define WIDTH         80

unsigned far *ptr, far *base;
char *m[] = {
   "This is a test of the small windows.",
   "This is a second line of the test.",
   "This is a third line of the test.",
   0
   };

unsigned far *find_screen_memory(int mode);
void do_window(int row, int col, int fore, int back, char *m[]);
void clhm(int mode);

int main(void)
{
   int back, fore, mode;

   mode = check_video_mode();
   if (!mode) {
      printf("Improper screen mode. Abort");
      exit(EXIT_FAILURE);
```

```
   }
   clhm(mode);
   system("dir /w");
   getch();
   ptr = base = find_screen_memory(mode);
   fore = BRIGHTWHITE;
   back = RED;
   do_window(10, 10, fore, back, m);
   getch();
}
/*****
do_window()

     Function that draws a window with the upper left corner
     at row-col coordinates and displays the message helf in
     m[]. The message can be in color.

     Argument list:    int row       the row position
                       int col        "  column   "
                       int fore      the foreground color
                       int back       "  background   "
                       char *m[]      the message

     Return value:    void

*****/
void do_window(int row, int col, int fore, int back, char *m[])
{
   unsigned far *s;
   unsigned attribute, *mptr, *hptr;
   int c1, deep, flag, len, offset, r1, wide;
   register i, j;

   wide = i = 0;
   r1 = row;
   c1 = col;
   while (m[i]) {              /* Find longest string */
      len = strlen(m[i]);
      if (len >= wide)
         wide = len;
      i++;
   }
```

Listing 14–3 continues

Listing 14–3 continued

```
deep = i + 2;
wide += 2;

hptr = mptr = (unsigned *) calloc(deep * wide, sizeof(unsigned));

if (mptr == NULL) {
   printf("Not enough memory. Abort");
   exit(EXIT_FAILURE);
}

attribute = ((back << 4) + fore) << 8;           /* Set attribute byte   */
                                                 /* Copy current screen  */
s = ptr = base + (row * WIDTH) + col;

for (j = 0; j < deep; j++) {
   for (i = 0; i < wide; i++, ptr++) {
      *mptr++ = *ptr;
   }
   row++;
   ptr = base + row * WIDTH + col;
}

row = r1;                                          /* Reset row and ptr */
ptr = s;

for (j = 0; j < deep; j++) {                       /* Do background */
   flag = 0;
   ptr = (base + (row + j) * WIDTH + col);
   *ptr++ = attribute;
   for (i = 1; i < wide; i++, ptr++) {
      if (j == 0) {
         *ptr = attribute;
         continue;
      }
      if (m[j - 1][i - 1] == '\0') {
         flag = 1;
      }
      if (flag) {
         *ptr = attribute;
      } else {
```

```
            *ptr = attribute + m[j - 1][i - 1];
         }
      }
   }
   getch();                          /* Pause to read message */
   row = r1;
   ptr = s;
   mptr = hptr;                      /* Restore screen */
   for (j = 0; j < deep; j++) {
      for (i = 0; i < wide; i++, ptr++, mptr++) {
         *ptr = *mptr;
      }
      row++;
      ptr = (base + row * WIDTH + c1);
   }
}
```

Global Definitions

The program begins with the usual list of #include files and several #defines for symbolic constants. The possible colors that can be used for the foreground and background of the message are presented in Table 14-2.

Table 14-2. Color Values

Foreground			Background		
0	Black	8	Gray	0	Black
1	Blue	9	Light Blue	1	Blue
2	Green	10	Light Green	2	Green
3	Cyan	11	Light Cyan	3	Cyan
4	Red	12	Light Red	4	Red
5	Magenta	13	Light Magenta	5	Magenta
6	Brown	14	Yellow	6	Brown
7	White	15	Bright White	7	White

Note that four bits are used for the foreground colors, but only three bits for the background color. This is why there are more foreground colors. If bit seven of the attribute byte is turned on, the foreground color is set to blink mode. Visually, the attribute byte looks like Figure 14-4.

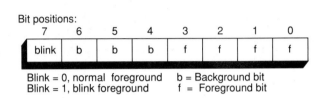

Bit positions:

7	6	5	4	3	2	1	0
blink	b	b	b	f	f	f	f

Blink = 0, normal foreground   b = Background bit
Blink = 1, blink foreground   f = Foreground bit

Figure 14-4. The Attribute Byte

If you want to have the foreground blink, simply turn on the high bit of the attribute byte. (With the exception of a blinking cursor on-screen, most people probably find a blinking display irritating.)

In Listing 14-3, BRIGHTWHITE with a value of 15 is assigned as the foreground color on a RED background. If you do not have color, simply use black letters on a white background.

Next two `unsigned int far` pointers are assigned. (Notice that the definition omits the default storage type `int` in Listing 14-3.) These pointers will be used to access the display memory. The next data definition defines the `m[]` array as an array of pointers to `char`. The pointers are initialized to point to the message that is to display on-screen. Next, several nonstandard functions used in the program are declared. (The source code for several of the functions is the same as that found in Listing 14-2, so it is not repeated in Listing 14-3.)

In `main()`, the first call is to the `check_video_mode()` function that is described in Listing 14-2. The purpose is to make sure that the display device is in the 80x25 text mode. If that is not the case, `mode` is 0, an error message is displayed, and the program ends by way of a call to `exit()`. If all goes well and `mode` has the proper value, the screen clears with a call to `clrscr_home()` (also from Listing 14-2) and the `system()` function is called.

system()

The system() function is an ANSI standard library function designed to perform an operating system command. The argument passed to system() is a character pointer containing the system command to be performed. In Listing 14-3, a command is passed to system() that does a "wide" directory of the current subdirectory. The only purpose of this command is to enable background information to display on-screen. If the screen is totally blanked, it is difficult to tell whether the program is working properly.

The system() call is followed by a call to getch() to pause the display while the directory is displayed. You might want to look at it for a moment so that you can compare the pre- and postwindow status of the display.

After a user presses a key, a call to find_screen_memory() determines the base address of video memory. (This function is examined earlier in the discussion of Listing 14-2.) The base address of video memory is then assigned into base and ptr for use later in the program.

A digression: Why isn't find_screen_memory() used to assign the base address of video memory in base as part of the function instead of returning the address as a far pointer? After all, base is a global variable and is in scope for find_screen_memory(). The reason is that if a variable is assigned as part of the function code, a programmer is forced to have a global variable named base in the program. This limits the flexibility of the function.

Next, the foreground and background colors are assigned and then do_windows() is called.

do_windows()

The do_windows() function does most of the actual work in the program. You should notice from the argument list for do_windows() that the size of the window is not specified. Rather than requiring a programmer to work with a fixed-size window, the size of the message determines the size of the window.

Determining the Size of the Window

The while loop scans the message array of pointer (m[]) to find the longest line of the message. After all elements of the array are scanned, wide equals the string length of the longest line. When the last element of the array is read, the NULL string terminates the while loop. Variable i equals the number of elements read plus one. After the loop, the depth of the window (deep) is defined to equal i plus 2 and the width to equal wide plus 2. This inserts an empty row above and below the message, and a blank column before and after each line of the message when it displays. The blank spaces "frame" the message and make it easier to read.

Allocating Memory for the Window Backing

With the width and depth of the window known, you can calculate the amount of memory required to store the current contents of the video display where the window will be placed. The call to calloc() allocates a deep by wide chunk of memory, each unit of which is an unsigned int in size. For example, if the window is 30 characters wide and 5 lines deep, 300 bytes of storage are returned by the call to calloc(). (The result is 300 bytes because each unsigned takes two bytes: 300 = 30 * 5 * 2.) The pointer returned from calloc() is cast to a pointer to unsigned int and assigned into hptr and mptr. If a NULL pointer is returned, there is not enough memory to create the window and exit() is called to end the program.

If the do_windows() function is used in other programs, it might be a good idea to have a return value of 0, informing the caller that the window could not be opened. If the window is opened, a return value of 1 tells the caller that the message was displayed successfully. This is a good solution because the program continues without the message. It leaves the choice of termination up to the programmer.

If the pointer returned from calloc() is not NULL, you can proceed to display the window. The next step is to set the attribute byte to be used for the window. The mechanics for the statement

```
attribute = ((back << 4) + fore) << 8;
```

are the same as those found in Listing 14-2, so they are not repeated here.

Copying the Contents of the Current Window

Next, the program initializes `ptr` to the proper offset in video memory where the window will be written. In calculating the index, the same method is used that was discussed following Listing 14-2. Two `for` loops are used to copy the video memory into the memory block returned by `calloc()`. The `j` loop counts the number of lines used by the window and the `i` loop counts the columns used by the window. The statement

```
*mptr++ = *ptr;
```

simply copies the contents of the video memory pointed to by `ptr` into the memory block pointed to by `mptr`. Keep in mind that two bytes at a time are being copied because each pointer is a pointer to an `unsigned int`. After the innermost (`i`) `for` loop finishes its first pass, the first line of video memory (where the window will appear) is stored in the block of memory returned by `calloc()`. After the outer `for` loop terminates, `deep` rows are copied into the memory block.

Notice how `ptr` is incremented on each pass through the (`j`) `for` loop. Because `row` is incremented on each pass, you move vertically down the screen. Also note that after both `for` loops terminate, `row` must be reset to its original value for use in subsequent calculations.

Writing the Window

With the previous contents of the window safely tucked away, this section of video memory can be overwritten with the window and its message. First, `row` and `ptr` are reset to their original values with the statements:

```
row = rl;
ptr = s;
```

where `s` is the starting memory address for the window.

Next two `for` loops are used to display the window and its message. The variable `flag` is used to determine whether a blank space is displayed or whether a character is displayed. Before the inner `for` loop is executed, `ptr` is set to the position for the next row to be displayed. The statement

```
ptr = (base + (row + j) * WIDTH + col);
```

has no impact on the first iteration of the loop because `j` is equal to 0. This leaves `ptr` unchanged from its starting position. Each subsequent pass through the loop, however, advances to the next row position on the screen.

Because a leading blank space should precede each message line, the statement

```
*ptr++ = attribute;
```

causes a blank space to be written using the background attribute. (There is no foreground character, hence no foreground color.) You now advance to the inner for loop.

The inner for loop (controlled by variable i) is responsible for displaying the message with foreground and background attributes. The if statement

```
if (j == 0) {
    *ptr = attribute;
    continue;
}
```

says, "If this is the first row being displayed, just show it as a series of blank spaces; do not display a message." This causes the first line of the window to appear as blank spaces.

The next if statement:

```
if (m[j - 1][i - 1] == '\0') {
    flag = 1;
}
```

checks to see whether the last character displayed was a NULL character. The reason for the strange indexing is that the j loop starts at 0, but you want to display message m[0] when j equals 1. In other words, the first message should be displayed on the second line of the window. If the last character was the NULL termination character ('\0'), the remaining characters should be displayed using just the attribute byte (that is, a blank space). If you have read past the end of the message, flag is set to 1.

The statements

```
if (flag) {
    *ptr = attribute;
} else {
    *ptr = attribute + m[j - 1][i - 1];
}
```

use flag to determine whether only blank spaces are displayed or whether both the message character and its attribute are displayed. The loop continues to display the characters for the line until wide columns are displayed.

The j and i loops continue until all rows and columns of the window have been displayed. The call to `getch()` simply pauses the display until the user presses a key.

Restoring the Original Display Screen

After a user views the message in the window and presses a key, two `for` loops are used to rewrite the original contents of the window back into video memory. This has the effect of erasing the window and restoring the original display screen. When the two `for` loops are finished, control returns to `main()`. The last call in `main()` is to `getch()` so that you can view the original screen after the window is erased. Another key press ends the program.

Suggested Improvements

There are two enhancements that could be added to the window system. First, you could incorporate the box function to draw a border around the window. Second, you could add a shadow to the box, similar to those used with the dialog boxes in the QC compiler. Drawing a box border would be fairly simple. Just enlarge the window by two more columns and two more rows, draw the box with whatever attribute you want, and then draw the window using the code in Listing 14-3.

The shadow effect is even more interesting and not very difficult. Figure 14-5 shows what needs to be added to create a 3D shadow effect.

Usually, the shadow is designed to look like a shadow created by the plane of the window. The shadow is drawn with a darker color than the window to add the illusion of depth. The illusion of depth is produced by creating a one-character offset to the window. This is shown as a GAP in Figure 14-3.

The shadow portion can be accomplished in several different ways. First, you can simply expand the block of memory used to store the original contents of the screen and write the shadow area (SHADOW in Figure 14-3) in black. Obviously, for this to affect anything, you must assume that the background is not all black to begin with. This is *not* the approach to shadowing that QC uses.

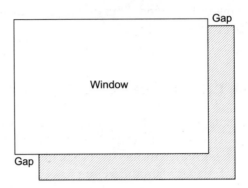

Figure 14-5. Adding a Shadow to the Window

If you look at the QC screen when a dialog box is present, you can still read the background characters that are in the shadow. This effect can be achieved by leaving the character bytes in the shadow unchanged, but rewriting their attribute bytes. This approach also uses less memory, because only the attribute bytes for the characters in the shadow are preserved.

For example, suppose that the window in Figure 14-3 is 50 columns wide and 10 rows deep. You would store one complete row (the bottom of the shadow) plus additional bytes equal to row −1, or 9. Therefore, using deep and wide, the required allocation is

```
sptr = (char far *) calloc(wide+(deep-1),sizeof(unsigned char));
```

Note that we cast the pointer from calloc() to a far character pointer this time. Now calculate the offset needed to get to the bottom gap:

```
offset = (rows + deep + 1) * 80 + 1;
```

This calculation places you at the GAP position at the bottom of the screen if you are using an unsigned int pointer. In order to use only the character elements, you must multiply offset by 2 to find the byte offset from base. The working character pointer is initialized by the statement:

```
wptr = (unsigned char far *) (base + offset * 2) + 1;
```

wptr now points to the first attribute byte in the shadow. Next you would use a for loop to store the current attribute bytes in sptr. The loop double-increments the loop counter so that you skip over the character bytes in the shadow. After all the attribute bytes in the bottom row are stored, you can recalculate offset using the `offset` formula above, decreasing `deep` on each pass through the loop. This stores all the attribute bytes in the shadow.

Now repeat the process, writing only the shadow attribute byte into the shadow positions. When it comes time to restore the screen, the process is started over using the contents of `sptr`.

Conclusion

You can add a lot of class to a program using the extended text graphics characters provided. Direct writes to video memory also can improve the speed with which the information is displayed. While character graphics are nice, `pixel` graphics are even better. Pixel graphics are examined in the next chapter.

15

Using Graphics

In this chapter, you learn about

Two types of graphics supported by QC

Graphics coordinate systems

Clipping

Viewports and windows

Presentation graphics

Graphics programming has made tremendous strides in the past ten years, especially on PC-type machines. Large-scale production and competitive pressure have reduced the cost of graphics systems substantially. At the same time, technological advances have dramatically increased the quality on all fronts (resolution, color, speed, etc.). Graphics programming is one of the more "fun" aspects of programming, and your imagination can have tangible (visual) results.

The thrust of this chapter is different from the other chapters in this book, because the amount of information makes it impossible to teach graphics programming in one chapter. (Indeed, it would be difficult to teach graphics programming in an entire book.) Therefore, the primary goal of this chapter is to teach you enough about QC graphics programming that you can ask the right questions. A secondary goal is to give you some guidance as to where you can find more complete answers to those questions.

Types of Graphics Programming Supported by QC

The term *graphics programming* refers to the programmer's ability to control all aspects of what is presented on the output device (usually the screen). Up to this point, I have discussed programs that use characters in one form or another. In Chapter 14, you learned how to use the IBM extended character set for text graphics. The actual representation of what was seen on the output device was controlled by the ASCII and IBM enhanced character sets that are etched into the hardware.

With graphics programming, you start with a clean sheet — literally! If you want to draw your own letters on the screen, you can. If you want to draw pictures, house plans, or statistical data plots, you can. Everything that appears on-screen is under your control.

QC graphics programming capabilities can be divided into two broad categories: *presentation graphics* and *general graphics*. Presentation graphics programming is concerned with presenting a visual representation of data. The idea that a picture is worth a thousand columns of numbers is the cornerstone behind presentation graphics. Presentation graphics is often concerned with a distillation of data.

What I call general graphics is a catch-all for the rest of graphics programming. General graphics programming is often used for modeling ideas (for example, computer-aided design, or CAD), representing images (houses, people, etc.), presenting abstract ideas (models of complex chemical compounds), and animation.

QC provides a library of graphics functions suited to both types of programming. Regardless of the type of graphics that interest you, it is important to understand some of the hardware constraints within which you must operate. That is the topic of the next section.

The Graphics Screen

The IBM PC and compatible machines support a wide variety of graphics capabilities. For the most part, the hardware of the output device influences how the graphics output looks. As you probably know, the display screen is comprised of small dots, called picture elements or *pixels*. You can create different images by turning these pixels on or off. The greater the number of pixels in a given space, the more realistic the graphics image. The greater the number of pixels, the higher the *resolution* of the graphics image.

Most PC's support two types of display screen operation: text and graphics. Table 15-1 presents a list of graphics display devices that are common to many PC machines along with the symbolic constants that QC uses to identify each mode. Chapter 14 discussed the text modes available under MS-DOS. This chapter concentrates on the modes that support pixel graphics.

Table 15-1. Graphics Display Devices

QC Symbolic Constant	MS-DOS Model	Type	Resolution
_TEXTBW40	0	T	40x25, 16 grey scale
_TEXTC40	1	T	40x25, 16 color
_TEXTBW80	2	T	80x25, 16 grey scale
_TEXTC80	3	T	80x25, 16 color
_MRES4COLOR	4	G	320x200, 4 color
_MRESNOCOLOR	5	G	320x200, 4 grey scale
_HRESBW	6	G	640x200, BW
_TEXTMONO	7	T	80x25, BW
_HERCMONO	8	G	720x348, BW *
_MRES16COLOR	13	G	320x200, 16 color
_HRES16COLOR	14	G	640x200, 16 color
_ERESNOCOLOR	15	G	640x350, BW
_ERESCOLOR	16	G	640x350, 4 or 16 color
_VRES2COLOR	17	G	640x480, BW
_VRES16COLO	18	G	640x480, 16 color
_MRES256COLOR	19	G	320x200, 256 color
_ORESCOLOR	64	G	640x400, Olivetti **
_DEFAULTMODE	-1	T	original mode **

*   This mode does not correspond to the MS-DOS mode value and is
      used to support Hercules graphics adapters.

**   This mode does not correspond to the MS-DOS mode value.

The most common display in service on the PC is the Color Graphics Adapter (CGA), followed closely by the Enhanced Graphics Adapter (EGA). Although there was some use of the Professional Graphics Adapter (PGA), it never caught on and was quickly replaced with the Video Graphics Adapter (VGA). The VGA system is rapidly becoming the new PC standard. Table 15-2 shows the highest graphics resolution possible with the most popular adapters.

Table 15-2. Common Graphics Adapters

QC Symbolic Constant	Adapter	Resolution
_MRES4COLOR	CGA	320x200, 4 color
_HRESBW	CGA	640x200, BW
_ERESCOLOR	EGA	640x350, 4 color
_VRES16COLOR	VGA	640x480, 16 color
_MRES256COLOR	VGA	320x200, 256 color

Recently "super" VGA adapters have appeared on the market. These adapters are capable of using an interlace mode to produce 1024x480 resolution. No doubt even higher resolutions are just around the corner. Even using an adapter with 320x200 resolution, however, you can do some pretty impressive graphics programming.

Resolution and Physical Coordinates

Each pixel has unique physical coordinates on-screen. No matter what type of data you are using (for example, `int` or `double`), that data must eventually be *mapped* into the physical coordinate space dictated by your graphics adapter. Suppose you have a CGA system and you want to use the four-color mode (`_MRES4COLOR`). Figure 15-1 shows how the hardware sees the physical coordinate space.

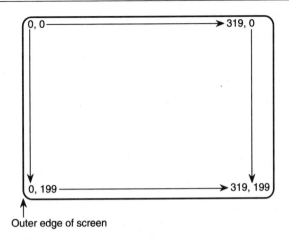

Figure 15-1. _MRES4COLOR Physical Coordinate Space

As you can see in Figure 15-1, the origin of the graphics screen is in the upper left corner. The largest x-y coordinates appear in the lower right corner of the screen. Although this coordinate system is "upside down" in the mathematical sense, it is dictated by the hardware used to drive the graphics screen.

Another thing to notice in Figure 15-1 is that the coordinate space maximums in the x-y direction are one less than the resolution of the screen. Although this may seem obvious to you, most programmers forget this detail and try to write a pixel to never-never land. Just remember that the maximum pixel coordinate is always one less than the resolution maximum.

Physical and Viewport Coordinates

Now that you know what determines the physical dimensions of the display screen, you need to understand viewports. Unless you tell QC otherwise, the viewport is the physical screen. This means that you can plot any and all values that fall within the resolution numbers of your physical screen. As shown in Figure 15-1, your viewport defaults to a rectangle bounded by 0,0 at the origin to 319,199 at the opposite corner.

Graphing within the limits of the physical screen is fine for many graphics applications, but it does not work well if your data includes negative values. Fortunately, QC supplies a function that allows you to cope (within limits) with such problems. The function is called `setvieworg()` and has the general form

```
struct xycoord far _setvieworg(short newx, short newy);
```

The structure named `xycoord` is declared in the `graph.h` header file. This structure holds the origin coordinates of the viewport that were previously used. The arguments to `setvieworg()` are the new x-y coordinates where you want to establish the origin.

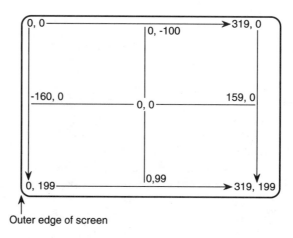

Figure 15-2. Changing the Logical Origin with `setvieworg()`

In Figure 15-2, I assume that the physical coordinates are for a 320x200 screen. If you perform the call

```
setvieworg(160, 100);
```

you are telling QC, "Go to coordinates 160,100 and, from now on, treat those coordinates as though they were coordinates 0,0." In other words, the purpose of `setvieworg()` is to map a set of physical coordinates into a new set of *logical coordinates*. (A logical coordinate system is any coordinate system you wish to use that is then scaled to fit the physical coordinate system dictated by the systems hardware.) This means that you can graph negative values to –160 for x and –100 for y. The tradeoff is that the maximum value for x and y must also decrease to 159 and 99 for x and y, respectively.

Listing 15-1 illustrates the effect that `setvieworg()` has on a graphics screen.

Listing 15-1. The DOTS Program

```
/*
    Generate random pixels until key is pressed
*/
#include <stdio.h>
#include <stdlib.h>
#include <graph.h>

#define TRUE    1


void graphics_mode(void),
     do_dots(void),
     set_org(char *s[]),
     end_graphics(int);


struct videoconfig myscreen;

int maxx, maxy;

int main(int argc, char *argv[])
{
   if (argc != 3) {
      printf("Usage: program orgx orgy\n");
      exit(EXIT_FAILURE);
   }
   graphics_mode();
   set_org(argv);
   do_dots();
   end_graphics(0);
}

/*****
                         do_dots()

    This function generates random x-y values and sets a!d pixel at those
    coordinates. In addition, the color used to set the pixel is also set
    at random. The program runs until a key is pressed.

    Argument list:     void
```

Listing 15-1 continues

Listing 15-1 continued
```
     Return value:      void


*****/


void do_dots(void)
{
   short int color, rx, ry;

   while (TRUE) {
      rx = (short) (rand() % maxx);
      ry = (short) (rand() % maxy);
      color = (short) (rand() % myscreen.numcolors);
      _setcolor(color);
      _setpixel(rx, ry);
      if (kbhit()) {
         break;
      }
   }
}


/*****

                              set_org()


     This function changes the origin of the viewport according to the
new coordinates passed as command line arguments. The arguments are
in x, y order.

     Argument list:    char *argv[]       command line arguments

     Return value:      void

*****/


void set_org(char *argv[])
{
   _setvieworg( atoi(argv[1]), atoi(argv[2]) );
}


/*****

                              graphics_mode()


     This function sets the graphics mode to the highest value possible
 for the video adapter in use. It also sets the two globals maxx and
```

maxy for the largest value consistent with the adapter.

```
   Argument list:     void

   Return value:      void

*****/

void graphics_mode(void)
{
   int i;

   i = _VRES16COLOR;               /* Start high... */

   while (!_setvideomode(i)) {   /* ...spin until we get a good one. */
      i--;
   }
   _getvideoconfig(&myscreen);
   maxx = myscreen.numxpixels - 1;  /* Set global x and y */
   maxy = myscreen.numypixels - 1;
}


/*****
                                 end_graphics()
```

This function resets the graphics mode to the default value at the end of a graphics program. If the argument is nonzero, the program waits for the user to press a key. Otherwise, it falls through.

```
   Argument list:     int pause       pause if 1, no pause if 0

   Return value:      void

*****/

void end_graphics(int pause)
{
   if (pause) {
      getch();
   }
   _setvideomode(_DEFAULTMODE);
}
```

Although this program is rather long, it is not complicated. The program begins by including the necessary header files and global variables. In main(), the program ensures that the user has supplied three command-line arguments. The first command-line argument is the program name (for example, dots), the second argument is the x coordinate that will be treated as the zero (origin) x coordinate, and the third command-line argument is the new y coordinate for the origin. If three command-line arguments are not passed to main(), an error message is displayed and the program terminates.

If three command-line arguments are supplied, graphics_mode() is called to set the graphics mode used in the program. This is done by setting i to the highest possible graphics mode and decreasing i until a nonzero value is returned by _setvideomode(). This works because _setvideomode() returns 0 if the video adapter does not agree with the mode being set. Eventually, _setvideomode() finds a compatible mode, the while loop ends, and i is the highest resolution mode consistent with the video hardware.

The call to _getvideoconfig() uses the mode in i to fill in the videoconfig structure named myscreen. (See Code Fragment 15-1 for a list of the members in the videoconfig structure.) The program now has access to information about the video hardware of the system. Next, the maximum values for the x and y coordinates are set in the global variables maxx and maxy.

Code Fragment 15-1. The videoconfig *Structure from graph.h*

```
struct videoconfig {
   short numxpixels;            /* number of pixels on x-axis */
   short numypixels;            /* number of pixels on y-axis */
   short numtextcols;           /* number of text columns available */
   short numtextrows;           /* number of text rows available */
   short numcolors;             /* number of actual colors */
   short bitsperpixel;          /* number of bits per pixel */
   short numvideopages;         /* number of available video pages*/
   short mode;                  /* current video mode */
   short adapter;               /* active display adapter */
   short monitor;               /* active display monitor */
   short memory;                /* adapter video memory in K bytes */
};
```

The next function to execute is set_org(), which establishes the logical origin at the coordinates supplied by the user as command-line arguments. Therefore, argv[] must be passed to the function. All set_org() does is convert argv[1] (the new x) and argv[2] into integer values and call _setvieworg(). The logical origin is moved to the new coordinates supplied by the user.

The next function called is do_dots(), which simply generates random x-y coordinates, as well as a random color value and plots the point on the screen. Consider how the program does this. The call to rand() generates a pseudorandom number between 0 and 32,767. The program takes that random value and applies the modulo operator using the maximum value of the screen. Because the modulus operator is used, the resulting value must fall within the required range. This is done for both x and y coordinates.

The color is set in the same manner. The random number is used with the modulo operator and the maximum colors supported by the video adapter, as stored in myscreen.numcolors. (See Code Fragment 15-1.) Again, the modulus operator ensures that the values fall within the required range. The call to _setcolor() tells QC the next color to be used when plotting a pixel. The call to _setpixel() tells QC where that pixel is displayed. As a result, the screen begins to fill with random points of different colors.

The function kbhit() stands for "keyboard hit". It scans the keyboard to see whether a key has been pressed. If no key is pressed, the function returns 0 and the break statement is not executed. If a key is struck, kbhit() returns the character, the break is executed and no more pixels are displayed. Note that kbhit() is different from other input routines, in that it doesn't wait for the user to enter something before continuing. It is a useful function for processing data while waiting for some activity by the user.

Finally, the end_graphics() function is called with a 0 argument. If the argument is nonzero, the function waits for the user to press a key before continuing. Otherwise, the function immediately ends graphics mode and resets it to text mode. Because the graphics screen disappears when control reverts to text mode, passing a nonzero argument is a good way to pause the program before exiting the graphics mode. In fact, you may want to keep the end_graphics() and graphics_mode() functions handy or perhaps even add them to your graphics library. (Refer to Chapter 13 for information on adding functions to your library using the LIB program.)

When you run the DOTS program, try running it the first time with the arguments 0 and 0. This shows how the screen looks when the physical and viewport coordinates are the same. Now run DOTS using half-resolution values for x and y. That is, if you have a CGA graphics adapter, call it with 110 and 100. You will see that all of the colors are limited to the lower right corner of the screen. (Figure 15-2 shows you why this is so.)

The sharp reader might be saying, "If I supply those new coordinates, do_dots() generates values that are too large for the screen to plot." True, but QC doesn't care. Values that fall outside the viewport are ignored, or "clipped". (Clipping is the topic of the next section.)

If you want to experiment with the DOTS program, make it smart enough to plot in the negative coordinate space when the logical origin is moved. Think of ways to make the program plot in only one or in all four sectors of the screen. (Hint: Would a fourth command-line argument using "1, 2, 3, 4, All" help solve the problem? Think about it.)

Clipping

The DOTS program in Listing 15-1 touches on the concept of *clipping*. In graphics, clipping refers to a program's ability to limit drawing to a defined region. Any attempt to draw outside the defined region is said to be clipped by the program. In other words, clipping restricts a display to a specified area of the screen. The visible portion that is not clipped is called the *viewport*.

The program in Listing 15-2 is a modification of the DOTS program from Listing 15-1. The only difference is found in the function clip_it().

Listing 15-2. Clip the DOTS Program

```
/*
   Generate random pixels until key is pressed
*/

#include <stdio.h>
#include <stdlib.h>
#include <graph.h>

#define TRUE    1


void graphics_mode(void),
     do_dots(void),
     end_graphics(int),
```

```
    clip_it(void);


struct videoconfig myscreen;

int maxx, maxy;

int main(void)
{
    graphics_mode();
    clip_it();
    do_dots();
    end_graphics(0);
}



/*****
                            do_dots()

    This function generates random x-y values and sets a pixel at
    those coordinates. In addition, the color used to set the pixel is
    also set at random. The program runs until a key is pressed.

    Argument list:     void

    Return value:      void

*****/

void do_dots(void)
{
    short int color, rx, ry;

    while (TRUE) {
        rx = (short) (rand() % maxx);
        ry = (short) (rand() % maxy);
        color = (short) (rand() % myscreen.numcolors);
        _setcolor(color);
        _setpixel(rx, ry);
        if (kbhit()) {
            break;
        }
    }
}
```

Listing 15-2 continues

Listing 15-2 continued

```
/*****
                            graphics_mode()

     This function sets the graphics mode to the highest value
     possible for the video adapter in use. It also sets the two
     globals maxx and maxy for the largest value consistent with the adapter.

     Argument list:    void

     Return value:     void

*****/

void graphics_mode(void)
{
   int i;

   i = _VRES16COLOR;                       /* Start high... */

   while (!_setvideomode(i)) {             /* ...spin until we get a good one. */
      i--;
   }
   _getvideoconfig(&myscreen);
   maxx = myscreen.numxpixels - 1;         /* Set global x and y */
   maxy = myscreen.numypixels - 1;
}


/*****
                           end_graphics()

     This function resets the graphics mode to the default value at the end of a
     graphics program. If the argument is nonzero, the program waits for the user
     to press a key. Otherwise, it falls through.

     Argument list:    int pause        pause if 1, no pause if 0

     Return value:     void

*****/
```

```
void end_graphics(int pause)
{
    if (pause) {
        getch();
    }
    _setvideomode(_DEFAULTMODE);
}
```

```
/*****
                            clip_it()

    This function clips the maximum viewport.

    Argument list:        char *argv[]        command-line arguments

    Return value:         void

*****/
```

```
void clip_it(void)
{
    int x1, x2, y1, y2;

    x1 = (int) ( (double) maxx * .2);
    x2 = (int) ( (double) maxx * .8);
    y1 = (int) ( (double) maxy * .2);
    y2 = (int) ( (double) maxy * .8);

    _setcliprgn(x1, y1, x2, y2);

}
```

The clip_it() function takes the maximum x and y values found by the call to _getvideoconfig() and resizes them to fit a smaller screen. If you look at the clip_it() function, you see that the program is shrinking each of the maximum dimensions by twenty percent and increasing the minimum values by the same amount. The result is a region that is smaller than the physical coordinates would allow.

Also note that `do_dots()` has not changed; it still generates dots that lie outside the viewport. The dots that are outside the viewport are clipped: they are not visible on the screen.

Using Graphics Windows

I mentioned earlier that the physical coordinate system poses a problem because it does not allow you to draw negative values. That problem is solved with the `_setvieworg()` function. Still, you cannot use data with fractional values (floating-point numbers) nor can you plot values that are larger than the screen resolution.

Obviously, QC also has solved these problems. The solution is to use the graphics windowing functions whenever the data cannot be represented with the nonwindowing functions. Typically, you use the windowing graphics functions whenever the data values are outside the physical coordinate values or when you need to work with noninteger data.

A number of windowing functions are used in a normal distribution program. The purpose of the program is to display a normal distribution curve (the "bell" curve). The user supplies a normal deviate value and the graph displays the bell curve, the plus and minus normal deviate positions on the curve, and the total probability associated with that normal deviate. Figure 15-3 shows a run using a normal deviate of 1.96. As you can see, about 95 percent of all values fall within a deviation of plus or minus 1.96 from the mean.

The code for the normal distribution program is shown in Listing 15-3. The program begins by including the required header files, and several #defines are used to set the number of iterations used to plot the curve. The STEP symbolic constant determines the increment value used for plotting different probability values. The Russian mathematician Chebyshev proved that at least $1 - 1/k^2$ percent of the data will lie within k standard deviations about the mean. When the normal distribution is used, virtually all values fall within three deviations from the mean.

The normal distribution has a mean of zero, and the standard deviation is called the *normal deviate*. The macro for ITER figures out how many passes through the loop are necessary to move from a normal deviate value of minus three to plus three. This range includes virtually all possible values for the normal distribution. Notice that as STEP

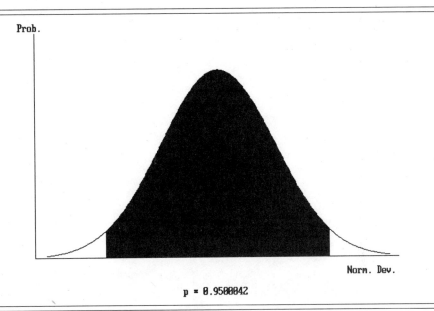

Figure 15-3. Normal Distribution Curve

decreases, ITER increases. Those familiar with calculus know that the smaller the step value, the closer the approximation to the true curve. However, if ITER becomes larger than the physical dimension of the x-axis, no increase in resolution is gained. The same pixel just gets plotted multiple times. Therefore, it makes little sense to increase ITER beyond the number of pixels on the x-axis; the greater the value of ITER, the longer it takes to draw the curve. The values shown in Listing 15-3 represent workable tradeoffs between good resolution and fast processing time.

Listing 15-3. Normal Distribution Curve

```
/*
    Plot the normal distribution curve, a normal deviate,and associated
    probability.
*/
#include <stdio.h>
#include <graph.h>
#include <math.h>
#define STEP    .02
#define ITER    ((3.0 / STEP) + 1) * 2
#define TRUE    1
#define BELL    7
```

Listing 15-3 continues

Listing 15-3 continued

```
double normal(double);

void do_window(void),
   do_area(void),
   do_normal(void),
   graphics_mode(void),
   end_graphics(int);
struct videoconfig myscreen;
double nd1, pstart, pend;


int main(void)
{
   char buff[20];

   for (;;) {                                     /* Get normal deviate */
      printf("Enter normal deviate: ");
      nd1 = atof(gets(buff));
         if (nd1 < -3.0 || nd1 > 3.0) {            /* In range?    */
         printf("Must be greater than -3.0 and less than 3.0 %d", BELL);
      } else {
         if (nd1 > 0) {
            nd1 = -nd1;
         }
         break;
      }
   }
   graphics_mode();        /* Set up graphics   */
   do_window();            /* Set up window     */
   do_normal();            /* Plot curve        */
   do_area();              /* Fill area         */
   end_graphics(1);        /* Cleanup           */
}



/*****
                          do_area()

   Function fills in the normal distribution probability between the plus and
minus normal deviate.

   Argument list:    void
```

```
    Return value:      void

*****/
void do_area(void)
{
    char answer[20], buff[20];

    _setcolor(4);
    _floodfill_w(0.0, 0.005, 2);
    sprintf(buff, "%8.7f", pend - pstart);
    strcpy(answer, "p = ");
    strcat(answer, buff);
    _settextposition(myscreen.numtextrows - 1, (myscreen.numtextcols / 2) - 6);
    _settextcolor(7);
    _outtext(answer);


}



/*****
                            do_normal()

    Function plots the normal distribution in the range -3.0 < nd < 3.0
    for the normal deviate.
*****/

void do_normal(void)
{
    int i;
    double nd, p1, p2;
    struct _wxycoord mycord;

    nd = -3.0;             /* Starting normal deviate */
    p1 = 0.0;

    _setcolor(2);          /* Draw some plain axes */
    _moveto_w(-3.2, 0.0);
    _lineto_w(3.2, 0.0);
    _moveto_w(-3.2, 0.0);
    _lineto_w(-3.2, 0.012);
    _settextcolor(7);
```

Listing 15-3 continues

Listing 15-3 continued

```
_settextposition(1, 1);

_outtext("Prob.");
_settextposition(myscreen.numtextrows - 3, myscreen.numtextcols  - 13);
_outtext("Norm. Dev.");

p1 = normal(nd - STEP);     /* Find the starting y value */
p2 = normal(nd);
_moveto_w(nd, p2 - p1);
nd += STEP;

for (i = 0; i < ITER; i ++) {     /* Plot the rest of the curve */
p1 = normal(nd);
p2 = p1 - p2;
_lineto_w(nd, p2);                      /* Another point on the curve     */
    if (nd >= nd1) {                    /* Past first nd?        */
        if (nd1 < 0.0) {                /* If the first one...   */
            pstart = p1;                /* ...set starting probability    */
            nd1 = fabs(nd1);            /* Now make it positive           */
        } else {
            pend = p1;                  /* Do the ending probability...   */
            nd1 = 200.0;                /* ...and don't come back here.    */
        }
        _lineto_w(nd, 0.0);             /* Draw the vertical normal deviate    */
        _moveto_w(nd, p2);
    }
    nd += STEP;                         /* Keep doing it...                */
    p2 = p1;
  }

}


/*****

                            do_window()

    Function opens a window consistent with the size needed to plot the normal
    distribution function.

    Argument list:     void

    Return value:      void
```

```
*****/

void do_window(void)
{
    _setwindow(TRUE, -3.5, -0.003, 3.5, .010);
}


/*****
                            normal()

    This function returns the probability associated with the normal
    deviate from the maximum ordinate of the normal distribution
    (for example, if x = 1.96, the return value from normal() is
    .9750021048). (The algorithm is from Collected Algorithms from
    CACM, #209, Vol.1, by Ibbetson and Brothers.)

    Argument:   double x       the normal deviate (sigma)

    Return value:  double       the probability associated with x for
                                the normal distribution.

*****/


double normal(double x)
{
    double w, y, z;

    if (x == 0.0)
        z = 0.0;
    else {
        y = fabs(x) / 2.0;
        if (y >= 3.0) {
            z = 1.0;
        } else {
            if (y < 1.0) {
                w = y * y;
                z = (((((((0.000124818987 * w
                -.001075204047) * w + .005198775019) * w
                -.019198292004) * w + .059054035642) * w
                -.151968751364) * w + .319152932694) * w
                -.531923007300) * w + .797884560593) * y * 2.0;
            } else {
```

Listing 15-3 continues

Listing 15-3 continued

```
            y = y - 2.0;
            z = ((((((((((((((-.000045255659 * y
            +.000152529290) * y - .000019538132) * y
            -.000676904986) * y + .001390604284) * y
            -.000794620820) * y - .002034254874) * y
            +.006549791214) * y - .010557625006) * y
            +.011630447319) * y - .009279453341) * y
            +.005353579108) * y - .002141268741) * y
            +.000535310849) * y + .999936657524;
        }
    }
  }
  if (x > 0.0)
     return (z + 1.0) / 2.0;
  else
     return (1 - z) / 2.0;
}


/*****

                          graphics_mode()

     This function sets the graphics mode to the highest value possible
  for the video adapter in use. It also sets the two globals maxx and
  maxy for the largest value consistent with the adapter.

  Argument list:    void

  Return value:     void

*****/

void graphics_mode(void)
{
   int i;

   i = _VRES16COLOR;                /* Start high... */

   while (!_setvideomode(i)) {      /* spin until we get a good one. */
      i--;
   }
   _getvideoconfig(&myscreen);
}
```

```
/*****
                        end_graphics()

    This function resets the graphics mode to the default value at the
    end of a graphics program. If the argument is nonzero, the program
    waits for the user to press a key. Otherwise, it falls through.

    Argument list:    int pause      pause if 1, no pause if 0

    Return value:    void

*****/

void end_graphics(int pause)
{
    if (pause) {
        getch();
    }
    _setvideomode(_DEFAULTMODE);

}
```

After the #defines are set, you see several function declarations and four global variable definitions.

In main(), the user is asked to enter the normal deviate to be used for the plot. The entered value is checked to make sure it falls within the plus- or minus-three standard deviation range. If it doesn't, the user must reenter the value until it does fall within plus or minus three standard deviations. The call to graphics_mode() is essentially the same function used earlier in this chapter. The only difference is that the maxx and maxy values were removed because they are not necessary in this program.

The call to do_window() defines the graphics window that you want to use. This function simply calls the QC function _setwindow() to set the size of the window used in the program. The function prototype is:

```
_setwindow(int v, double lx, double ly, double rx, double ry);
```

where v is the view orientation. If v is 1, the view places the smaller numbers for the y-axis at the bottom of the display screen. This orientation is consistent with the way most people view things. If v is 0, the values of y increase as you move from the top of the screen toward the bottom, reflecting the physical coordinate system. v is set to True because it simplifies the program. (You could do things "upside down", but it complicates things.) The remaining arguments define the size of the window by setting the minimum and maximum values for x and y.

You could do away with do_window() and simply call the QC function _setwindow() directly. The choice is more a matter of style than substance.

At this stage in the program, you have determined the graphics mode to be used and have a window in which to plot the data. The do_normal() function plots the data on-screen. The call _setcolor(2) sets the color value for drawing the axes on-screen. (In the EGA or VGA modes, the value 2 corresponds to green.)

_moveto_w() and _lineto_w() Functions

The _moveto_w() function is used when you want to move to a specified location on-screen. The _w at the end of the function name tells you that this function is designed for use with a graphics window. Because you are using a window, the coordinates are doubles that represent the x and y coordinates of the new location.

The _lineto_w() function draws a line from the current screen position to the coordinates specified in the arguments in _lineto_w(). Once again, the _w tells QC that a line is being drawn in a window, so the arguments are double data types. Notice how _moveto_w() and _lineto_w() work. The sequence

```
_moveto_w(1.0, 1.0);
_lineto_w(5.0, 5.0);
```

draws a line from coordinates (1, 1) to (5, 5). The _moveto_w() function is a "pen up" command; no drawing is done. The _lineto_w() function is a "pen down" command, and the line is drawn from the current screen position to the coordinates given in _lineto_w().

In do_normal(), the vertical axis is labeled "Prob." by setting the text color (_settextcolor()), the position where you want to print the axis label (_settextposition()), and finally, by calling _outtext() to display the label on-screen. Next, you again call _settextposition(), but this time you use the row and column information held in myscreen. Placing the horizontal axis in this manner ensures that the text ends up in the proper position, regardless of the video display device. (The same method is used in do_area().)

The rest of do_normal() is concerned with drawing the bell curve based on values returned from normal(). The normal() function takes the normal deviate value and returns the cumulative probability for that normal deviate. (This function comes from my *C Programmer's Toolkit*, published by Que Corp.) Because you are interested in the point probability, you must subtract the previous probability from the current value returned by normal() (that is, p1-p2). The call to _lineto_w() plots from the last probability value to the current probability value. You do this sequence ITER times.

The if statements within the for loop are used to draw the vertical lines at the normal deviate positions. (See Figure 15-3.) This allows you to see where the normal deviates fall within the bell curve.

After the curve is drawn, do_area() is called to fill in the area under the normal curve for the normal deviates. First you call _setcolor() to change the color for the fill. The call to _floodfill_w() is used to fill a bounded area with the color just set with _setcolor(). The arguments to _flood_fill_w() are

```
flood_fill_w(double x, double y, int bcolor);
```

The x and y values are like a _moveto_w() call in that the current screen position is set to these coordinates. The variable bcolor is the boundary color used to define the area to be filled. _flood_fill_w() works by coloring pixels with the "flood" color moving from x and y outward to the point where it sees a bcolor pixel. In other words, QC starts a left-right, up-down scan, setting pixels to the flood color until it runs into a bcolor pixel. Therefore, _flood_fill_w() lets you "paint" a bounded area of the screen with a color, regardless of its shape.

Using *sprintf( )*

The QC graphics library does not include a printf() function that lets you print formatted numbers on-screen. Only text (character string data) can be written to a graphics screen. Therefore, if you want to display numbers on a graphics screen, you must first convert them to ASCII characters, place them in a string, and then use _outtext() to display the text in the display window.

The sprintf() function has the following prototype

```
int sprintf(char *d, const char *c, ...);
```

The second argument, called the control string, contains the usual format conversion characters you want to use (for example, %d, %10.8f, etc.). The first argument is a character array that will receive the formatted output. This means that instead of writing the output to the screen as is the case with `printf()`, the output is written into the character array d. It is your responsibility to make sure that d is large enough to hold the data plus the null termination character.

The three periods (...) in the prototype are called an *ellipsis* operator and are used to denote that one or more arguments of unspecified data is present in the list of function arguments. The reason it is used in the `sprintf()` prototype is that there is no way of knowing in advance how many arguments are required by the control string. (`sprint()` calculates the number of arguments by counting the number of % conversion characters in the control string.) Therefore, the ellipsis operator is used in function prototypes whenever a variable number of arguments is present.

After the call to `sprintf()`, you build a second string that contains p =. The call to `strcat()` *concatenates* (adds together) the second string and the contents of the string built by `sprintf()`, to produce the message you want to display. The call to `_settextposition()` places the cursor at the row-column location on-screen where the output will be written. Next, the color used for printing is set with `_settextcolor()`, and then `_outtext()` is called to display the argument string.

Lastly, `end_graphics()` is called to return the screen to the normal text mode before the program ends. However, because `end_graphics()` is called with an argument of 1, the function waits for the user to press a key before returning the display to the text mode. This allows the user to view the output before flipping back into text mode. After the user touches a key, the screen is set to text mode and the program ends.

The example shown in Listing 15-3 falls somewhere between general graphics and presentation graphics. This is because the graphics drawing routines used are at the pixel level, but the purpose is to convey visual information about specific data. Indeed, almost the same visual information could be provided if you used the presentation graphics functions provided by QC. The next section shows you how to use the functions found in the QC library.

Presentation Graphics

The QC library includes a powerful set of graphics routines designed to eliminate the "grunt" work of doing presentation graphics. The set of presentation graphics includes pie charts, bar and column charts, line graphs, and scatter plots. The type of chart you use depends in part on the data being graphed.

Stocks and Flows

Most data falls into one of two categories: *stock* or *flow*. A stock variable is one that is measured at a point in time. Stock variables do not have a time subscript associated with them. A flow variable is one that is measured over a unit of time and requires a time subscript. For example, if someone asks how much your car costs, you might say, "Ten thousand dollars." If I ask you what your income is and you reply, "One hundred dollars," I'm still not sure what your income is. Is it $100 per hour, per day, per week, per month, or even, per year? Clearly, income is a flow variable because it needs a per unit time stated with it to make sense.

On the other hand, the price of something is its value at a point in time, so it does not need a time subscript to make sense. Therefore, price is a stock variable. All measures of price or wealth are stocks and all income variables are flows.

With respect to presentation graphics, some charts are better at showing stock variables, whereas others are better at showing flows. Pie charts are good for showing how something is subdivided at a point in time. For example, companies often show how total company revenues are allocated to income and expenses using a pie chart. Corporate sales by product line is another common use for a pie chart. In both examples, a stock variable is divided into parts using a pie chart.

Bar charts also are good for stock variables. Frequency distributions often are graphed as a bar chart. Because frequency distributions are measured at a point in time, they depict stock variables.

Column charts, on the other hand, are better at showing the movement of one or more variables through time and, therefore, lend themselves to flow variables. You probably have seen a column chart that shows company sales over the past five years. Because column charts show the data over time, they are best suited to flow variables. Line charts and scatter diagrams are used to find time trends in data and are most suitable to flow variables.

The first step in using QC's presentation graphics is deciding which type of graph to use. If you keep the "stock versus flow" concepts in mind, you find that the choice is often dictated by the data and by what you want the data to show.

A Presentation Graphics Program Example

There are so many options available when using the presentation graphics library that the best way to start is to plunge in with a complete sample program. Listing 15-4 presents a program that reads the data from an ASCII file and displays it using a scatter diagram.

Listing 15-4. Scatter Diagram Program

```
/*
   Read data from an ASCII file and do scatterplot
*/

#include <stdio.h>
#include <stdlib.h>
#include <string.h>
#include <float.h>
#include <graph.h>
#include <pgchart.h>


#define MAXLINE    90
#define FALSE      0
#define TRUE       1

void get_sizes(char *, float far *, float far *),
   get_room(float),
   graphics_mode(void),
   end_graphics(int);

struct videoconfig myscreen;
float set, values, far *xptr, far *yptr;
float minx, miny, maxx, maxy;              /* For scaling */



int main(int argc, char *argv[])
{
   int i;
   i = read_file(argc, argv); /* Open and read data    */
   if (i == 0) {
      exit(EXIT_FAILURE);
   }
```

```
   graphics_mode();           /* Set up graphics     */
   do_chart();                /* Set up window       */
   end_graphics(1);           /* Clean up            */
}

/*****
                       do_chart()

    This function does all the work to set up a scatterplot chart.
    See discussion in text for each variable.

    Argument list:    void

    Return value:     int      0 on error, 1 if ok

*****/

int do_chart(void)
{
   chartenv env;

   _pg_initchart();
   _pg_defaultchart(&env, _PG_SCATTERCHART, _PG_POINTANDLINE);

   strcpy(env.maintitle.title, "Who Knows What");
   env.maintitle.justify = _PG_CENTER;
   env.maintitle.titlecolor = 6;

   strcpy(env.subtitle.title, "Sample X versus Sample Y");
   env.subtitle.justify = _PG_CENTER;
   env.subtitle.titlecolor = 6;

   strcpy(env.xaxis.axistitle.title, "Sample X");
   strcpy(env.yaxis.axistitle.title, "Sample Y");

   env.xaxis.axiscolor = 3;
   env.yaxis.axiscolor = 3;

   env.chartwindow.border = TRUE;
   env.chartwindow.bordercolor = 3;

   env.datawindow.border = FALSE;

   env.xaxis.autoscale = FALSE;
```

Listing 15-4 continues

Listing 15-4 continued

```
    env.yaxis.autoscale = FALSE;

    env.xaxis.scalemin = minx *.9;       /* No points on axis */
    env.yaxis.scalemin = miny * .9;
    env.xaxis.scalemax = maxx * 1.1;
    env.yaxis.scalemax = maxy * 1.1;

    env.xaxis.scalefactor = 1.0;    /* MAY NEED TO CHANGE THESE */
    env.yaxis.scalefactor = 1.0;    /*               "          */
    env.xaxis.ticinterval = 1.0;    /*               "          */
    env.yaxis.ticinterval = 5.0;    /*               "          */
    env.xaxis.ticdecimals = 0.0;    /*               "          */
    env.yaxis.ticdecimals = 0.0;    /*               "          */

    env.yaxis.grid = FALSE;
    if (_pg_chartscatter(&env, xptr, yptr, (int) set)) {
      _setvideomode(_DEFAULTMODE);
      _outtext("Error: can't do it");
      return 0;
    }
    return 1;
}



/*****

                              read_file()

    This function reads the input data file. The input file is an ASCII text
file with the following format:

        n, total\n       n = total cases, total = total values

        x1, y1\n         First x and y values
        x2, y2\n
        . , .\n
        xn, yn\n         Last x and y values

Notice that each line ends with a newline (you pressed Enter at the end of
the line). It should be clear that if n = 10, there will be 11 lines in the
file, including the first line. By using ASCII, it is easy to change the data.


        Argument list:    int argc         command-line argument counter
```

```
                    char *argv[]              "              vector

    Return value:      int      0 on error, 1 if ok

*****/

int read_file(int argc, char *argv[])
{
    char buff[MAXLINE];
    int i;
    FILE *fpin;

    if (argc != 2) {                              /* Right arguments? */
        printf("\nUsage: program datafilename\n");
        exit(EXIT_FAILURE);
    }

    minx = miny = FLT_MAX;                        /* For scaling */
    maxx = maxy = FLT_MIN;

    if ((fpin = fopen(argv[1], "r")) == NULL) {    /* Open the file   */
        printf("\nCannot open %s\n", argv[1]);
        exit(EXIT_FAILURE);
    }

    fgets(buff, MAXLINE, fpin);
    get_sizes(buff, &set, &values);   /* How many values?    */
    get_room(set);                    /* Allocate memory for it  */
    for (i = 0; i < set; i++) {
        if (fgets(buff, MAXLINE, fpin) == NULL) {
            printf("\nData end prematurely");
            return 0;
        }
        get_sizes(buff, &xptr[i], &yptr[i]);
        if (xptr[i] >= maxx)
            maxx = xptr[i];
        if (yptr[i] >= maxy)
            maxy = yptr[i];
        if (xptr[i] <= minx)
            minx = xptr[i];
        if (yptr[i] <= miny)
            miny = yptr[i];
    }
    return 1;
```

Listing 15-4 continues

Listing 15-4 continued

```
}
/*****
                            get_room()

    This function gets enough room to store the data held in the ASCII data
    file.

    Argument list:      float set        number of x-y pairs

    Return value:       void

*****/


void get_room(float set)
{
   xptr = (float far *) calloc( (size_t) set, sizeof(float));
   yptr = (float far *) calloc( (size_t) set, sizeof(float));
   if (xptr == NULL || yptr == NULL) {
      printf("Out of memory.\n");
      exit(EXIT_FAILURE);
   }
}



/*****
                            get_sizes()

    This function converts the ASCII input data to floating-point data. The
    function assumes that a comma separates each x-y pair and that the line ends
    with a newline character so that fgets() works.


    Argument list:      char *s           pointer to line buffer
                        float far *v1     pointer to x storage
                        float far *v2     pointer to y storage

    Return value:       void

*****/

void get_sizes(char *s, float far *v1, float far *v2)
{
```

```
char tbuff[MAXLINE], *tptr;

strcpy(tbuff, s);
tptr = strchr(tbuff, ',');
if (tptr == NULL) {
        printf("Improper data format\n");
    exit(EXIT_FAILURE);
}
*tptr = '\0';
*v1 = (float) atof(tbuff);
*v2 = (float) atof(tptr + 1);
}
```

```
/*****
                        graphics_mode()
```

This function sets the graphics mode to the highest value possible for the video adapter in use. It also sets the two globals maxx and maxy for the largest value consistent with the adapter.

```
    Argument list:      void

    Return value:       void

*****/

void graphics_mode(void)
{
    int i;

    i = _VRES16COLOR;              /* Start high ... */

    while (!_setvideomode(i)) {   /* ... spin until we get a good one. */
        i--;
    }
    _getvideoconfig(&myscreen);
}


/*****
                        end_graphics()
```

Listing 15-4 continues

Listing 15-4 continued

```
    This function resets the graphics mode to the default value at the end of a
  graphics program. If the argument is nonzero, the program waits for the user
  to press a key. Otherwise, it falls through.

  Argument list:     int pause        pause if 1, no pause if 0

  Return value:      void
*****/

void end_graphics(int pause)
{
   if (pause) {
      getch();
   }
   _setvideomode(_DEFAULTMODE);
}
```

The various functions are discussed in the following sections.

read_ file( )

The read_file() function is responsible for opening and reading the file that contains the data to be graphed. To make it easy on you, the data file is a garden-variety ASCII data file that can be created with almost any text editor, including the QC editor. The format, however, is rather strict. Figure 15-4 illustrates the way the data are entered into the data file. Note that only the numbers (starting with pair 6,12) appear in the file.

The file is organized as two columns of numbers in x-y sequence. The first two numbers are not part of the data set, but rather, tell how many cases, or rows, of data are contained in the file. In Figure 15-4, the digit character 6 on the first line says that there are 6 x-y pairs in the file. The 12 is simply two times the first number (6). Therefore, the second number tells how many total values are contained in the file. Obviously, this second number is not needed, but was added to maintain the symmetry of the file and to simplify its processing.

Each line in the file ends with a newline character. This is added to the file when you press the Enter key, even though it normally does not appear on-screen as a visible character. The newline is required so that fgets() can be used to read the file one line at a time, picking up x-y pairs.

Columns

x   y

6, 12

1, 20

2, 33

3, 11

4, 25

5, 55

6, 38

Figure 15-4. ASCII File Format

Finally, each x and y value is separated by a comma. With the QC compiler, you can have a blank space after the comma and it should pose no problem. If a different compiler is used, however, it may be necessary to remove the blank space. Some compilers have atof() functions that quit when a nondigit character is read. The ANSI standard states that blank spaces are ignored, but still there are some atof() functions that don't meet the standard.

The first thing read_file() does is check that the proper number of command-line arguments were supplied when the program was started. The argument count should be two: one for the program name and one for the file name of the data file. If two arguments were not given, the program displays an error message and aborts. If two arguments were given, the program attempts to open the file for reading.

get_sizes()

The first call to fgets() reads the first line of the data file and calls get_sizes(). There are three arguments to get_sizes(). The first argument is a pointer to the character array that holds the line just read from the disk data file. The second argument is the lvalue of the variable set. The third argument is the lvalue of values. Because lvalues are passed, in effect you are passing pointers to get_sizes().

Once inside get_sizes(), the call to strcpy() copies the line read from disk into tbuff[]. You copy the string passed to get_sizes() because you alter the string in this routine. Because no further processing is done on the string, you could omit this step.

strchr() is a standard library function that searches a character array (tbuff[]) for a given character (in our case a comma). If a comma is found, tptr points to the comma. If no comma is found, tptr is a null pointer. The if test checks for the null pointer and aborts the program if tptr is null. If the pointer is not null, the program writes a null termination character into the string where the comma was. This has the effect of creating a substring out of the first number of the line just read from the disk.

Next, the substring is converted to a floating-point number by calling atof(). atof() returns a double, so the result must be cast to a float before you assign the result into v1. Because v1 is a pointer to the variable passed to get_sizes(), you end up storing the number at the lvalue of set back in read_file(). Because the first value in the file tells how many rows of data are in the file, you now can use set to control how many lines must be read from the disk file.

The statement

```
*v2 = (float) atof(tptr + 1);
```

creates a second floating-point number from the rest of the string and assigns it into v2. Because v2 is a pointer to values back in read_file(), the floating-point value is stored in value.

Notice how the second floating-point number was created. Because tptr points to the comma, adding 1 to the pointer (that is, increasing the lvalue by 1) points to the first digit character of the second value held in the buffer. atof() converts the rest of the string into the corresponding floating-point value.

Finally, you fall through a series of if statements to set the maximum and minimum values for x and y (that is, minx, maxx, miny, and maxy). These variables were initialized to FLT_MIN and FLT_MAX in read_file(). The values for FLT_MIN and FLT_MAX are found in the float.h header file. These values are used to set the vertical and horizontal scales for do_chart().

Now, back to the next line in read_file().

get_room()

After the first call to get_sizes(), control returns to read_file(). You now know how many numbers are in the data file. The function get_room() attempts to create enough space to hold two set-sized blocks of storage. The call to calloc() creates set storage units, each of which is large enough to hold a `float`. The QC presentation graphics functions require that these data arrays be defined as `far` pointers to `float`; therefore, the casts are necessary for the two pointers. Variables `xptr` and `yptr` are global `far` pointers to `float`, as defined near the top of the program.

If either pointer is null, an error message is given and the program aborts. Otherwise, control returns to `read_file()`.

The `for` loop in `read_file()` reads all the rows (or cases, for you statisticians), using `set` to control the number of iterations. On each iteration, `get_sizes()` is called to fill the x and y values. Note that you must pass the `lvalue` of the arrays to `get_sizes()`, so you can use the address-of operator before the array names. You also can use `xptr` and `yptr` as long as you increment them with each pass through the `for` loop. I use the array method because it makes the code more clear.

If `fgets()` returns a null pointer before reading `set` data sets, an error probably occurred. Instead of aborting the program at this stage, I return a value of zero. The program is then aborted in `main()`. I did this because you might want to change the logic and attempt to display the part of the data that was processed successfully.

Assuming all went well in `read_file()`, a 1 is returned to `main()`. All of the data is now in place, and you are ready to graph it.

do_chart()

As you might expect, `do_chart()` is the real workhorse of the program. The statement

```
chartenv env;
```

is the `typedef` that defines a large structure of type `chartenv` (the chart environment). Within this large structure are many smaller structures, each of which controls one aspect of the chart. Virtually all of the code in `do_chart()` is concerned with filling in the structure members of these substructures. If you want to see the `typedef` for `env`, place the cursor in the source window on the word `pgchart.h` of the `#include` directive, press Atl-V-I (View an Include file), and press Enter. You may be asked whether you want to save the source file before seeing the `pgchart.h` header file. Answer Yes and the header file appears in the source window.

The call to `_pg_initchart()` is responsible for filling in many of the default values for the chart environment. The next statement

```
pg_defaultchart(&env, _PG_SCATTERCHART, _PG_POINTANDLINE);
```

has the effect of telling QC, "Take my chart environment (env), fill it in with the necessary default values for a presentation scatter chart (_PG_SCATTERCHART), and use both points and connecting lines on the chart (_PG_POINTAND LINE)." You can change the type of chart simply by changing the symbolic constants in `_pg_defaultchart()`. The alternatives are shown in Table 15-1.

Table 15-1. `_pg_defaultchart(end, type, style)`

Type	Style
_PG_PIECHART	_PG_PERCENT
	_PG_NOPERCENT
_PG_BARCHART	_PG_STACKBARS
_PG_COLUMNCHAR	_PG_PLAINBARS
_PG_LINECHART	_PG_POINTANDLINE
_PG_SCATTERCHART	_PG_POINTONLY

As you can see from Table 15-1, each type of chart has a set of two possible styles that can be used with it. For example, a bar chart can have either stacked or plain bars. The same is true for column charts. You can make fairly rapid changes to the overall look of a chart by changing the symbolic constants used when `_pg_defaultchart()` is called.

The statement

```
strcpy(env.maintitle.title, "Who Knows What");
```

copies the title of the chart ("Who Knows What") into the primary title field of the chart environment. The first argument to `strcpy()` is typical of most elements in the env structure. Because the dot operator appears twice in the first argument, you know that the env structure contains another structure named `maintitle`. This structure has a member named `title`. `title` must be a character array because you are copying the chart title into this member.

As you can see from the next two statements

```
env.maintitle.justify = _PG_CENTER;
```

```
env.maintitle.titlecolor = 6;
```

the `maintitle` structure allows you to set the color of the title and justify

it. We chose to center the title, but you can also right- (_PG_RIGHT) or left-
(_PG_LEFT) justify the title. If you are not using a color graphics adapter, just
leave the titlecolor statement out of the program. The actual color you see
depends on your graphics adapter. (The 6 above on a VGA or EGA adapter
is magenta. Note that this number is one greater than the normal IBM color
scheme. Therefore, black is 1, 2 is blue, 3 is green, and so on.) You also can
control similar information about the subtitle used on the chart.

The remaining statements simply initialize other members of the
various structures, and the intent of each is clear from its name. (Again,
Chapter 14 in *C for Yourself* explains each structure and its members.)
However, the statements

```
env.xaxis.autoscale = FALSE;

env.yaxis.autoscale = FALSE;
```

need some explanation. If you choose not to take advantage of automatic
scaling of the chart (as indicated by the preceding statement), you are
required to fill in the scalemin, scalemax, scalefactor, scaletitle, ticinterval,
ticformat, and ticdecimals for each axis. I chose to do this for several
reasons. First, it shows how to override the default settings. Second, I
forgot to set the scalefactor member when I first ran the program and got
runtime overflow errors. It seemed like a good idea to point this out so that
you don't spend time trying to figure out what you did wrong. Third, I
don't like a graph to run to the edge of the screen, and that is what happens
with automatic scaling.

The different scaling factors you see in Listing 15-4 were set for the
sample data file I used to test the program. Obviously, your data set will
be different, so these values must be changed. The scalefactor members
for the x- and y-axis should reflect the size of the numbers you are plotting.
The minimum and maximum values for x and y are set in read_file().
However, I set scalefactor to 1.0 and assume it is acceptable. In "real life,"
you should check the minimum and maximum values and set scalefactor
accordingly. If you are plotting the national debt, the scale factor might be
one trillion. If you are plotting annual income, the scale might be in
thousands. If the scale factor is too large, the graph will be all "scrunched
up." If the scale factor is too small, some of the data points might be
clipped. The scaling factor is dictated by the data.

Also note that I set the datawindow.border structure to FALSE. This
means I do not want a line drawn around the area in which the data are
plotted. On the other hand, chartwindow.border is set to TRUE so that the
entire chart is surrounded with a line. You might set these to opposite

states to see the effect it has on the graph.

After all the initialization statements are set to their proper values, the program calls `_pg_chartscatter()` to actually draw the chart.

The `end_graphics()` function was discussed earlier in this chapter. You call it with an argument of 1 so that the program pauses for the user to view the chart.

Conclusion

There is no way to convey properly the amount of work that is being done in the background by the QC presentation graphics functions. If you tried to use the low-level graphics functions to reproduce the output in Listing 15-4, it could take hours — maybe even days! You should experiment with the different structure members in the `env` structure to see what impact those changes have on the output. You should list the `pgchart.h` header file on the printer and make notes on the listing as you experiment.

The goal of this chapter was to make you feel fairly comfortable with the way QC expects you to approach graphics programming. With this background, you might want to try modifying some of the graphics programs found in the *C For Yourself* manual supplied with the QC compiler.

Appendix A

ASCII Codes

This appendix contains the American Standard Code for Information Interchange (ASCII) codes. The table also includes the decimal, hexadecimal, and binary representations for the ASCII character set.

Decimal	Hex	Binary	ASCII
0	0	00000000	NUL
1	1	00000001	SOH
2	2	00000010	STX
3	3	00000011	ETX
4	4	00000100	EOT
5	5	00000101	ENQ
6	6	00000110	ACK
7	7	00000111	BEL
8	8	00001000	BS
9	9	00001001	HT
10	a	00001010	LF
11	b	00001011	VT
12	c	00001100	FF
13	d	00001101	CR
14	e	00001110	SO
15	f	00001111	SI
16	10	00010000	DLE
17	11	00010001	DC1

18	12	00010010	DC2
19	13	00010011	DC3
20	14	00010100	DC4
21	15	00010101	NAK
22	16	00010110	SYN
23	17	00010111	ETB
24	18	00011000	CAN
25	19	00011001	EM
26	1a	00011010	SUB
27	1b	00011011	ESC
28	1c	00011100	FS
29	1d	00011101	GS
30	1e	00011110	RS
31	1f	00011111	US
32	20	00100000	(space)
33	21	00100001	!
34	22	00100010	"
35	23	00100011	#
36	24	00100100	$
37	25	00100101	%
38	26	00100110	&
39	27	00100111	'
40	28	00101000	(
41	29	00101001	)
42	2a	00101010	*
43	2b	00101011	+
44	2c	00101100	,
45	2d	00101101	-
46	2e	00101110	.
47	2f	00101111	/
48	30	00110000	0
49	31	00110001	1
50	32	00110010	2
51	33	00110011	3
52	34	00110100	4
53	35	00110101	5
54	36	00110110	6
55	37	00110111	7

56	38	00111000	8
57	39	00111001	9
58	3a	00111010	:
59	3b	00111011	;
60	3c	00111100	<
61	3d	00111101	=
62	3e	00111110	>
63	3f	00111111	?
64	40	01000000	@
65	41	01000001	A
66	42	01000010	B
67	43	01000011	C
68	44	01000100	D
69	45	01000101	E
70	46	01000110	F
71	47	01000111	G
72	48	01001000	H
73	49	01001001	I
74	4a	01001010	J
75	4b	01001011	K
76	4c	01001100	L
77	4d	01001101	M
78	4e	01001110	N
79	4f	01001111	O
80	50	01010000	P
81	51	01010001	Q
82	52	01010010	R
83	53	01010011	S
84	54	01010100	T
85	55	01010101	U
86	56	01010110	V
87	57	01010111	W
88	58	01011000	X
89	59	01011001	Y
90	5a	01011010	Z
91	5b	01011011	[
92	5c	01011100	\
93	5d	01011101	]

94	5e	01011110	^
95	5f	01011111	_
96	60	01100000	`
97	61	01100001	a
98	62	01100010	b
99	63	01100011	c
100	64	01100100	d
101	65	01100101	e
102	66	01100110	f
103	67	01100111	g
104	68	01101000	h
105	69	01101001	i
106	6a	01101010	j
107	6b	01101011	k
108	6c	01101100	l
109	6d	01101101	m
110	6e	01101110	n
111	6f	01101111	o
112	70	01110000	p
113	71	01110001	q
114	72	01110010	r
115	73	01110011	s
116	74	01110100	t
117	75	01110101	u
118	76	01110110	v
119	77	01110111	w
120	78	01111000	x
121	79	01111001	y
122	7a	01111010	z
123	7b	01111011	{
124	7c	01111100	|
125	7d	01111101	}
126	7e	01111110	~
127	7f	01111111	DEL

Index

T

Y